WORK AND FAITH
IN THE KENTUCKY
COAL FIELDS

RELIGION IN NORTH AMERICA

Catherine L. Albanese and Stephen J. Stein, editors

Work and Faith in the Kentucky Coal Fields

Subject to Dust

Richard J. Callahan, Jr.

INDIANA UNIVERSITY PRESS
Bloomington and Indianapolis

This book is a publication of

Indiana University Press
601 North Morton Street
Bloomington, IN 47404-3797 USA

http://iupress.indiana.edu

Telephone orders   800-842-6796
Fax orders   812-855-7931
Orders by e-mail   iuporder@indiana.edu

Manufactured in the United States of America

Library of Congress Cataloging-in-
Publication Data

Callahan, Jr., Richard J., date
   Work and faith in the Kentucky coal fields
: subject to dust / Richard J. Callahan, Jr.
      p. cm.—(Religion in North America)
   Includes bibliographical and index.
   ISBN 978-0-253-35237-8 (cloth : alk.
paper)   1. Kentucky—Religious life and
customs.   2. Coal miners—Religious
life.   I Title.
   BT555.K4C35 2008
   277.69'082—dc22   2008013740
 1 2 3 4 5 14 13 12 11 10 09

Song lyrics:
"Kentucky Miners' Wives Ragged Hungry
Blues"
By Annt Molly Jackson
© Copyright 1967 STORMKING MUSIC
INC. (BMI)
All rights reserved. Used by permission.

"The Dream of the Miner's Child"
Written by Rev. Andrew Jenkins
Used by permission of Shapiro, Bernstein &
Co., Inc.
All rights reserved. International copyright
secured.

"I Hate the Company Bosses"
By Sarah Ogan Gunning
Used by permission of Folk-Legacy Records,
Inc.

All other song lyrics are in the public domain.

Title page illustration: No. 203 Mine Camp,
Jenkins, Ky., 1913. Item 137, The Jenkins,
Kentucky Photographic Collection,
1911–1930, 2001AV01, University of
Kentucky Archives. Used by permission.

In memory of Helen G. Callahan

Pillars holding up the roof in the No. 206 Mine, Jenkins, Ky. Item 122, The Jenkins, Kentucky Photographic Collection, 1911–1930, 2001AV01, University of Kentucky Archives. Used by permission.

Contents

Foreword

In this volume Richard Callahan introduces a topic that has received too little attention from students of American religious history. He immerses the reader in the social and cultural realities shaping the religious world of the coal miners of eastern Kentucky in the years when coal mining emerged as a major industry in southern Appalachia. This account views that context principally from the standpoint of the miners and their families instead of from the vantage point of the owners of the mines and economic historians. As a result, the reader will discover the religious role and power of work in that mountain culture and the variety of ways in which labor led to reflection on a series of spiritual questions.

This is not conventional religious history with its predictable focus on clergy and theologians, creedal statements, and sacred texts. Callahan does not ignore those traditional topics, but he concentrates his attention on the realities at the center of life for the coal miners and their families as conditions were dictated by the coal industry. The unbending mine schedule set fixed daily routines for miners and their families. Constant physical danger surrounded those working in the mines and obsessed those whom they loved. Psychological and financial challenges confronted those who depended on the mines for their livelihood and for their housing. The frequency and the nearness of accidental death by mine tragedies haunted all in coal towns. These realities shaped the life and work of coal miners in the Appalachian mountain region and gave rise to particular religious patterns.

Callahan describes the religious world that emerged in the southern Appalachian mountain region as contrasting sharply in many respects with contemporary religious patterns in the late nineteenth and early twentieth centuries. In fact, religion in the region was intentionally different from what mountain folks called "railroad religion," a term linked negatively to representatives of the large Protestant traditions that were organizing denominationally throughout the nation. Many—perhaps most—of the local Appalachian preachers that Callahan identifies were also miners during the week and thorough products of the mountain society and culture. Their spiritual messages reflected the realities shaped by work in the mines and by the surrounding context. They gave voice to the spiritual concerns that arose from the coal world. These preachers often enjoyed an independence and autonomy that were not characteristic of denominational clergy. They also regularly exercised diverse spiritual gifts that set them apart, including healing, speaking in tongues, and other remarkable skills seemingly confirming the presence of the Holy Spirit. These "gifts" also distinguished miner preachers from the clerical representatives of more established denominations, a contrast that is a central theme in this volume.

Callahan's linkage of work and religion in this mountain region provides a useful model other historians might follow when writing about different social groups defined by their particular vocations. Work and labor inescapably affect and reflect values. Among the most graphic sections of this volume, for example, are the accounts telling of the ways in which the workers in eastern Kentucky responded in sermon and song to the tragedies that often befell those working in the mines. A power of expression and of faith filled the sermons and testimonies delivered by miner-preachers. When mining replaced subsistence farming as the principal livelihood in the region, miners reshaped the commitment evident in the faith they inherited from the past and fitted it for their new circumstances. The lyrics of hymns and religious songs also gave voice to the strength they obtained from their labor.

Hence from this study we learn a great deal about the ways in which the residents of eastern Kentucky employed the religious idiom of their Appalachian culture to address the issues that were central to their existence—the need for work, the hardships linked to labor, the omnipresence of danger, the reality of death in their midst. Callahan also shows the ways in which these same mountain folk adapted to the changing world that they inhabited, a world that was invaded by the emerging Holiness movement on the religious side as well as by organized labor unions on the economic side. We learn about the ways in which the traditions of mountain religion joined forces with the growing Holiness-Pentecostal movement to give voice to the ultimate concerns of residents in the region around the turn of the twentieth century. We also learn about the ways in which competing unions seeking to organize mine workers experienced both success and failure as they addressed the ultimate questions that governed life for those in the coal towns. Callahan provides an account of the ways in which two unions—the National Miners' Union and the United Mine Workers of America—competed in their attempts to organize coal miners in the region. Success for the UMWA ultimately hinged on religious judgments held widely by miners in the region, judgments reinforced by Holiness (and Pentecostal) principles.

Finally, this immersion in the world covered by the dust from the coal mines is highly suggestive with respect to other research that needs to be done by historians. How do daily realities confronting other workers in different vocations and diverse locations shape their spiritual strivings? To what extent does work determine the spiritual voice of those who labor?

Catherine L. Albanese
Stephen J. Stein
Series Editors

Acknowledgments

This book is the result of conversations, inspirations, and provocations over the course of many years. It is impossible to recognize everybody who influenced my thinking or writing, but some require special notice. First, I would like to thank my teachers at the University of California, Santa Barbara, for their patience, encouragement, and wisdom. Professors Catherine L. Albanese, Wade Clark Roof, Richard Hecht, and Charles Long have all been wonderful friends in addition to their important roles as teachers. Their influence on me is profound. Likewise, I wish to thank Eugene Gallagher, Garrett Green, and Lindsey Harlan, the teachers who first introduced me to the field of religious studies at Connecticut College. My perspective on the study of culture was forever changed by Erika Brady, Michael Anne Williams, and Lynwood Montell, my teachers in folklore and folklife at West Kentucky University.

At Indiana University Press, Stephen J. Stein, Dee Mortensen, Miki Bird, Laura MacLeod, Elaine Otto, Beth Marsh, and Michael Lundell each deserve my gratitude for their helpfulness and patience.

A number of organizations have helped to fund my research. A Humanities/ Social Sciences Research Grant from UCSB allowed me to do initial exploration in the field and the archives. I also benefited greatly from a fellowship with the Pew Program in Religion and American History at Yale University. At the conference that concluded my year as a Pew Fellow I received helpful comments on my work from Jon Butler and Stephen J. Stein. Extensive work on the manuscript was made possible by a summer stipend from the Research Council at the University of Missouri–Columbia.

Some of the ideas and material in this book were presented at annual meetings of the Appalachian Studies Association, the Society for the Scientific Study of Religion, and the Western Region of the American Academy of Religion. I benefited from the feedback that I received in each of these forums. At various times throughout the course of this project, especially in its early stages, I had several conversations in particular with established scholars in the fields of religious studies and Appalachian studies that made me feel that what I was doing was indeed important. For that inspiration I would especially like to thank Dwight Billings, Stephen Foster, Helen Lewis, Ann Taves, and David Chidester. Colleagues in the Young Scholars of American Religion Program at Indiana University–Purdue University Indianapolis were exceptionally smart conversation partners on all things related to American religious history, and they also provided feedback on chapter 2. I would like to thank each of them individually: Jonathan Baer, Jim Bennett, Catherine Brekus, Wendy Cadge, John Giggie, Becky Gould, Tommy Kidd, Amy Koehlinger, Luis Murillo, John Schmalzbauer, Sarah Taylor, Peter Williams, and Anne Wills.

Three archival sources were invaluable to my research: the Appalachian Collection in the King Library's Special Collections at the University of Kentucky; the University of Kentucky Library's Social History and Cultural Change in the Elkhorn Coal Field Oral History Project, 1987–88; and the Appalachian Oral History Project, especially the part of the collection housed at Alice Lloyd College in Pippa Passes, Kentucky. At the University of Kentucky, Kate Black was especially considerate in directing me to sources and pushing me to explore a range of materials. I also want to acknowledge the resources of the Southern Appalachian Archives at Berea College's Hutchins Library.

There are many scholars who have become important guides and friends through their work, though I do not know all of them personally. They have shaped my thinking and ways of seeing and therefore ought to be recognized here. They are John Berger, Pierre Bourdieu, Henry Glassie, Avery Gordon, Archie Green, Robert Orsi, Kathleen Stewart, Michael Taussig, and Raymond Williams. Although they do not all appear in the body or the footnotes of my text, they have been very much a part of my writing.

A few friends deserve special mention for their insights and critical comments on my work: Trish Beckman, Anna Bigelow, Courtney Bender, Darryl Caterine, Lisle Dalton, Steve Friesen, Paul Johnson, John Lardas, Elaine Lawless, Katie Poole, Leonard Primiano, Elijah Siegler, and the late Ninian Smart. I am also indebted to my parents and my grandmothers for their patience, encouragement, and aid both emotional and material throughout my years of writing and revising this book. During that time, both of my grandmothers passed away. I will miss them both greatly. This volume is dedicated to the memory of my paternal grandmother, Helen G. Callahan.

Finally, I would like to thank my wife, Melissa Click, for all of the ways, tangible and intangible, that she has helped me through this process. She has provided a constant ground, helpful criticism, welcome distraction, and emotional support. Trey is lucky to have her for a mother. For all this and more, I thank her.

WORK AND FAITH
IN THE KENTUCKY
COAL FIELDS

INTRODUCTION

I'm afraid today a lot of…people, they're not taking a good long look at this, of where their ancestors and fore-fathers, of where they come from, and what it's cost, up through these years, to have a way of life that we have to enjoy in this great country of ours. It's cost men's lives. It's cost men's lives in the battlefields. It's cost men's lives in the coal fields, because they demanded a better way of life. They demanded something for their children. There was a lot of 'em that died with that very determination. It cost them their lives, and it cost them a lot of things.

—TALMADGE ALLEN, coal miner and
preacher, Floyd County, Kentucky

IN 1931 A REIGN OF TERROR settled over the counties of Harlan and Bell in eastern Kentucky. In May, following a series of violent confrontations between out-of-work coal miners, United Mine Workers of America organizers, and dep-utized mine guards who worked for the interests of mine owners, the governor declared the area a state of terror and lawlessness and sent in the National Guard to maintain order. Any "order" that resulted, however, appeared to be tilted in favor of coal operators, furthering the ongoing disenfranchisement of mine workers. Unable or unwilling to continue its efforts at organizing miners under such conditions, the UMWA soon left the eastern Kentucky coal fields. The

National Guard followed. In their wake they left ongoing tensions and unre-solved conflicts. Desperate for change, a small group of unemployed miners turned to the recently formed National Miners' Union (NMU) for support, orga-nizing a local chapter in July. The controversial union only deepened class divi-sions in Bell and Harlan counties. Mining families continued to face firings, evictions, and violence throughout the summer and fall.

In November, a group of NMU members met in a small Baptist church in the town of Wallins Creek. Their local president, a preacher who worked as a miner, spoke up:

> The time is presented to you in the days when the Children of Israel was under bondage, when Moses went to lead them out.... We have the same opportunity presented to us, laboring men, by the National Miners' Union to walk out as the Children of Israel did, and if you don't drown these Capitalists and this Capital-ism, it is your own bad luck. You can't blame any one but yourself.[1]

The NMU was a Communist organization, a term that meant little or nothing to eastern Kentucky miners. Rather, miners at the November meeting regu-larly drew upon the Bible to characterize the union in prophetic terms. It was not coincidental that the meeting was held in an independent Baptist church or that the local union president, Billy Meeks, was a preacher. He was followed by several other miners who spoke of horrible conditions of labor and who saw in the union the promise of an end to their suffering—and in some cases re-demption.

The NMU did not have a long life in eastern Kentucky. By February 1932, less than a year after the union's first appearance in the area, the majority of its eastern Kentucky members quit when they learned that its Communist national leaders did not believe in God. But despite this outcome, for the period that the NMU was active, its eastern Kentucky members articulated a religious orien-tation to labor resistance that continued, if somewhat less radically, in the subse-quent organizational efforts of the United Mine Workers of America in 1932 and later. To this day miners' labor concerns—and issues of labor more generally—intertwine at a basic level with religious expression, sentiment, and imagination in the coal fields of central Appalachia where eastern Kentucky lies. Throughout the hills one finds memorial monuments to men who died while working in the mines. Local preachers are a common sight at UMWA rallies and strikes. It might not be too far off to say that in the eastern Kentucky coal fields, the labor movement is, in fact, a form of religious expression that has emerged from the struggle to express and meet particular human concerns in the context of industrial capitalism. Indeed, union and nonunion miners alike articulate an orientation to the world that merges religious idiom and material reality through the experience of daily work. For the most part, however, scholars have paid scant attention to the religious expressions that emerged specifically from the labor of mining and the world that miners inhabited. Those studies that have taken the context of industrialization into account are notable for their tendency to focus on extraordinary religious practices—serpent handling comes to mind—as compensation for poverty or social disempowerment.[2] They remain focused almost exclusively on institutional forms of religion, and these they subordinate to economic and psychological factors. But what of the issues of work itself and the ways that people have engaged and imagined the obstacles and promises specific to their livelihoods? How have people and communities worked through their circumstances with the religious and cultural resources at their disposal to forge new meanings, orientations, and practices in relation to pressing material contexts?

The problem is not isolated to eastern Kentucky or central Appalachia in particular. One could make the case that a history of religion in the United States can be written that takes *work* and *labor* as its guiding themes. Nor is this just an American story. In one way or another, all over the world, human beings and societies have labored to survive, to create, and to prosper. The meanings and values of these labors have always been open to conflict and reconsideration, especially as modes of production and exchange transform social and material landscapes and widen (or shrink, as the case may be) boundaries of community and influence. Each context is specific in its nuances, impacts, outcomes, responses, and innovations. Yet the process of orientation and reorientation to self, world, and society through the medium of material production (which is so closely intertwined with cultural production) is fundamental to human experience the world over. Indeed, philosopher Hannah Arendt has argued that these terms—work and labor—are essential and enduring categories in the constitution of human beings and societies, which suggests that they are also essential categories for the study of religion.[3]

Yet American religious history, the context within which the present study is situated, has all but ignored work and the issues of work as a central argument and organizing principle running through the nation's story.[4] When scholars bring religion and work (or labor or economic struggles more generally) together into their conversation, they tend to treat each as an independent variable. The *and* in "religion and work," which keeps the two terms separated, is emphasized, with "religion" occupying one data set in the form of doctrines, institutional affiliations, or organizational structures, and "work" occupying another data set in the form of attitudes, economic or demographic trends, policies, or (again) organizational structures. Work itself as an orienting concept or symbol through which to think about religion and human significance has rarely been taken up. Perhaps this is due in large part to the way that religion itself has been conceived in both American historical scholarship and the academic study of religion more generally, a topic that has been the subject of a great deal of scholarship over the past decade.[5]

Furthermore, reexaminations of historiography have illustrated that the dominant scholarship on religion in America has cast too narrow a net.[6] Even with the current attention to pluralism, Protestant, Catholic, and Jew have remained favored categories. Although beginning to widen, scholarship until recently has rested largely upon institutions, doctrines, theologies, and major thinkers. But these do not exhaust the American religious experience. They barely begin to cover it. The majority of religious actors in America have been those ordinary people who did not write theological tomes, did not contribute to elite doctrinal debates, and did not often record their own histories. They may or may not have belonged to churches—a large number of Americans have always been "unchurched." Yet even many of these remained religiously concerned and active in other ways.

The movement to retell the history of religion in the United States has tended to focus on new questions as well as new venues. Rather than understanding religion simply as what happens in church, some scholars now take an anthropological approach or one associated with the discipline of the history of religions, using different methods and sources to seek out ways that people have made religious sense of their worlds. According to historian Robert Orsi, these new questions redirect scholars "away from traditions—the great hypostatized constructs of 'Protestantism,' 'Catholicism,' and so on—and likewise away from the denominational focus that has so preoccupied scholars of American religions, toward a study of how particular people, in particular places and times, live in, with, through, and against the religious idioms available to them in culture."[7] Such an approach regards religion as an activity rather than as a reified institutional structure or intellectual enterprise. It therefore draws upon such relatively new approaches to the humanistic sciences as cultural studies, social history, and folkloristics. It tends to be ethnographically oriented, even when the study is historical, because what the scholar seeks to describe and understand are the interpretive tactics and strategies by which situated human beings have improvised and acted within their dynamic and changing circumstances. Above all, it is open to unexpected locations and manifestations of religious activity.

One of the most profoundly powerful structures shaping and transforming everyday life in American history has been the development of industrial capitalism and its expansion into every corner of the social world of the nation. Indeed, the story of capitalism's power to expand and transform the parameters of existence—structures of exchange, sources of value and authority, forms of kinship, modes of labor, patterns of movement and settlement, desires and possibilities—is not limited to the United States.[8] It is now the world's story. Where once upon a time human communities focused their religious thought and activities around the hunt or the harvest, more recent world history must take into account the manner in which capitalism, world trade, and a market economy have oriented new religious problems and questions. To cite Robert Orsi again, "Americans have been compelled to make and remake their worlds and themselves endlessly, relentlessly, on constantly shifting grounds, in often brutal economic circumstances, and religion has been one of—if not *the*—primary media through which this work of making and remaking has proceeded."[9] The particular circumstances that provoke religious response in this setting are varied and differ according to the ways in which modern material and social forces are felt in particular communities. One community might be particularly impacted by migration, while another might find the restrictions of an unfriendly legal system to be a significant structuring limit to its potential. In contrast, yet another community might benefit from modern trends and find the world opened to new and unforeseen possibilities. In each of these cases, however, material circumstances inform the parameters of thought, imagination, and practice. Religion, where it is vital and dynamic, is to be found emerging from such circumstances. The form it takes is often unexpected, often drawing upon a vast array of cultural idioms that traditional approaches to the study of religion would have trouble making sense of, and often speaking to practical concerns as much as to transcendent ones.[10] To be clear, this approach does not *reduce* religion to material forces but rather understands religion as human activity that is embedded within them. Human beings live in social and material worlds, and their religious practices inform and are informed by them, giving shape to hopes and fears, anxieties and promises, and the urgent meanings of the present as well as the potentials of the future. Religion ties the extraordinary to the ordinary, in other words, and the particular to something more encompassing.

American religious history has generally neglected the central Appalachian region. Appalachia has been treated as a special case that sits outside of the flow of national history and instead represents a "folk" or regional anomaly.[11] Although American popular culture signifies the Appalachian hills most regularly and ambivalently by images of *religion* (snake handling, foot washing, extemporaneous preaching, innocent and uncorrupted ways of life) and of *economy* (poverty, labor unrest), these two issues are rarely brought together except in causal interpretations that tend either to cast the religious thought and practices of the region—characterized as "fatalistic"—as the psychological result of poverty or, conversely, to see poverty as the result of "fatalistic" religion and culture.[12] In either case, Appalachia is a problem to be solved, rather than a representative case of American cultural development and performance. As Deborah Vansau McCauley, one of the few historians of Appalachian religion, has written, "American Protestantism in particular has historically and consistently interpreted the worship practices, belief systems, and church traditions of mountain people as the religion of a subculture of poverty and the product of powerlessness and alienation."[13] To further understand how late nineteenth-century Protestant views of religion and society in Appalachia have powerfully structured subsequent inquiries—defining the lay of the land, so to speak—it is helpful to review how Appalachia emerged in American consciousness as a distinct and identifiable region.

Appalachia on Our Religious Mind

According to historian Henry D. Shapiro's innovative *Appalachia on Our Mind*, Appalachia was born during the 1880s. The context of its birth was not "a reinterpretation of a newly discovered fact," Shapiro has argued. "Rather it followed from the recognition that the well-known realities of southern mountain life were not consonant with new notions about the nature of America and American civilization which gained currency during this period: that America was, or was becoming, or ought to become a unified and homogeneous national entity, and that what characterized such an entity was a coherent and uniform national culture."[14] Following the powerful symbol of the Union's victory in the Civil

War, the United States began to heal its wounds and tried to dilute regional differences by reimagining itself as a unified body. The symbol of national unity and the material reality of modern transportation and communication systems such as the railroad and the telegraph combined to effect a real change in the conception of national space. With the aid of these technological developments, American citizens were more readily able to think of themselves as inhabitants of a unified national community, even as the nation grew larger and larger.[15] Local places subordinated their identity under the idea of the nation as a whole, while infrastructural interconnections throughout the nation increased the ease and speed with which people could traverse the landscape. In the midst of this, according to cultural historians such as Shapiro and Allen W. Batteau, artists and writers represented Appalachia—or rather the idea of Appalachia in the mind of the American public—by the elaboration of what they saw as the area's "colorful" regional differences.[16] By the 1880s the southern mountains had come to signify a complex and sometimes contradictory web of meanings in popular imagination, all of which had at least one thing in common: that the region, its people, and its culture were radically different from the rest of America. Appalachia stood out from the united nation, and the newly developed and widely popular urban middle-class magazine industry, including *Harper's, Lippincott's,* and the *Atlantic,* represented the difference most thoroughly in articles on "local color" and travel writing.[17] It was these sources of "cultural production" that tooled the techniques by which Appalachia came to be regarded as "Other" and an isolated "wilderness." Popular and scholarly writing on the region by the late nineteenth century interpreted its Otherness both geographically and temporally; because of geographic isolation, the story went, the mountains had become a "retarded frontier" that had remained outside of the stream of progress enjoyed by the rest of the country.[18] Some accounts had the people of the region stuck in time 150 years ago, still speaking Elizabethan English.[19] When "suddenly the 'retarded frontier' was rediscovered" in the 1880s, social worker Olive Dame Campbell wrote in 1925, two types of people rushed in, "those who saw the natural resources and sought them regardless of the interests of the natural owners; and those who with missionary zeal rushed in to educate and reform."[20] The otherness of the mountains, used as a literary device for the romantic imagination, also "became a major justification for the swift acquisition of mountain land and resources by outsiders" when the timber and coal industries began to buy up property and build infrastructures in the 1880s, according to Ronald D. Eller. Eller notes that the themes of "uplift" and "Americanization" used by missionaries and industrialists highlighted the fact that, for them, the "otherness" of Appalachia meant that the religious and economic progress shared by the rest of the nation had somehow passed the region by.[21]

Various interpretations of religion and society in the region have either implicitly or explicitly drawn upon this "invented" Appalachia and participated in the maintenance of its construction.[22] Both scholarly and popular treatments in the twentieth century have incorporated the isolationist, retarded frontier model that directed early twentieth-century missionary work in the mountains. The effect has been that they have often continued the discussion about the southern mountains that was begun during the late nineteenth century, taking the mountains as a problem that needed solving without examining critically the site from which the problem was being posed. In other words, studies of religion treated the dominant Protestant denominations of the United States and industrial progress as the norm and wondered why Appalachia did not follow the patterns of American life. The focus, then, was on churches and doctrines.

When, in recent decades, scholars have turned their attention to the interaction between religion and the industrialization, they have tended to follow suit. Such studies point to the important place of religion in the transformations of society, economy, and labor in Appalachia at the dawning of the twentieth century. Yet they tend to suffer to a greater or lesser extent from two problems. First, they remain too focused on churches and institutionalized religion. That is surely a part of the story, but religion reaches beyond churches and, especially in settings of profound change like the one in question, finds expression in new and unusual venues as individuals and communities encounter and create new worlds and their attendant possibilities. Second, and extending from the first, these studies assume too much of a differentiation between religion and other aspects of life. This book seeks to learn from these studies but to go beyond them to explore the religious dimensions and expressions emergent from the intersections of life and work.[23]

In addition to the focus on work, a few other concerns have influenced my perspective and approach in the writing of this book. First, I have been thinking about religion as itself a kind of work, always in process as it is produced and reproduced in particular settings. Religion does not exist without people practicing it, and those people are always embedded firmly in concrete historical, social, material, and cultural settings. They are individuals with their own particular histories informing their relationship to the world around them, and they are members of communities that live among other communities. All of the dynamics that go into the construction and maintenance of boundaries between self and other; all of the forces shaping social and cultural patterns and perceptions; all of the structures, strategies, and tactics of power that impact the contours of life in a particular place and time—all of these things, and more, go into the manifestations and meanings of religion as it is lived. Religion, as it appears in the lives of real people, then, is always at the intersection of tradition and innovation, a work in progress that draws from historical and institutional idioms but at the same time remakes them for particular purposes. This process is not unique to religion; it is the work of all cultural forms. However, it is important to recognize that religion is not a thing apart from this process.

Understanding that religion is always performed and practiced in particular settings leads to my second interest, which is the relationship between religion and everyday life. The concept of "everyday life" has a multifaceted scholarly history, shaped by studies of folklore and folklife, sociology, Marxist critical theory, and ethnographic approaches to historical research.[24] Everyday life is mundane; it is sometimes repetitive and it is made up of the ordinary routines, experiences, and locations in which persons carry out their common individual and social existences. It is therefore often overlooked in studies of religion, which tend to focus on the extraordinary and exceptional as the domain of religious concern, as in the dichotomy between *sacred* and *profane* that is central to important theories of religion. If the everyday is the profane, then it is the opposite of religion, according to theorists such as Emile Durkheim and Mircea Eliade.[25] Yet, of course, religion, as it is lived, is lived in and through daily life. And in this setting, it is messy, ambivalent, and sometimes inconsistent, at odds with the often highly structured ideals presented by doctrines, theologies, and the portraits of traditions painted by scholars.[26] So my interest in the intersections of religion and work is more specifically conditioned by a focus on the ways that work structures everyday life and how that life is imagined and articulated in religiously significant ways, while it also shapes the way that religion is imagined and practiced.

Third, in the context of working people's everyday lives, I have been interested in the place and role of the body and the senses in the process of mediating the world as experienced. This concern has led me to pay special attention to the way that coal miners understood and represented their daily life and work through talk about their pains and nerves, the dustiness of mining, and the way that coal "gets in the blood." The individual knows his or her world through the senses, an obvious statement but one that has not always informed the way that scholars approach religion.[27] In the case of manual laborers, whose daily lives are filled with hard work, bodily sensations are all the more relevant. Through the body the individual not only knows the world but makes the world, and is a part of the world in and through which he or she makes him or herself. Likewise, in cultures of work, communities of workers share the sensual experiences of their labor: senses are thus not only individual and subjective but also shared by others who know what it means to do the same work. I have found Raymond Williams's notion of "structures of feeling" useful as a way to think about the ways that a particular material social and cultural setting can structure feelings and perceptions in ways that are not always able to be fully articulated and rationalized at the time, but that nonetheless are shared and "known" by those living in that setting. In this book, I have looked to the importance of the sensual body and its centrality in miners' representations of work and life as one avenue to explore the ways that material conditions can give rise to religious expression and as a key to understanding the significance of religious practices such as Pentecostal-Holiness religion to tactile, embodied experience in the coal fields.

Dust

The subtitle of this book, *Subject to Dust,* is borrowed from one miner's tape-recorded oral history of life in the eastern Kentucky coal fields in the 1920s and 1930s. I chose it for its multiple interpretive possibilities that make it a potent metaphor for imagining the world of coal mining, its religious potential, and the work of recovering the history of religion in the everyday life of working people in the United States.[28] On the one hand, it is a concrete, empirical description of the appearance of a coal town: it is subject to dust from the constant blasting, chipping, and transporting of coal. Coal towns were notoriously covered in coal dust, as were the miners who dug the coal. It was impossible to escape the significance of dust in descriptions of work and life in the coal fields. Focusing on the dust was a way of remembering and representing the concrete, tactile, material dimension of the work of mining. It also suggests the overwhelming presence of industrial coal mining as it overtook all aspects of life in the first decades of the twentieth century in the eastern Kentucky mountains.

Further, "subject to dust" resonates with a theological perspective common in the Appalachian mountains, recognizing the physical world as mortal, limited, and ultimately reducible to dust. It is a point of view that contrasts sharply with "modernist" theologies in its devaluation of the material world in favor of a more real, more enduring spiritual reality that lies beyond death and contingency. But it is also a statement of the awareness and acceptance of the limitations of the world that gives meaning and significance to the hardships of working life.

Finally, it can be read as a remark on history: the stories and lives of coal miners and other working people are themselves subject to dust, crumbling and blowing away, and therefore they risk not being represented in historical work—not least in histories of American religion. Likewise, the sources required to access and recover the lives of working people are also subject to being overlooked and forgotten. The largest difficulty for a study of this type is the scarcity of sources. As social historians and students of everyday life know, the lives of ordinary people are often notoriously difficult to recover. They did not write books, nor did they keep detailed records. In some cases they might have written letters or a diary, but those are rarely preserved. In the case of eastern Kentucky, the high degree of illiteracy and a culture based upon orality make the situation yet more difficult. And, of course, coal miners rarely had the time or inclination to write very much down. Even the indigenous organized churches have kept little in the way of records, again because they are orally based and have few resources. Any recovery of the world of miners, then, as opposed to industrialists and missionaries, must seek different sources.

I have drawn from primary sources when they have been available, including newspapers, missionary reports, travel writing, and local histories. In many cases I have had to read these texts "against the grain," evaluating their descriptions for their biases. For example, it is crucial to understand the background recited above in which missionaries and local color writers were situated when they produced their descriptions, interpretations, and evaluations of religious practices and beliefs in the central Appalachian mountains in order to appreciate more fully the perceptions and assumptions out of which those texts were woven. Their biases do not disqualify the sources from usefulness. On the contrary, knowing the context of production opens up the texts, revealing them to be not "objective" descriptions but particular arguments, cultural practices in the work of cultural interpretation. No text, of course, is anything but this. Approaching historical resources in this vein, then, is ultimately not about weeding out the "objective" from the "biased," but rather situating perspectives in a field of relations that acknowledges effects that social location has on perception and understanding.[29]

Besides these written sources, however, I have also looked to songs, stories, and narratives documented by folklorists as a way to access eastern Kentucky's culture. These are important resources for two reasons. First, they can help to fill in gaps where primary sources are absent. In many cases these are the only cultural expressions available that were produced by the people themselves. They offer a glimpse into the way that people made something of their worlds in symbols and in practice. And this leads to their second import: history can tell us what happened, but folklore, folklife, and song give access to something more than what happened. They reveal what sorts of idioms were available to people to express the significance of events, persons, and emotions. They can, at times, allow entrance into the internal world that newspaper reports, for instance, sometimes do not permit. It is through such items as these that scholars can begin to explore the links between different aspects of life, to see the connections that people were making between their religious imagination and their daily life.

I have also been fortunate that eastern Kentucky and Appalachia more generally had something of a cultural awakening in the 1970s. Suddenly intrigued by their own heritage and traditions, and wanting to document them as a resource, many colleges and other institutions in the southern mountains began oral history projects. Armed with notepads and tape recorders, students and researchers headed into the hills and coal camps to collect life histories and stories. I have been able to make extensive use of some of these collections. Two in particular have been especially helpful: the Appalachian Oral History Project, carried out by the combined forces of Alice Lloyd College, Appalachian State University, Emory and Henry College, and Lees Junior College; and the Social Change and Cultural History in the Elkhorn Coal Field Oral History Project, 1987–88, contained at the Louie B. Nunn Center for Oral History at the University of Kentucky Libraries.

The use of oral history has some inherent problems associated with it, which have been discussed at length by oral historians and folklorists.[30] For my purposes, the biggest concern has been the relationship between memory and reality. Since the oral histories I use were recorded in the 1970s, it might be said that they actually say more about eastern Kentucky consciousness and uses of the past during the late twentieth century than they do about the realities of life in coal mining and coal towns in the 1920s and 1930s. To that, I offer no objection.

In fact, I have been intrigued, listening to the tapes, by exactly that: they tend to construct history in very interesting ways, treating the preindustrial farms as an idealized past while seeing the development of the coal industry as a fall from that paradise, a real historical moment of worldly decline that is also religious metaphor. For most miners, the coming of the United Mine Workers of America and its president, John L. Lewis, was nothing less than salvation from slavery, degradation, and sin. It is not uncommon to hear Lewis linked with Jesus Christ in oral histories. So there is the real problem of memory versus "reality." And yet those constructions of memory are part and parcel of those people whose lives were transformed by the coal industry itself, working in its mines under the ground. Those memories are a part of "what happened."

I have tried, wherever possible, to compare oral histories with documents from the time to ensure that they do, in fact, have something to do with the period. This has been a useful method and one that I think ensures that what I am hearing in oral histories, though not coming from the mouths of miners in the 1920s and 1930s, is consistent with the expressions of the time. There will always be some distance and difference here, but that is the case no matter what the sources. As the history of scholarship on eastern Kentucky and Appalachia attests, even primary documents produced contemporaneously with the events under consideration are located in fields of power, their authors selecting and interpreting what they see and say in that context. I have chosen to consider oral history sources much as I would other sources; the relation of the source to the "reality" is never a direct correspondence, but is always shaped by mediating factors whether they be ideology, experience, social location, space, time, or other forces or circumstances. The work of the scholar is to come to know, as best he or she can, the social and cultural worlds that are the subject of the study, including the matrices of power and influence, so that he or she can make educated guesses and informed interpretations about the relations of the sources to each other and to representations of events.[31]

Oral history sources also raise the issue of the differences between regional vernacular speech and grammatically and syntactically "proper" English. Some readers are sure to note instances of this in some quotations. Rather than interrupting the flow of the text with repeated use of "[sic]," which is both judgmental and cumbersome, I have chosen to transcribe the words of eastern Kentucky residents as they were spoken. Some locally written documents occasionally also contain "nonstandard" English, and again in these cases I have treated the local vernacular as a legitimate, long-standing pattern of language use. Also in keeping with my decision to respect the vernacular, I use the term *Holiness* to refer to phenomena that are usually associated with Pentecostalism. In central Appalachia, "Holiness" includes a range of behavior and belief within the Holiness-Pentecostal spectrum.

Overview of the Book

In what follows, I attempt to situate religion in the context of the transformation of eastern Kentucky patterns of life from subsistence farming to coal mining—most Appalachian residents who went into coal mining came from a background of subsistence farming. In exploring this history I have focused my attention on white miners native to central Appalachia. Although this demographic was the largest among eastern Kentucky coal miners, African Americans and European immigrants also made up relatively substantial numbers of mineworkers at various times during the period of industrialization. Their stories are important, and the history of eastern Kentucky coal mining would be misrepresented without including their experiences and the intersections and exchanges between all the peoples that made up the industry. This book is not intended as a general study of coal miners or coal mining society, however, and is more limited in its scope. Central Appalachia is often represented as a homogeneously white Protestant region, but coal towns defied this description. Much work is left to be done recovering the history of diversity in the mountains.

Chapter 1 provides an overview of religion in Appalachia. After surveying historical roots of Appalachian religious culture and the development of a distinctive tradition of organized worship and churches in the region, I turn to explore the wider central Appalachian mountain culture, particularly paying attention to practices that are usually classified as "folk belief" or "superstition." These practices reveal a religious culture deeply embedded within material life and practical concerns, linking world and spirit in a powerful, sacramental manner. It directs attention beyond churches to discover some of the ways that religion appeared in everyday life. Chapter 2 brings us into eastern Kentucky specifically. Drawing from oral histories and building upon the work of previous studies, this chapter begins by recovering the patterns of life and work that made up the world of subsistence farming. Here *work* is an important center in individual, community, and cosmic patterns. The chapter continues with a look at the ways that economic changes at the turn of the century were expressed on a religious register.

The everyday life of coal towns is the subject of chapter 3. This chapter teases out the anxieties and desires contained in this new world of diversity, capitalism, and industrial power, and it traces disruptions, transformations, and continuities of older rural patterns of life and orientation. The chapter ends with a look at the changing topography of organized religion in coal towns and commercial centers. Chapter 4 moves to an exploration of religious expressions that emerged from that coal mining world, in particular those relating to the embodied experience of the work of mining coal. Again drawing upon oral histories, songs, folklore, and other primary sources, this chapter pays special attention to images of bodies, the play of the senses, and social obligations as miners navigated and articulated the forces of industrial mining through religious idioms.

These expressions had an organized form, too, in the Holiness and Pentecostal churches that grew in popularity in the coal fields during this time. Chapter 5 is a more synthetic and speculative discussion about Holiness religion's emergence and popularity in the coal fields. Holiness crystallized the structures of feeling of the industrial mining lifeworld, I argue, and provided a powerful outlet for symbolic engagement with and resistance to the dilemmas posed by material and social realities of industrial mining. As a highly sacramental expression of traditional mountain religious culture, it focused on the body and its limitations as a point of access to the Holy Spirit and a reality beyond the visible world. It was also thoroughly modern, emerging from and attending to the particular context of industrial life.

Finally, in chapter 6, I cover the complex religious meanings of the labor movement that emerged in the 1930s. The Communistic National Miners' Union took on religious meaning for many miners, and their narratives and testimonies offer insight into the ways that the issues investigated in the prior chapters connected to organized labor. But the National Miners' Union (NMU) was not liked by everyone, and the revelation of its atheistic leanings led to its downfall. This chapter ends with a discussion of the possibilities and limits of religious resistance expressed by the brief life of the NMU. The story of religion and work, of course, continued far beyond the 1932 date that marks the end of this study, but 1932 seemed a good place to stop. By this time the massive transformations of daily life had taken place, and the dynamics that went into the reception of the NMU illuminate the possibilities of the religious significance of organized labor. The NMU serves as a particular case study, as one of the first occasions of organized resistance to industrial power in eastern Kentucky. After 1932 the legal landscape changed nationally for organized labor, and the United Mine Workers of America engaged in a long and often violent effort to organize eastern Kentucky's coal fields.[32] This story, and other intersections of work and religion including the continuing issue of "foreign" religious agencies who targeted native mountain mining families for various types of assistance and uplift, deserve their own careful study.

I have lived with the history of eastern Kentucky's coal miners for many years now, and come to know their voices and labors as they have drawn me into their world. In this book I hope to move readers into this world. I cannot speak from the world of the coal mines, of which I am not a part, but instead I try to allow miners and their families to speak, and I work to fill in the gaps, to the best of my ability, so that together the reader and I may move into their labors and, I hope, come to know them and ourselves anew.

ONE

APPALACHIAN MOUNTAIN RELIGION

HIGHWAY 119 IN SOUTHEASTERN KENTUCKY runs roughly parallel to the Virginia border from Pineville, the seat of Bell County, through Harlan and Letcher counties to Jenkins, built as a company town by Consolidation Coal Company. There it merges with Highway 23 and continues northeast through Pike County to Pikeville. This is coal country. Highway 119 connects town after town that together have played a central role in the history of coal mining in the area. Small side roads spur off of Highway 119 and wind through the tightly clustered mountains through towns that owe their origins to coal: once company-owned coal camps and coal towns, they were built for the sole purpose of housing miners and their families in the 1910s and 1920s. Similar-looking houses, arranged close together, line each side of the road in rows. As you drive along Highway 119 and these densely forested side roads with hills and kudzu-covered trees closing in on every side, here and there a coal tipple looms out from the greenery or stands silhouetted against the mountain backdrop. The tipples appear simultaneously to be a break in the natural landscape and yet a part of it, their chutes extending into the trees like tentacles and disappearing into the wooded hillsides. It is not uncommon to find yourself stuck behind a slowly moving truck loaded with heavy coal as it struggles to climb the mountain road, or to be stopped at a railroad crossing where coal-laden train cars creep by, dominating the rhythm of movement. Coal mining is as much a part of these hills as the trees.

The road also takes you past small, unassuming churches, usually located off the side roads in the smaller towns or situated in the stretches of road that wind between them. These are not the large stone churches that stand solidly down-town in larger places like Harlan or Pineville. They are more humble, usually one-room structures and made of wood. There is little that explicitly marks their sacred purpose other than a simple sign designating each as "Old Regular Baptist," or "Primitive Baptist," or "Holiness." They seem to belong here, perhaps because of preconceptions produced by countless images of the Appalachian mountain culture in popular media, or perhaps by the way that they fit in with the architecture of houses and the peaceful surroundings.

Here and there, too, hanging by a nail from trees on the side of the road, are hand-painted signs on wood with prophetic messages: "Jesus is coming" and "Death is coming, Jesus saves." They appear as you come around a corner or emerge from the dense foliage as you approach, declaring a silent warning that points beyond this moment in time and place toward a larger drama.

In the midst of the churches, the signs, and the small family cemeteries that also dot the roadside, the drive down Highway 119 and its side roads evokes a complex and densely structured sense that here nature, the human, and the divine interweave, producing a haunting sense of the everydayness of life, death, and mystery. Nature is close here, present to the eyes, nose, and ears, not distant. The dominating industry does not separate people from nature in the way that factories might, but rather brings them right into it—right inside mountains. Coal mining, it might be argued, is a classic example of the domination of nature by human beings. But the impact of mine accidents and the treacherous steepness of roads that wind across and around the hills green with thick foliage make it clear that nature has not entirely been tamed here. Meanwhile, the churches and graveyards, and especially the prophetic and somewhat eerie signs, produce an aura of haunted presence: this place, as Flannery O'Connor once said of the South in general, is "Christ haunted."[1] The landscape in southeastern Kentucky, both human and natural, shimmers with the presence of something just beyond the visible.

But there is more to the haunted nature of the coal fields. It has a source in human history that helps to energize its power. Pulling into the town of Benham, for example—another company town, this one built as a "model town" that was planned and designed from the outset in 1910 to provide for all the needs of International Harvester's employees—you can visit the Kentucky Coal Mine Museum, housed in a large stone building that was once the town's company store. Immense chunks of coal stand on the sidewalk before the museum, concretely displaying the material and symbolic source of Benham's history. Behind the museum is a grassy park with an old train car and a brick wall that lines the hillside. This is the Coal Miners' Memorial Park. Each brick in the wall has a name on it, and each name commemorates the life of a miner who died in the line of work or a person who wanted to memorialize those who died. Many eastern Kentucky towns have such memorials. In Lynch, another "model town," it is a black rock with over 300 names inscribed on it, set atop a stone base in front of United States Steel's Mine Portal 31. Harlan's memorial stands before the courthouse downtown, reminiscent of a tombstone with two large light-colored stone slabs flanking a shiny black stone. Engraved with a picture of a miner, the stone announces that it has been placed here "In Honor of the Harlan County Coal Miners Who Sacrificed Their Lives While Supporting a Family and a Nation." The flanking pillars are inscribed with a seemingly unending list of names.[2]

If the South is Christ-haunted, then eastern Kentucky is additionally haunted by the ghosts of coal mining. The land, the monuments, and the narratives of place all speak to the omnipresence of coal as a bearer of life and death, where culture and nature, life and livelihood, meet. The life stories of people who live in these mountains are so frequently shaped by references to coal mining that it quickly becomes clear that the coal industry is more than a source of employment. It structures a sense of place and orientation. For those who live here, the names listed on memorials to coal mining fatalities are names of ancestors and relatives who are recalled and honored at annual family and community reunion meetings. The dead are present in their absence, haunting the landscape and drawing attention—by the manner of their deaths—to the very everyday matters of work, even as they provoke awareness of *something else*. That *something else* points to a world beyond this one and to the invisible powers that shape and run through this world—powers that may have their sources in things social or economic no less than in things spiritual. The boundaries between these forces are unclear as they intertwine, shaping and leaving their traces on the daily lives of those who live in southeast Kentucky's coal fields.

As this description suggests, the sacred and the everyday are not easily separated here. The everyday world of work, dominated since the beginning of the twentieth century by industrial coal mining, has defined the contours of experience and textured the way that the sacred is imagined and expressed. In order to understand this aspect of the religious life of the eastern Kentucky coal fields, it will be necessary to know something of the history of religion in the area prior to industrialization and something of how it shaped the culture. There is never a definite "starting point" to history; there is always something that came before that influences the possibilities of how people will respond to and interact with new events, crises, or discoveries. Industrialization, no more or less than anything else, took place in the context of already established, densely textured social and cultural arenas that provided idioms, ideas, and gestures by means of which people would engage the changing dynamics of their situation. Moreover, the new context of industrialization could not help but inform further cultural and social developments. Industrial coal mining set the new context in, through, and against which the people of eastern Kentucky acted and thought religiously as they experienced the world, other people, and themselves. It is important, therefore, to explore the history of Appalachian mountain religion as background to understanding the religious resources that made up miners' responses to industrial coal mining.

Appalachian Mountain Religion

Eastern Kentucky lies in the midst of the regional cultural area known as southern Appalachia, which is distinct from the Bluegrass region of Kentucky to its west geographically, historically, and culturally. Whereas Appalachian Kentucky is mountainous, the Bluegrass is flat; where the latter enjoys high social and financial capital, the former conjures images of poverty and ignorance in the popular imagination. Popular stereotypes of Appalachian Kentucky are for the most part products of the twentieth century and derive from the devastation that has resulted from the region's economic dependence upon the coal industry. However, the image of the mountains as a place set apart and distinctly different from the rest of America—economically, socially, culturally, and religiously—first emerged in the late nineteenth century, just before the incursion of industrial capitalism into the area.[3]

The geographical area of the Appalachian region is meaningful not only because it delineates a place but also because the place's physical features have helped to create a cohesive social and cultural identity. Europeans began settling these lands in the eighteenth century, but by the middle of the nineteenth century more accessible westward routes bypassed the obstructing mountains and left them a low priority, even ignored, by developments in transportation, communication, and commerce that were uniting other regions across the nation. The southern Appalachian region, though never completely isolated, remained remote enough that by the 1880s visitors to the area described it as a "retarded frontier" where inhabitants led a peculiar way of life, unchanged over the prior century or more.[4] Religion was cited as one of the primary signifiers of the area's distinctiveness, along with dialect. Indeed, by the late nineteenth century Appalachia was home to a style of Protestant worship that looked quite different from those varieties practiced in much of the rest of the United States. It would be a mistake to conclude, as many observers of the nineteenth and twentieth centuries did, that the religion and culture of the mountains was simply ignorant, "backwards," or frozen in time.[5] It was more complicated than that. In the hills, through a combination of historical developments and ways of inhabiting the landscape, the residents of the region formed a repertoire of practices—ways of talking and doing—that continue to inform their cultural and religious environment today. The seeds of this culture can be traced to those first European settlers of the Appalachian region in the late eighteenth century, though subsequent factors shaped how those seeds would grow.

The white mountain population originated from three primary ethnic backgrounds. These were Germans, who came primarily from the Palatine area to southern Pennsylvania in the early eighteenth century; Scotch-Irish from Ulster in the north of Ireland, who also initially settled in Pennsylvania and the Middle Colonies; and English, especially Nonconformist dissenters from the Anglican church in Virginia. Each of these groups moved southward and westward as their populations grew, establishing themselves throughout the middle and southern colonies. The coming of the Wilderness Road, blazed by Daniel Boone in 1770, opened the door for their westward migration through the Appalachian mountains. The Scotch-Irish were the first to take this route in substantial numbers, supplemented by a smaller number of Germans, both of whom followed the Wilderness Road from Pennsylvania and settled in the valleys or continued westward out of the mountains. Some English were also among this early group. After the Revolutionary War, German and Scotch-Irish immigration along the Wilderness Road route slowed as westward-bound travelers favored a more northerly path through Ohio, a route protected from Indian attacks with the requisitioning of English forts. Migration into the mountains after 1790 came mainly from eastern portions of Virginia and was strongly made up of dissenters from Anglican authority who sought refuge in the mountains.[6]

Each of these groups brought with them distinctive but related religious traditions that shaped what would become the region's religious culture. The Scotch-Irish were Presbyterians, whose Calvinistic theology and traditions of sacramental revivalism profoundly impacted the religious culture of southern Appalachia. The English were Nonconformists, Puritans who dissented from the Church of England and emphasized decentralized, congregational-style churches and local governance. The Germans included members of the Reformed church and Lutherans, but many were from more radical Pietist and Anabaptist backgrounds that stressed personal religious experience, perfectionism, and practices such as foot washing and baptism by full immersion. All of these parties shared left-wing Protestant foundations. Puritans, Presbyterians, and Reformed were Calvinist, while Pietists and Anabaptists thought that Calvin had not gone far enough in his reforms of Christianity, thus setting the stage for the development of a regional religious culture whose self-identity thrived on the boundary work of distinction and separation.

Not long after these peoples began settling into the mountains, a period of activity began that was crucial to the formation of Appalachian mountain religion and to American religious history in general. It came to be known as the Second Great Awakening, and its southern frontier counterpart—the Great Revival—began west of the mountains in Kentucky around 1801. Historians credit the Second Great Awakening with spreading a common evangelical style across American Protestantism, "democratizing" Christianity and restructuring the landscape of religious authority in the country through the use of widespread revivalism.[7] It also created an environment that allowed the various ingredients of Appalachian religion to mix together into a particular regional religious culture.

Revivalism was familiar to the Scotch-Irish, whose Presbyterian background in rural Ulster included a yearly cycle of late-summer sacramental revival meetings.[8] They continued this practice in the middle colonies and carried it with them into the mountains. It was also familiar to the Baptists. Revivals took place in the form of protracted camp meetings that often lasted for weeks at a time. Set up outdoors and attended by people from near and far, camp meetings drew both sinners and saved; they were social events as much as religious ones. Their widespread popularity and accessibility among both churchgoers and non-churchgoers alike helped to foster a common language and repertoire of gestures and idioms that pervaded Appalachian society. The hallmarks of camp meetings were the emotional, dramatic preaching and the experience of individual conversion. Both quickly entered the vernacular of Appalachian religion. According to revival rhetoric, human life was to be understood as an individual drama of sin and salvation, culminating in the radical transformation of the conversion experience. Preachers, taking their initial cues from scriptural texts, launched into stylized improvisations that were said to be inspired by the Holy Spirit. They stressed highly tactile, visceral images that worked on the emotions of their audiences, the sinfulness of human nature, and the inability of individuals to save themselves from the fires of eternal damnation. Alternately, they spoke of the saving grace of Jesus and the Holy Spirit that would provide the comforts and safety of eternal salvation and heavenly reward for the saved. Those who experienced conversion—being convicted of their sinfulness and feeling the weight of their mortality, followed by an assurance of salvation signaled by the *felt* presence of grace in the form of the Holy Spirit lifting their burdens away, often accompanied by tears of joy—were able to affirm their place among the saints (the preferred term for the elect). Conversion was followed by full-immersion baptism in a running stream.

At camp meetings this drama of salvation played itself out in public performances before hundreds, perhaps thousands. Even those who were not "religious"—not regular attendees of a church—learned and shared this dramatic structure of imagination that shaped an understanding of the human journey in which salvation could come through no cause or decision of one's own, at any place, at any time (though nearly always in adult life). The potential for such perfection always existed, but always just beyond the power of the will. Appalachian revival culture, therefore, was a model of human humility in the face of greater power, yet at the same time it instilled a constant awareness of that power and the possibility that it could break through into the world. On the other hand, temptation was also always present, calling one away from the life of perfection. Revivalism taught that the drama of salvation was often episodic and that the converted might still "backslide" into a world of sin and alienation from the Spirit.[9] The righteous life required discipline, alertness, and community.

In this context, to be a "Christian" took a meaning that is common in Appalachia but foreign to mainstream American Christianity. The Christian tradition dominated and shaped religious and cultural life in the mountains. In that sense, almost everyone was "Christian," insofar as the symbols, idioms, and concepts of Christianity—regionally articulated—intertwined with and shaped the wider culture. However, in Appalachia, attending church or reading the Bible or quoting scripture or praying to Jesus did not entitle an individual to call him or herself a "Christian." That term was reserved for the saved who had experienced conversion and been baptized. Mountain churches rejected the idea of infant baptism and with it the idea that one might be "saved" or a "Christian" from birth. Indeed, it was rare to hear of conversions at an age younger than adolescence, and a great many people did not experience salvation until late adulthood. It is common today to hear people in eastern Kentucky say that they are not Christian, despite occasional or even frequent church attendance. I will return to this point later when I explore a wider meaning of *religion* than that found in churches.

As for organized religion in the mountains, the Great Revival and its camp meetings mixed and redistributed the traditions brought by the original cast of settlers.[10] By emphasizing the power and presence of the Holy Spirit as the source of religious authority, the charismatic and inspired preachers of protracted camp meetings legitimized the religious authority of ordinary people, those without formal religious training, so long as their preaching appeared to be inspired by the Spirit and in keeping with the Bible. Many of the early white residents of the mountains were Presbyterians, but the Presbyterian Church did not fare well in the mountains. It was a highly organized institution that waited for settled and established communities to call upon a presbytery—the governing body—when they desired a minister.[11] Their ministers were seminary trained and ordained. In contrast, Baptists and Methodists, instigators and products of the revivals themselves, early on embraced untrained preachers. Their ranks swelled throughout the South, including the mountains where they were joined by a growth of independent, nondenominational local churches.

Over the course of the nineteenth century, the religious culture of Appalachia increasingly diverged from that of the rest of the country. The story of Old Regular Baptists provides a good example of this process and illustrates some of the concerns that have shaped mountain religious culture. Exploring this history has the additional advantage of being particularly relevant to the development of religion in eastern Kentucky where the Old Regular Baptist church dominated the religious landscape at the time of the introduction of industrial coal mining. Although the Old Regular Baptists are only one "subdenomination" of Baptists within the mountains, they are in many ways representative. Their differences with other Baptist subdenominations, independent nondenominational churches, and other churches in Appalachia illustrate the contours of religious concern that bound the regional culture.

The New Salem Association of United Baptists, the original of all Old Regular Baptist churches, formed in 1825 in eastern Kentucky. It was made up of churches in Letcher, Floyd, Perry, Breathitt, and Pike counties.[12] An "association" was a group of individual churches that fellowshipped with each other and met yearly to check up on each others' doctrine and practice; governance was left in the hands of individual churches, though in the case of a disagreement within an association, a church might be "disassociated" or choose to disassociate itself. The United Baptists were formed of the union in 1801 between Regular Baptists and Separate Baptists who had earlier split over doctrinal issues related to atonement. Regulars had held a doctrine of predestination or "particular" atonement, preaching that only an elect few were predestined to be saved, and the particulars of who was saved and who condemned were preordained by God. Separates, on the other hand, had held to "general" or "universal" atonement preaching that salvation was possible for all. When they came together in the atmosphere of the Great Revival, they agreed upon a modified Calvinist doctrine that represented the general theological position that was more or less shared throughout Appalachian religious culture: they retained the doctrines of total depravity and the perseverance of the saints, but compromised between Calvinist and Arminian positions on atonement and free will.[13] While strict Calvinism held that human beings could do nothing to affect their salvation—election or damnation was predestined—Arminians put the onus of salvation on the freely made choice of the individual. The modified doctrine of the New Salem Association said that human beings could do nothing to save themselves, that only God's grace could initiate the call to salvation. However, once called by the experience of grace and the Holy Spirit, human beings made the choice to cooperate in their salvation or reject it. Thus the New Salem Association's middle way (shared by Appalachian religious culture more generally) emphasized the presence of the Holy Spirit and its evidence through subjective felt experience and emotional expression in singing, shouting, tears, and energetic preaching.

In practice, the worship style was strongly related to that of the Great Revival. But revivalism's logic and many leaders of the Second Great Awakening embraced an Arminianism that the New Salem Association rejected. As Baptist churches multiplied throughout the nation, they tended to embrace a doctrine of general or universal atonement. These General Baptists formed state organizations, keeping with the ideal of local congregational autonomy but increasingly widening the boundaries of association statewide through the early nineteenth century. The effect was a gradual centralization of organization, even as central organization remained in tension with Baptist ideals of local control. By 1814 the General Missionary Convention of Baptists was organized, later to be called the Triennial Convention. The Triennial Convention formed the foundation for the nationalization of Baptists, which by 1845 issued in the Southern Baptist Convention.

Against this background, the 1825 date of the founding of the New Salem Association of United Baptists is important because it calls attention to three important developments in the differentiation of Appalachian Baptist history from the direction that Baptists were moving nationally. First, Appalachian Baptists chose not to associate with larger, nonmountain, national Baptist organizations in existence at the time. Their associations remained limited and local, and they privileged congregational independence. The formation of the New Salem Association can be seen as a reassertion of local association and rejection of larger national ties. Second, Appalachian Baptists declared their opposition to a theory of general atonement, embraced by the Triennial Convention as revealed by its missionary motives. Third, the same missionary movement that was helping to shape the national Baptist denominations and their priorities (which were shared by other American evangelical Protestants) stirred an antimission sentiment that was heavily represented in Appalachia. The subdenominations that would become Old Regular Baptists, Primitive Baptists, and their variations came down strongly in opposition to missions, saying they were human inventions that were not biblical. In part their reasoning derived from their anti-Arminian theology, which was against missions for two reasons. First, it said that human beings could not offer salvation; only God could. Second, it said that only God could call an individual to preach or teach, and missionary organizations would have human beings appointing missionaries. But their reasoning was deepened by the realization that churches with missionary agendas would spend much of their time fund-raising and dealing with worldly distractions that would get in the way of the work of worship. The New Salem Association embraced the antimission position, though it did not find the need to make a formal statement about missions until its annual meeting of 1856, then again in 1876 when the minutes recorded that the Association "declare non-fellowship with all modern institutions such as Missionary Baptist, Bible and Tract societies, Sunday School Union."[14]

In 1854 New Salem changed its name from United Baptists to "Regular United Baptists," perhaps re-embracing the old title "Regular" as a way of differentiating themselves from the increasing embrace of Arminianism by other forms of Baptists (followed as it was two years later by a formal statement of opposition to missions). In 1874 the New Salem Association became "Regular Baptists," dropping "United" from their name. The title "Old Regular Baptist" first appeared in the minutes of 1892, but was likely in use earlier to further distinguish themselves from other Regular Baptists who, though otherwise the same, were holding revivals and Sunday schools.[15] This same year they reiterated their modified Calvinist view of atonement, urging their associated churches to stay away from the both the doctrine of absolute predestination, which leaves salvation outside of the realm of human agency and implies that sinners were predestined by God to sin, *and* the Arminian doctrine that the work of humans ("creatures") is essential to salvation.[16] They formalized this doctrine in 1905, but according to Deborah Vansau McCauley it was already a generally accepted theological position throughout Appalachian mountain religion by that point. Even those revival-centered and missionary churches in the mountains that held to doctrines of general or universal atonement shared a related understanding of the workings of grace and did not embrace a fully Arminian view of atonement.[17]

The story of the Old Regular Baptists provides some insight into the dynamics that went into the creation of a distinct Appalachian religious culture. It suggests that this culture was not born of simple isolation or ignorance. Rather, it was formed in relationship with larger developments of American religious history, on the ground and in particular contexts, through strategic choices of differentiation. It was, to use Catherine L. Albanese's term, a "contractive" religious culture that defined itself as maintaining the "old time" (or primitive) religion in the face of corrupting change and for whom boundary maintenance was important.[18] The culture was shaped as much by the fear of losing local control—and local identity—during this profoundly dynamic period of American religious history as it was by purely theological issues. Over the course of the nineteenth and twentieth centuries, southern Appalachian churches continued to feel the tension between their own desire for local control and self-determination in worship practices, on the one hand, and attempts by forces from outside of the mountains to draw them into national forms of worship and organization. Typically siding with the North during the Civil War, mountain churches nevertheless rejected Northern bureaucracy and formalism in religion and actively opposed the efforts of such groups as the American Home Mission Society that sought to bring Appalachians into their fold. Northeastern "Yankees" were a threat culturally and religiously to the inhabitants of the mountains, just as they were to the South in general. Yet mountain churches continued to resist Southern Baptist control as well.

A distinctive Appalachian religious culture was probably identifiable by the 1840s. By then, Baptists and Methodists were the mainstream denominations in the South. No longer the rebellious upstarts they had been, Baptists and Methodists settled into the patterns of established American denominations. They preferred educated, trained preachers, and religious leadership became a paid profession. The emotional dynamics of worship in turn were toned down, perhaps remaining lively in comparison with the staid liturgical churches but nothing like they were in their earlier revival period. In contrast, churches native to Appalachia, regardless of name, whether antimissionary or accepting of missionary practices, were distinguished by their continued emphasis on the active presence of the Holy Spirit in the world, preachers who were "called by the Spirit" and not seminary trained, and emotional worship that often included shouting and tears. Moreover, throughout the nineteenth and twentieth centuries, mountain churches embraced worship practices, understood to be Gospel ordinances, that Protestant churches elsewhere did not. These included foot washing as part of the Lord's Supper communion service, baptism by full immersion in a river or stream, anointing the sick with oil, and in many cases the laying on of hands and healing through prayer.

By the 1870s—and continuing through the 1890s—writers visiting the mountains, such as Will Wallace Harney, James Lane Allen, and William Goodell Frost, reported their observations of "a strange land and a peculiar people" in scholarly and popular publications, drawing attention to the ways in which Appalachian society and culture differed from the majority culture of the nation.[19] In particular, the religious practices and beliefs of the mountains caught the attention of both scholars and representatives of America's dominant Protestant denominations. These observers, in an age of social reform and missionary development, noted the variety of distinct mountain practices already mentioned and commented on illiterate preachers, dramatic testimonies of sudden conversions, and "funeralizing" customs. Churches were located far apart, they remarked, and mountain residents only worshiped once a month or so. They also reported the general disorganized structure of worship services, which seemed to begin and end at arbitrary times. Moreover, preachers, who were unpaid, often preached at more than one church. At any given worship service there might be several preachers present. The churches did not belong to nationally organized denominations, although they called themselves Baptist or sometimes Holiness. Visitors to the mountains invariably noted that on doctrinal and theological issues the mountain churches tended to be Calvinistic; some were called "hardshell" to signify their unbending stance on predestination. All of these examples, and more, reflected the existence of an identifiable regional religious culture in the mountains. By the end of the nineteenth century, the churches of rural eastern Kentucky shared little with the nationally organized denominations that came to dominate American religious history over the course of the nineteenth century and that began to establish themselves in the Kentucky mountains in the late nineteenth and early twentieth centuries in the towns that arose in the context of industrialization.

The churches that made up Appalachian mountain religion could be as diverse as their local independence might imply, but, as indicated, they also shared idioms, gestures, and common theological and doctrinal concerns (over which they might disagree vigorously).[20] Churches tended to be very small and independent bodies that engaged with and emerged from local populations. Preaching by unpaid, "untrained" preachers was a vocation, not an occupation or source of livelihood. Individual churches might join together into "associations," which met yearly to check up on each others' doctrine and practice, but governance was left in the hands of individual churches. In the case of disagreement within an association, a church might be "disassociated"—and it was not unusual for such splits to occur, for new churches to be formed, and even for new associations to come into existence. The arguments that mountain churches had with each other—over such issues as general versus particular election, the limits of free will in salvation, or the necessity or inappropriateness of missions—held mountain religious culture together in a shared community of discourse even as these conflicts formed distinctions between various churches and subdenominations.[21] It is helpful to read these splits and disagreements as part of an ongoing dynamic process of religious practice in the mountains. Appalachian mountain religion, as a regional religious tradition, is not one monolithic thing but a shared repertoire of idioms, gestures, and concerns that has bound together an internally diversified style of worship and religious identity.

A river baptism in the hills of eastern Kentucky. Item 28, Cora Wilson
Stewart Photographic Collection, PA58M25, University of Kentucky
Archives. Used by permission.

Religion in Everyday Life

The church traditions of Appalachia were a powerful source of the idioms and
gestures that gave shape to the Appalachian religious imagination and its expressions. But the residents of eastern Kentucky lived lives that exceeded the bounds
of their church activities in this land where church services were irregular occur-
rences and the majority of people were not church members. There continues to
be a religious dimension of the everyday culture of the mountains that informs
and haunts daily life. Religion was never confined solely to churches in Appala-

chia, as it never has been anywhere.[22] A quick look into the cultural history of Appalachia presents a picture of a world shot through with both natural and supernatural forces. Life in the hills included many cultural practices relating to the perceived supernatural order that might not have been specifically acknowledged or even sanctioned by church doctrine but that nevertheless were part of people's everyday lives and experiences. Studies of mountain culture, however, have tended to categorize these practices as "folklore" or "superstition," divorcing them from the study of religion proper.[23] Indeed, even the most thorough and sympathetic full-length study of religion in Appalachia to date, Deborah Vansau McCauley's *Appalachian Mountain Religion: A History,* treats religion primarily as it relates to church history. As critically aware as she is of the ways that the concerns of non-mountain Protestants have shaped perceptions of religion in the southern mountains, her text relegates mountain religion to its organized forms, tracing the origins and growth of the doctrines and practices of churches in the mountains. This is surely an important story to tell, yet it leaves much of the religious dynamics of everyday life outside of the "official" story of mountain religion. Appreciating the breadth and depth of Appalachian religious life means also paying attention to cultural practices that existed alongside and outside churches through which people also placed themselves in relation to natural, supernatural, and social powers. Many of those practices had roots in the Protestant traditions that also cohered in the mountain churches. Some of them extended the logic, symbols, or metaphors of organized worship and theology in creative ways. And some derived from the mountain setting where nature and nature's powers were always close at hand. In most cases, mountain people drew from all of these available resources as they navigated their way through the world.

If the church in Appalachia was a biblically based association of the saved, much of the rest of the rural mountain population lived in a world in which the Bible also held a central place. In other words, biblical idioms were not limited to their institutional point of origin, and they moved freely across the boundaries of the church into everyday life. But the Bible was understood within Appalachia somewhat differently from its understanding by mainstream Christians in America. Over the course of the nineteenth century, the forms of American Protestantism that came to dominate the nation's religious landscape saw the Bible more and more as a book of moral lessons. But among rural southern Appalachians it continued to be something of a technical manual for working and surviving in the material world. It helped people to understand events in the natural, supernatural, and social worlds and gave them directions for action. One eastern Kentucky resident noted that her father "lived by the Bible. He used it as a basic of life." His was not an ordinary, organized form of religion, however. "He had a religion," she continued, "but you couldn't say he was a Roman Catholic, or a Protestant, or a Methodist, or anything like that. And like I say, he used the Bible as a basic for all things; very seldom you talked to him what he wouldn't bring [up] something that he'd read in the 'Good Book.'"[24] Even among the nonliterate, who were the majority of the population, the Bible's stories circulated orally, and its verses and phrases entered everyday conversation.[25] Beyond its use as a book of stories, lessons, or truths, the Bible sometimes served as a magical book as well, opened at random to give direction in times of crisis or disorientation. Some of its verses worked like charms with magical healing effects themselves, able to stop blood from flowing to heal a wound.[26] The specific verse or verses used in this practice were usually passed along according to strict rules—for instance, only from grandmother to granddaughter in secrecy—that were also part of the cure's efficacy. The most common bloodstopping charm was Ezekiel 16:6, "And when I passed by thee and saw thee polluted in thine own blood, I said unto thee, when thou was in thy blood, 'live, and grow as a plant in the field.'" Some bloodstoppers substituted the name of the bleeding person for "thee." Another known charm was "God made the ocean, God sent the flood, God calms the ocean, God stops the blood."[27] "Fire" or "burn" doctors made a similar use of charms to "talk out fire," which meant to heal burns. A common technique called for the doctor to slowly wave his hand over the burn, as if pushing the burn away, while repeating three times, "There came an angel from the east bringing fire and frost. In frost, out fire. In the name of the Father, the Son, and the Holy Ghost." Other versions substitute *salt* for *frost*. Similar charms have been found in England, where many Appalachian folkways originated.[28]

For many in Appalachia, the Bible recorded the creation, and therefore the order, of the world and the story of human beings finding their way in the world in relation to God's design for them. If the world was made by God, as the people of the rural hills claimed, then God also provided tools and signs by which human beings could survive. Some of these were recorded in the Bible. Others were learned by observing the natural world to learn its patterns and signs. Conceptions of a God-given cosmic order were related directly to Appalachian farming and gardening practices that made heavy use of moon phases and signs of the zodiac to yield a better harvest. "Well, it must have been in th' plan when th' world was made," said one mountain farmer. "Because you know in Ecclesiastes it says, 'There's a time for everything. A time to be born and a time to die. A time to plant and a time to harvest.' That's God's book, you know, so that's the reason."[29] Her words were representative. For Appalachians, some plants—those that grew below ground—grew better when planted under a full moon; others grew better above ground when planted under a new moon. The zodiac, found in many almanacs throughout America, but also passed along through oral tradition in the mountains, mapped constellations of stars onto the human body and the "bodies" of plants as well. The reasoning worked along the lines of what anthropologists call "sympathetic magic": like affects like. Cabbage, for instance, was best planted during the month when the signs were "in the head," because cabbage resembled the human head. Beets, on the other hand, were planted "in the feet." Humorous outcomes could result from the logic of signs: potatoes should *not* be planted in the feet, or they would form lots of toes.[30]

This sympathetic logic extended from natural correspondences between stars, moon, and plants to cures for bodily ailments. The Bible told of plants and herbs created by God to help with disease and healing, so that mountain residents justified biblically the practice of herbal healing that lasted well after medical doctors were available.[31] Some foods or roots were considered appropriate for certain ailments based upon their shapes or qualities that resembled the ailment or part of the body that needed curing. Again, this was a way of relating to the natural and material world that assumed a logic of correspondence and analogy, suggesting an order in God's creation that was not based upon analytic reason but upon observable likeness. Extending the logic further, charms came into play for both luck and healing. Often the charm resembled, or was in some way connected to, its intended effect. Sometimes the relationship between symptom and cure was not obvious. For example, putting a hole through a dime and wearing it on a string around the neck was a preventative for nosebleed.[32]

In the mountains, healing was and continues to be a religious activity, whether articulated through Christian belief or vernacular conceptions of the natural design of things. Some forms of healing required special knowledge, learned through apprenticeship or passed along orally within families.[33] Herbs, for instance, were available to all who knew how to utilize them efficaciously. Other kinds of healing could only be accomplished by those with special access to supernatural powers. Faith healing is an example. While faith healers claimed that the power to heal did not come from themselves but from the Spirit, nevertheless some individuals were known to have better access to the Spirit's healing powers. Churches that practiced faith healing called forth the Spirit through intense prayer and preaching, working up the congregation's energy and calling the Spirit down. In that case it was not the individual but the community of the saved that accessed and bore witness to the Spirit's healing powers. But even more mundane forms of healing and medical work were often loaded with religious significance. They worked on the boundaries between well-being and disease, tied to life and death. Midwives were especially important figures in rural Appalachia in this regard. They not only assisted in childbirth—an event that was as potentially dangerous as it was charged with sacred importance—but also treated illnesses of all types. Midwives often understood their work as a religious calling, something that they were destined to do and that was their purpose in life. They pointed to biblical passages referring to midwives and identified with them.[34]

The idea that an individual had a particular purpose in life, whether explained as a calling or a special blessing, was deeply tied to the conception of the world as ordered by God's design. It was also related to the Christian idea of a calling or vocation, and like the Appalachian modified Calvinism it implied a variety of predestination that was not at the same time a fatalism. Some believed that a person's character and both physical and emotional qualities, while changeable to some degree, were set in large part at birth or in the womb. Birth signs supplied information about the nature of the newborn: placenta covering the head, for instance, signified that a child would have special abilities to read signs and see the future. Other marks on the body were said to indicate something of a person's innate character. Interaction with the child also had serious implications for his or her future development—and this meant while the child was in the womb as well as after he or she was born. In some cases the consequences were merely physical. For instance, a mother's cravings could leave a mark on her child's skin in the form of the object she craved, such as cornbread or cucumbers or candy. In other cases, a child might acquire the mother's cravings herself. More profoundly, a mother's frightening, unusual, or shocking experience, some believed, could effectively mold her unborn child's personality with characteristics associated with her experience. The mother's behavior while pregnant would affect the child to no small degree.[35]

As all of the foregoing examples suggest, for many in Appalachia the world was made up of signs that could reveal deeper patterns and structures of life and reality if read correctly. On the one hand, these signs resembled a kind of "folk science," derived from careful observation of causal laws or hypothesis relating to inferred laws. But the meaning of these signs went further than that. They also signaled the pervasive sacramentalism of mountain religious culture. Nature itself pointed to deeper mysteries that lay behind or beyond the visible world, but sacramentalism also derived from the Scotch-Irish Presbyterian and German Pietist influences on Appalachian culture. Pietism taught that the Spirit could be experienced in this world, known not only intellectually but *felt*. That is, one could encounter the divine in the world, and mountain churches gave evidence to believers that the Spirit did enter the world and make itself felt. Anabaptist rituals of foot washing and baptism that became common worship practices of mountain churches were material actions that gave access to this experience of the Spirit. Moreover, the yearly sacramental revivalism of the Presbyterians, whose Calvinism was such an important foundation of mountain religion, also insisted that the supernatural world—the world of divine power and the Holy Spirit—could be accessed through material means. Although Calvinists rejected Roman Catholicism's "superstitions," early American Scotch-Irish Presbyterianism and the mountain religion it influenced continued the practice of communion, calling it "the Lord's Supper" or simply "sacrament." As Southern historian Samuel S. Hill has explained, the Appalachian sacramental orientation declares "that mundane matter somehow reveals God in or through itself." It is a "cosmic theology," a "theology of 'the ordinary disclosing the extraordinary,'" in which "some kind of synergic relation exists between spiritual and physical."[36] Appalachians might not use the term *sacrament* to describe all of the ways that this concept traces throughout mountain culture. But this sense that divine power was accessible through the world influences the wider, non-church culture as well, mixing with the sense of nature's power and mystery to produce what might usefully be viewed as a deeply sacramental culture where natural and supernatural often blurred.

The interpenetration of the visible and invisible worlds is a prominent feature of Appalachian religious cultures. Religious studies scholar Charles H. Lippy has noted a general sense in central Appalachia "that the world of everyday life is a realm of power, an arena where supernatural forces of good and evil are operative," and a related "understanding that life transpires simultaneously on two levels of reality, the 'here and now' and the hereafter."[37] It comes as no surprise, then, to know that tales and experiences of ghosts were common in the mountains and that people often talked about "haints," or places that were considered to be either haunted or filled with some sort of supernatural power.[38] Indeed, the world was full of omens and portents pointing beyond the present to give warning about impending doom. Dreams and visions, even odd feelings in the body, no less than material signs, were a regular part of Appalachian life that offered access to the invisible world. In many ways, this world resembled that of early New England, another deeply Protestant culture that read natural and social history as divine drama. Historian David Hall has shown that colonial New Englanders lived in a world of signs and wonders, where earthquakes and thunderstorms were interrogated for divine meaning.[39] Appalachians were similar. In both places the world was inhabited by active invisible forces of both good and evil.

In a culture that scanned the world for signs to reveal the deeper meanings of everyday life, stories and talk took on the important religious function of transforming the simple facts or events of life into interpretations of their significance. People "made something of things" by telling about them, giving them meaning or significance by linking them to other stories, to other events, or by framing their stories in idiomatic ways. In the sacramental mountain culture where people read God's plan and the invisible world through the everyday, talk and rumor and story resonated on several levels. Comments on the everyday, on interactions or behaviors or natural events, could both be simple talk *and* resonate with larger implicit structures that point beyond the material world. One powerful idiom that could inform the significance of otherwise "everyday" comments was the dramatic plotline of the episodic human journey from sinner to saved, with its familiar detours and backsliding. Heard against this background, a person's successes and failures were potential insights into the state of his or her character and soul, and stories or comments about them were potential moral lessons to others. An individual's own difficulties might call forth reflections on God's designs and that person's relationship to them. Then again, the same stories might be read against a different plotline, that of the state of the world and the larger battle between good and evil that would ultimately end on the day of judgment. In this drama everyday events were signs revealing cosmic history, in which difficulty and tragedy were signals of the world's decline that some said would precede the ultimate battle of good and evil at the end of history. Conversely, an unusual occurrence in the right time and place could instill hope or revelation. In the words of anthropologist Kathleen Stewart, describing another central Appalachian setting, "In a world in which things happen and people scan things for *signs,* the uncanny can lie gathered in the ordinary, the sacred can penetrate the profane, and a visit can become a visitation."[40] Seemingly mundane happenings might, and often did, take on profound (often religious) significance that called forth a host of connected, and contested, responses.

If religion cannot be separated from everyday life, then the history of religion in eastern Kentucky's coal fields quite clearly has been shaped by the forces that have shaped the everyday lives of the people who live there. Likewise, as people have responded to those forces, remapping their worlds and their understandings of themselves and others, they have done so through and against available religious resources. They have creatively adapted religious idioms to new situations or rejected them or even created new ones. Religion may be, as Karl Marx would have it, a comfortable yet oppressive illusion that keeps people from changing the conditions they live in. No doubt that is true in some instances. But religion can also be a force for concrete change, presenting an ideal picture that condemns the current reality and motivates its transformation. Or religion can offer forms of resistance to power, underlying a refusal to change not out of ignorant blindness but by choice, positing an authority greater than worldly authorities. Religion can also, more simply, yet profoundly, provide comfort and hope in the face of anxiety or despair when otherwise life might seem too difficult. Religion does all of these things and more.

In central Appalachia, nothing has impacted all aspects of life in the twentieth century—including religion—more than the coal industry. It transformed the landscape, economy, demography, and image of the mountains. But how did people on the ground, in their daily work and worries, meet and shape these changes religiously? How did the experiences—physical, existential, social, and otherwise—of their new work and environments transform religious expression?

The questions move away from exclusive focus on churches and into everyday religious articulations. In the context of interpreting the religious history of coal miners, it is important to note the centrality of embodied experience. Appalachian mountain religious culture places great emphasis on the body and its senses as the primary locus of religious experience. The sensual body is the center of the experience of conversion, evidence of the Spirit, health and disease, and dreams, visions, and ominous feelings. Likewise, the experience of capitalist labor is an embodied experience. The effects of economic and social change wrought by the development of the coal industry, no less than the bracing physical labor of coal mining, were primarily *felt* as well as thought about by miners and their families. Just as health, family, social relations, and nature were always central to Appalachian mountain religious culture, so too would miners articulate the changes that industrial mining brought to these aspects of life in religious ways. As the world changed and they changed with their world, performances of religion expressed and informed the real material situation in which people lived their daily lives. Conversely, their material setting produced religious innovations. The majority of those who became miners began, during the period of development, as subsistence farmers; the next chapter explores the world in which they lived.

TWO

PATTERNS OF LIFE AND WORK

God knew that it would take brave and sturdy people to survive in these beautiful but rugged hills. So He sent us His very strongest men and women, people who could enjoy life and search out the few pleasures that were contained in a life of hard work.

—VERNA MAE SLONE,
What My Heart Wants to Tell, viii

UNTIL THE COAL INDUSTRY transformed its landscape and economy forever at the turn of the twentieth century, subsistence farming was the primary mode of livelihood in eastern Kentucky. Industrial mining was established in Virginia and West Virginia and in pockets of eastern Kentucky by the end of the nineteenth century. But most of what would become the southeastern Kentucky coal fields was still inaccessible to industry, lacking adequate trade routes to bring supplies in or coal out of the area efficiently. With the construction of railroad lines in the first decades of the new century, coal mining operations and coal towns began springing up almost overnight. The coming of coal companies greatly accelerated a process that was already under way, more slowly, in the Kentucky mountains, as a household-oriented economy was being transformed into a market economy.

The family farm stood at the center of the preindustrial eastern Kentucky economy. According to census reports from Perry, Floyd, and Harlan counties from the years 1860, 1870, and 1880, nonfarming occupations added up to less than 1 percent of the total population.[1] The little occupational diversity that did exist was geographically localized in developed towns. Professionals like lawyers, politicians, and some merchants, making up a portion of the minority 1 percent, tended to reside in county seats that were home to the courthouse and bank. Town centers during this time were not yet the bustling nodes of trade that they would become once railroad lines penetrated the Kentucky hills, but they were nevertheless centers of legal and economic power that connected the mountain communities to national markets. The majority of eastern Kentucky's mountain residents lived away from town centers, settling sparsely in hollows ("hollers") between the hills, along creek beds, and, less desirably, on hillsides. For most, county seats were only relevant on "court days," the twice-yearly occasions when the court of law was scheduled to meet, and election days. Appalachian folklore is filled with stories of the carnivalesque atmosphere of these special times when everyday life was interrupted for the sociality that came with the crowds that gathered in town. It would seem that more horse trading and drinking took place than the civic duties for which these days were set apart.[2] Most of the time, though, most people in eastern Kentucky worked at the chores of farming, the dominant mode of production that patterned a way of life.

There is evidence of tenant farming throughout the nineteenth century, but mountain farms were largely owner-operated and can best be thought of as extensions of the home. Kentucky's commercial farming was located, by the mid-nineteenth century, in the western part of the state.[3] In the mountains, farming was not a specialized occupation within a larger diverse economy but was instead part of a generalized home-based subsistence economy. The entire family shared in the labor, and the produce they raised sustained them. The mountain family farm's primary crop was corn, owing to its low risk, low investment, and ability to grow in the wide range of topographical settings found in the hills. Indeed, the limited supply of bottom land drove farmers to cultivate hillsides, leading to humorous stories in oral tradition that tell of mountain farmers falling out of their cornfields and rolling down the hills.[4] Peas, beans, and potatoes were also common staple crops. Farms often included a variety of livestock, too, usually chickens, pigs, and a few milk cows, and sometimes some sheep, for food and clothing. Any surplus that remained after the needs of the home were met might be traded or sold at the local store, but surplus production was not the goal. There was simply no market for surplus produce. Geographically, the mountain economy was largely cut off from the growing national economy. A number of small stores existed throughout the mountains, many of them located at river forks that made them accessible both to wholesalers who used the waterways to transport goods and to mountain residents who used river and creek beds as roads. These stores usually supplied general dry goods, unspecialized, offering for sale or trade those things that could not be produced at home and on the farm. Because the mountain economy was predominantly one of household subsistence, however, not sales and profit, money was scarce, and small-scale merchants were constantly on the edge of financial failure. They usually maintained a farm alongside their mercantile endeavors, and at times switched primacy between these occupations.[5]

Home life in the mountains therefore typically centered around the work of farming, but it also included a host of other activities involved in the production of items that were otherwise not available from merchants. Household chores fell generally along the lines of gender—men made chairs and other woodwork, for instance, and perhaps worked with iron, while women spun yarn, wove cloth, and sewed clothes. Kitchen utensils, brooms, beds, baskets, and other items were all the products of home manufacture.[6] Much of the work in the fields was shared by men and women, children and adults alike. Nevertheless, the husband was considered the head of the household, and his authority lay at its center. Historian Robert S. Weise has characterized the ideology that governed behavior in nineteenth-century eastern Kentucky as "household localism," referring to "the perception that political, economic, social, and religious sovereignty resided in the individual household and particularly in the male household head." Household localism privileged male authority, as well as whiteness, but at the same time it acted as a social equalizer among white men. With the household as the basic economic and political unit, families stressed their independence and self-rule. Independence, in this context, meant the ability—and responsibility—of men to provide for themselves and their families without outside aid. Independent did not necessarily mean individualistic, however, as households depended upon neighbors and extended networks of kinship to survive.[7]

In this environment, to live was to work. Oral histories reveal lives in which time and space were structured by the daily chores of farm and home, which also produced character—identity and worth. The work was seemingly endless; there was always something more to be done, it seemed, and much of it involved the entire family. Mountain residents remember childhoods spent rising early to milk cows and working through the day hoeing corn, picking beans, and digging potatoes.[8] Far from the idle life of the romantic imagination, the household economy of the mountain farm in eastern Kentucky produced a life of constant hard work.

Work

In the rural mountain setting of the household farm, work was both a matter of survival and, for many, a way of being in the world that tied daily life to a larger order of truth and meaning. It is significant that work emerges from the stories and oral histories of eastern Kentucky and Appalachian natives not only as a fact of life but also as a way of placing oneself and others in the world. To work was to be human, and to be human was to work. Through the daily routines of work, farming families wove themselves into the world and came to know themselves. For people who believed that the Bible taught them about the nature and order of the world, ideas about the importance and ubiquity of human labor had a source in Genesis where it is written that soon after the creation of the world human beings fell from a state of paradisiacal leisure. As the result of the greed and transgressions of Adam and Eve, all subsequent humans were condemned by God to labor for their survival forevermore in this world. This was the story of the creation of work, its reason and its source, built into God's design. Referencing the authority of this biblical explanation, eastern Kentuckians therefore understood work to be a fundamental aspect of the human condition. Work was an obligation, but not a choice, and had moral as well as material ramifications. James F. Collins, a miner from Letcher County, echoed many others in recalling that in the rural mountains, "we believed that it was a man's duty to work by the sweat of his face to earn his bread" (paraphrasing Genesis 3:19).[9]

But work was a fact of human life that held an ambivalent meaning. Despite the implication in Genesis that work was a punishment, work was also a form of creation, an active engagement with the world that made one a part of it and helped to make the world one's own. In work, people created themselves and adapted themselves to the world's order. It could therefore be a joy rather than a burden. Verna Mae Slone understood work in this manner, saying that "of all the things my father taught me, I am thankful that I learned from him the enjoyment one could obtain from work." Work was so central to Slone's understanding of the natural state of human affairs, and so regular a presence in her life, that she claimed that she was fully grown before she learned that there were people who did not like to work. Slone felt that working on the farm in particular, cultivating crops and tending to her chores, actively tied her to the sacred powers that ordered all life. "All good things come from God," she said. "But you seem so close to Him, one with nature, when you plant the tiny seeds, in faith that they will grow. Later there is the joy of gathering and storing away these results of your partnership with nature."[10] For many, like Slone, farm work had the potential of an almost sacramental logic in tying the everyday to a wider sense of divine order. For the most part, however, work tied the individual and community to a larger order in practical, habitual ways.

Daily work also contained a rhythm that situated the individual in time, ordering the day, the week, the season, and the year. Tied together by the cycles of the seasons, community grew from the shared experience of work and celebrated its routines. Verna Mae Slone again provides an example. In her autobiography, she recalled that the seasonal life of corn cultivation began as early as January or February each year with the job of "grubin," which entailed "digging the young sprouts that were beginning to grow around where the trees had grown." After clearing and preparing the area, she and her family "dug in" the corn in rows. Once it had grown to a foot tall, the corn was thinned and weeded. A few weeks later, it was weeded again. This second weeding, known as "laying it by," was a time of "wild celebration" for Slone's family and tied the household to a wider social world as adjoining farms competed against each other to see who could finish their hoeing first. Neighboring farms, then, and farms throughout the hills shared the seasonal patterns of work and made human significance of them by making them social events. "Our hills are so close," Slone recalled, "many different family groups could see and hear each other." She continued, "When the last 'hill of corn' was hoed they would begin to yell, beating their hoes together or against rocks, thumping on the dinner bucket, anything to make a noise. Someone at the house would ring the dinner bell, telling all their friends that they were through with their corn. An extra good dinner or supper, as the case might be, would be cooked, and everyone had at least one whole day's rest. Even the mules got this one day without working."[11]

In September they gathered the fodder, and in November they harvested and stored the corn, a complex process that involved cutting, stripping, curing, and hauling. The fall was time for canning or otherwise preparing fruits and vegetables for winter storage.

Describing other household chores and activities, Flora Rife, born in the eastern Kentucky hills in 1904, also suggested that life on the farm integrated aspects of self, family, and work life into a daily rhythm:

> We all helped. We all hoed corn. We all planted beans. We picked beans, we helped in the garden. We done everything. We fed the stock. . . . You'd get through in an hour and a half or two hours of the morning. . . . You had the rest of the day, the boys did to chop wood and to get ready for the cooking and the girls pieced quilts and sew and darn [sic]. And where they'd go and shear their sheep, you know, they'd take that wool and us children would get to card it, and then we'd twist it with our fingers into little fine stems of strings and yarn.[12]

That link between work and social production, blurring or negating any distinction between them, was an important aspect of the local household economy and the culture of eastern Kentucky. Work linked individual and family to community. To the farming community, work also implied obligations and responsibilities that carried a moral weight and provided the basis for emotional as well as social expression. Family members provided the labor for daily chores, but tasks such as harvesting, butchering, or house building that required more hands commonly brought the neighboring farms and community together for "workings." People would gather to pool their labor and then eat together, play music, and socialize.[13] One mountain farmer remembered workings and "bean strings"—when families would gather to help each other string beans—as times "as fun as movies are today."[14]

Through such daily work, many eastern Kentucky farm families learned and enacted the values of community and reciprocity, lessons they applied toward interpreting scripture and through which they evaluated theological arguments. Conversely, scripture helped them to interpret their labors. From daily life, through stories of others and shared experiences, to worship and theology, mountain residents came to know the world through work and gave their experiences language and meaning through religious idioms. Folklorist Henry Glassie found a similar orientation toward work and life in rural Northern Ireland, where he noted that "in some cultures first things command attention, posing puzzles to the mind. . . . [But here] the topic is less prime order than it is the ways people operate within that order to build and destroy human associations." Eastern Kentucky's religious culture likewise did not question the origins of the world. Their concerns, in a strictly theological sense, were with issues of salvation and free will. They were questions about humanity and destiny and how those terms related to present actions. In a more everyday sense, however, the practical problems had to do with making do with what was given in creation, fitting the self to the world's order and working on the world to make it serve the needs of the people. "The first principle is crucial but not a question. God made the world. The question concerns free will more than God's plan, culture more than conditions," Glassie explains. "How do people create within creation? The world is in order. It is the ordeal of people to adapt. . . . At work on the world, in the world, they learn their way." Everyday life—from planting to harvesting to social relations—taught lessons, however incomplete, about the world's order and the human place in it.[15]

Learning their way in the world through working on it, people found that the world spoke to them if they knew its language. Seasonal cycles of planting and harvesting determined what work needed to be done, but action was further guided by signs such as the phases of the moon, the zodiac, and the behaviors of insects and leaves on the trees.[16] Likewise, the earth that provided food and the materials for clothing and shelter also provided herbs to heal diseases. To many in rural eastern Kentucky, it was all part of a grand design created by God in which human beings played a particular role as the benefactors of what God provided. But for them, none of those things were handed to people without effort, giving work a significant role in the human place within that design.

As biblical language, cosmic patterns, and the experiences of life on the farm blended together, the boundaries between material and spiritual practice blurred. In other words, the daily life of rural farming shaped organized worship and theological expression as much as religious idioms—drawn from sources like the Bible, folklore, doctrinal statements, theological arguments, personal testimonies, and worship practices—informed interpretations and stories of daily life. In a study of an Independent Baptist Church in Appalachian Virginia, folklorist Jeff Todd Titon found that his subjects often used metaphors that grew out of the work of farming to express religious concepts. They emphasized especially the metaphor of *husbandry*, which Titon suggested linked farmers to their farm, to their spouse, and to their God.[17] It is worth noting the gendered implications of this term, evoking the ideology of household localism that defined rural eastern Kentucky's subsistence farms. Husbandry might be understood as both a responsibility and a term of authority, closely connected to the idea of *dominion* that appears in Genesis when God created human beings and gave them dominion over all the earth. Extending the metaphor, *home* was also a central symbol to mountain farmers, whose livelihood was focused on the household economy and whose image of heaven was likened to that of a home. Homecomings, then, achieved sacred significance when extended family returned home once a year, often but not always associated with a church or the wider community. As the terms *home* and *husbandry* imply, kinship was of utmost importance. Kinship was a theme that ran through both eastern Kentucky life and worship. Members of mountain churches referred to each other as "brother" and "sister," suggesting that church membership was considered an extension of kinship or a form of fictive kinship, tying the church community to the home economy and structures of authority. Mountain songs and hymnody further advanced the image, picturing heaven not only as *home* but also as a reunion with departed kin. "By-and-by we'll go and see them / On the other bright shore," went one song, successive verses begging fathers, mothers, brothers, sisters, Christians, neighbors, and others to "meet me / on Canaan's happy shore."[18] Mothers and children, husbands and wives would be reunited in heaven's eternal rest, where work would no more be required. The significance of kinship was put into practice in the care and upkeep of family cemeteries and in yearly memorial services (often held in conjunction with homecomings). Kinship was also the primary organizational structure around which social and economic life in the hills turned. Areas of settlement and patterns of obligation were built around family ties in the preindustrial mountains, and political power and authority were held and maintained almost exclusively through lines of kinship.[19]

Given the apparent fluidity and coherence with which subsistence farming and the world's order intertwined, it can be tempting to reconstruct the rural life of the preindustrial mountains in such a way as to make it appear as a seamless whole in which every part had its place, to assert a kind of social and cultural functionalism. Indeed, since the late nineteenth century, the Appalachian region has served as a repository for such romantic imaginings of premodern and preindustrial folklife.[20] But it would be a mistake to take this coherence as an indication that there was no conflict or competition in the southern mountains before the intrusion of industrial capitalism.

Historian Robert Weise found that household localism could create competition both between and within families. Households "represented a fundamental site for the exercise of power, particularly male power," he noted, "and with power invariably comes conflict."[21] Indeed, there was plenty of conflict, as Verna Mae Slone indicated in a description of a typical "working": "I'm not going to say that everyone got along together in love and fellowship," she said. "There were quarrels and disputes, even ending in fights and gun battles. Some men were killed." Negotiating conflicting desires and perspectives was a form of social work that was no less important than physical labor, carried out in relation to patterns of life expressed as the proper order or ideal and its breaches. As Slone continued her description, the mountain ideal became clear. Violence in Appalachian society, she said, "has been told and written about, but I hope to show you another life, one that was more real and more true: people who joined together to help their neighbors."[22]

The reciprocal and cooperative patterns of life that mountain residents often remember fondly in oral histories, and that lie at the root of romantic portrayals of preindustrial folklife, should therefore be thought of as an ideal. It is the "more real and more true" sense of order that provided a model by which people could measure their lives and their dreams.[23] As in any society, there were deviations from the ideal, times when the sense of order—both cosmic and social—was tested and the potential for alternative, even oppositional, orientations was also possible. It is helpful to understand the idea of a shared mountain culture, then, not as consensus but as a shared language, a shared system of symbols, even if contested, that shaped the possibilities for conceptualization and communication. For instance, the importance of *work* as a constitutive element of being fully human was revealed as much in cases in which that ideal was violated as those in which it was achieved. To be sure, there were those who did not relish the hard work of farm life and those who shirked their responsibilities. People who were lazy and did not pitch in were considered to be of "no account," irresponsible, and therefore lacking in social value. One mountain resident described a family that he called "a bunch of 'seben sleepers'" who "were considered trash-sorry people." A seben sleeper, he explained, was "somebody that laid in bed when they ought to be up and out working."[24] Similarly, an individual or family who appeared to be greedy or unwilling to help with shared work stood a good chance of being marginalized by the larger community and socially classified as worthless. As one person put it, "There were people, as I think it over, we [called] 'sorry' if they didn't work. For the man that doesn't provide for his family the term 'sorry' was the lowest term you could label him."[25]

Idleness was not to be tolerated, but when God designed and created the world, he set aside a day of rest that was to be honored. "Old and young fear above all things the breaking of the Sabbath," wrote mountain resident Emma Bell Miles.[26] Sunday marked off the weekly rhythm of hard work with a day of worship and socializing. Although it is difficult to recover the history of church-going in preindustrial eastern Kentucky, what evidence exists indicates that it was a highly social affair.[27] Services at a given church might only have been offered once a month, but when they were offered they were often all-day events.

Oral histories reveal that church was a popular place for boys and girls to meet and perhaps begin courting. Worley Johnson from Harlan County, for instance, remembered that people used to go to church whether they were church members or not. In the eyes of the Old Regular Baptists' modified Calvinism, everyone but the saved was a sinner, and many sinners still desired to worship.[28] On the other hand, Johnson said that he and other boys were drawn to the independent church near them, and went every Sunday, precisely because it was the place to meet girls. According to Johnson, the *good* girls were mostly church members: "I seen whole strings of girls go into the creek" to be baptized, he said, "whole strings, they just kept on dippin' 'em in the water and turnin' 'em out."[29]

Church, then, may have served functions profane as well as sacred, but as the local institution that formally made explicit the connection between everyday behavior and the ideals and order of God's design, it was a focal point for the maintenance of social values among members and nonmembers alike. It did this in direct and indirect ways. Indirectly, its meetings served to bring the dispersed community together periodically. Catching up with those they had not seen during the course of the week or longer, people discussed their families, their crops, and their lives and perhaps shared a meal together after the service. The church service therefore provided a location and a reason for visiting, and its role as a nexus of communication between households cannot be underestimated. The custom of visiting between churches widened the communication network. If a particular church was not meeting for worship one week, its members and participants might travel to another accessible church for services. At these gatherings, news traveled and a sense of community grew.[30] At the same time, community members could police each other's behavior and activities, drawing and maintaining the boundaries of acceptability as they shared stories, spread or quashed rumors, and voiced desires or aggravations.

The church intervened more directly into the maintenance of social order as well. During the service a preacher might single out a particular person whose behavior was socially disruptive or ran contrary to community morals; in extreme cases such a person might be banned from participation in the church.[31] In making distinctions between sinners and the saved, churches were in the business of asserting and policing ideals, even if they claimed that individuals had little or no power over their state of salvation. The church ministered to all people, but clearly considered becoming a "Christian"—by undergoing the experience of conversion—as the ideal. That is, at least in its language, it privileged the saved. But the church also functioned as social leveler and mediator between its members, a role that found its clearest expression at yearly association meetings. There, elders representing independent churches that held loose organizational ties with each other met to regularize doctrine and practice. Their first order of business was to see that the church could be declared "at peace." This meant that the members of every church in the association had to resolve all differences with one another before any further business could continue. Thus church members who harbored ill feelings toward one another for any reason had to work out their quarrels or put them aside.[32] The basis of this practice was doctrinal, stemming from the understanding that the will of God was known to individuals within a communal worship setting, where all were in agreement about God's will.[33] But the result was socially powerful. Churches in this way directly impacted social relations and remained closely tied to the everyday world of interpersonal and community relations.[34]

Among their many roles, then, churches also acted not unlike a legal system in rural eastern Kentucky. Indeed, for those who were members it was important to resolve differences through the church, under the will of God and the community of the saints, rather than through the humanly constructed courts. But the ideal of a community at peace reached out beyond the converted. While the church, on the one hand, was oriented away from the ordinary world toward the special community of the saved and its hope for a world to come, it was also firmly grounded in this world and spoke to both saint and sinner. The social control exerted by the church, therefore, was carried out within a community of people, both saved and unsaved, "Christian" and other, who knew each other and who could work out their differences in direct confrontations. The language of the church was shared by members and nonmembers alike and blended with wider cultural conceptions of the world's order and people's place in it.

Both organized worship and the patterns of everyday life were structured in a similar cultural style, as ongoing performances of an episodic drama dynamically defined along a continuum of sin and salvation, order and disorder. God provided the tools and the way to overcome obstacles, according to this perspective, but difficulties would always lie in the path—whether they were temptations, illnesses, or natural disasters. Converted Christians might slip back into sin, just as a healthy body might slip into disease or a season's crop might not yield a good harvest. Widespread acceptance of such limitations and contingencies in the mountains led a host of visiting observers in the late nineteenth and early twentieth centuries to comment upon the "fatalistic" nature of Appalachian culture, which they said derived from religious ideas of predestination and resulted in the lack of industry or desire to improve.[35] But these observers failed to realize that in the mountains religion was itself a form of *work*—an ongoing work of interpretation and orientation, in thought and imagination as well as in behavior and interaction with the world. Acceptance of limitations was a rational and reasonable orientation to the world, experienced time and time again as people worked with, but did not have control over, natural forces like weather and illness. God's creation provided tools and signs with which to do one's best. Likewise, to be a human being was an ongoing process. Knowing God's design and humanity's place in it required constant observation, scanning for signs and adjusting knowledge and practical action. Practices of planting by the signs, anticipating future events from the behavior of animals and insects, healing through herbs and biblical charms, and an intense interest in interpreting scriptural passages for guidance in everyday life were the practical elements of a religious cultural style. Each of these suggested that life was uncertain but that there were patterns that could be observed and techniques that were available for working with the variety of forces that infringed on daily life. Emma Bell Miles understood this when she wrote of her community in the Tennessee mountains that a person from the area "learns to see Nature not as a thing of fields and brooks, friendly to man and docile beneath his hand, but as a world of depths and heights and distances illimitable, of which he is but a tiny part." She went on, "Inevitably, he comes to feel, with a sort of proud humility, that he has no part or lot in the control of the universe save as he allies himself, by prayer and obedience, with the Order that rules."[36]

But the order was changing with time, driven by a number of economic, social, and demographic factors. Perhaps most famously, the mountains' vast supplies of natural resources came to the attention of national markets in the 1880s, and local businesspeople seized the investment opportunity signaled by the demand. Land speculation corporations blossomed from county seats, buying the rights to lumber and minerals in league with investors from the northeastern states. Before there was even a railroad with which to transport the promised resources out of the hills, speculators were banking on the potential that one would soon be built.

As a money economy grew in eastern Kentucky with increased speculation and development, self-sufficiency became harder to manage. Population growth added to the trouble as families found it more and more difficult to parcel their land into plots for new generations.[37] Confronted with the need for land to live on and to farm, but without the security of inheritance, some turned to tenant farming, entering into relations with wealthy landowners who offered a share of the harvest or a wage to tenants who worked their land or essentially became their employees. The growing money economy that accompanied the spread of commerce throughout the hills, however, posed a problem that tenant farming alone would not solve. Duty required that a man provide for his family, but farming did not offer enough. Now a man—indeed, a family—needed money. A different sort of work was required in order to earn money—signified by its designation as "public work" as opposed to just plain work.[38] *Work* was the term in the mountains for the labor required for living: tending to the family, raising food, taking care of housing and clothing—the products of which were the production and reproduction of life itself. *Public work,* on the other hand, was work for somebody else, outside of the household economy, in exchange for money. Historian Crandall Shifflett uses the term *additive labor* to designate these cash-earning jobs, and while it is difficult to say for how long additive labor was a part of Appalachia's economy, the voices of oral history explain that it became more and more necessary at the turn of the century as capitalist patterns of exchange transformed material and social relations.[39] By its very nature, public work entailed the alienation of labor from subsistence or immediate need, and the money economy allowed this relationship to grow increasingly abstract and mediated by nonlocal, unnatural forces.

Public work came in many forms. According to one mountain resident, some farmers in the early twentieth century, transforming the subsistence farm to a commercial one as they retooled their labor toward a growing money economy, would plant ten to fifteen acres of corn and then hire hands to harvest it for twenty-five to fifty cents a day. That was the only way many people could make money, he claimed.[40] Both farmer and hired help would thereby earn the cash that was becoming more useful just as subsistence farming was beginning to become more difficult. As railroads and mines began developing, other men worked at laying railroad tracks or constructing the houses or buildings that would make up coal towns. Roads that needed repairing—a growing concern since transportation was at a high premium at this time—also required part-time workers. Some made money not by working for other people but by picking ginseng or hunting possum for pelts and selling these to merchants and traders. There was always somebody who would buy "anything that had fur," according to Henry McIntosh, a miner from Perry County.[41] McIntosh found another way to enter the cash economy through moonshining, a venture that became the basis for widespread stereotypes of mountain residents in images that endure to the present day.

Some Kentucky farmers discovered that through the process of fermentation and distillation they could convert their crops of corn into a more valuable and marketable product. In its wider context, however, moonshining could bring individuals into conflict with both prevailing social values and the law. The market for moonshine indicated both the shifting patterns of exchange and the ambivalence of the mountain moral economy during these transitional times. The texture of the social world was changing.

Religious Articulations of Socioeconomic Change

More than finances were at stake as traditional patterns of life met the emerging money economy. Tensions and conflicts wrought by economic and social change registered in a religious key. The world of the subsistence farm wove together individual, community, and cosmos into a coherence that presented a dynamic order. An individual might always fall away from the ideal, but the order was understood to exist just the same. But how would the community react to someone who appeared to oppose the order completely, who actively rejected it and participated in its destruction? Against the background of the traditional patterns of life and work, the culture of the market in which speculators and business people participated, with its lack of concern for familiar values and obligations, appeared to some rural eastern Kentuckians as exactly that—an active disruption of the perceived order of things, causing rifts in the social world that had serious repercussions. To gain at another's expense was one thing, but to gain beyond reason while others found it more difficult to provide for themselves and their families resulted in overt uneasiness and animosity. Anyone who engaged in such behavior might be classified by Appalachian and eastern Kentucky folklore as a witch. A witch was in league with the devil, having formed a pact or made a deal to reject actively the "proper" order of God's creation. Implicit was the assumption that cosmic order entailed a moral dimension and, therefore, responsibility on the part of persons to behave in accord with that order if creation was to run smoothly. Witchcraft accusations were sometimes levied against individuals who were perceived as not being integrated into the social life of the community, gaining at the expense of others, or using unnatural means for their own empowerment.[42] Appalachia, of course, was not isolated in this regard. Anthropological literature tells us that witchcraft accusations have been a part of many traditional cultures and often signal perceived imbalances of power and material gain in the context of rapid economic and social transformation.[43]

While I have come across no evidence that land speculators or businesspeople in particular were named as witches as eastern Kentucky underwent rapid transformation after 1880, another appellation that appeared in that context should draw attention. In these cases, at least two local men who actively aligned themselves with the forces of change were known by the name "Devil."

The first to arouse interest is "Devil" Anse Hatfield, the infamous feudist. Feuding has long been a standard trope for stereotyping mountain culture. But in closely reading the records and social history of one of the most notorious feuds, between the Hatfields and the McCoys in the Tug Valley on the Kentucky/West Virginia border, historian Altina Waller found that the dispute had very little to do with deep-seated patterns of violence and Civil War hostilities—a common interpretation. Instead, it had very much to do with newly emerging structures of power and authority in the period leading up to industrialization.[44] As Waller related, the feud was a clash between a traditional mountain culture, in which disputes were worked out face-to-face within a community of people who knew each other and shared customs of authority and mediation, and a newer orientation that was more connected to distant sources of authority such as town and state courts, legal land titles, and a money economy. Anse Hatfield, whose family had settled in the Tug Valley in the 1830s, stood at the center of those emerging tensions.

After a successful stint in the Civil War, Anse returned to settle down in the Tug Valley, only to find that he would have a difficult time making a living in the farming lifestyle that his family had known. Population had grown, tillable land was scarce, and new laws restricted the amount of wild game that Tug Valley residents could hunt. Anse was not content to work as a laborer on someone else's land, but in the early 1870s he found himself positioned to take advantage of changes coming to the area. He entered the burgeoning timber marketing business, selling timber from his own land and that of his brothers. By entering the timber trade, Anse departed from more than the farming economy. He also departed from the local moral economy, aligning himself with nonlocal authorities and forces of modernization. The market for timber brought competition and an accompanying suspicion between neighbors and within families, and it was considered by many to be a business fraught with dishonesty and risk.[45]

Legal battles over land rights and property borders added to the tensions. Devil Anse, aggressively seeking timber rights and profits, was involved in several lawsuits. Rather than working out disputes in a neighborly fashion, he used the legal system to his advantage and thus further situated himself outside of the obligations and authority of the local community. According to Waller, his "economic maneuvering" and "exercise of economic power" classified him as an outsider to his neighbors.[46] Over time, Devil Anse came to represent, in the Tug Valley, a way of acting and interacting that threatened traditional patterns of life and the livelihoods of those who refused to give up those patterns. Ultimately, the causes of the Hatfield and McCoy feud lay in the disjunctures between traditional and capitalist economic activity, as well as between local and state-sanctioned authority, and the tensions that ensued.

Waller's analysis is rich, and in portraying the social ramifications and expressions of the incursion of money, land speculation, and nonlocal legal structures on mountain culture, she also exposes the place of religious difference as it played through changing orientations to value and accumulation. The dominant form of organized religion in the Tug Valley in the late nineteenth century was the Primitive Baptists, according to Waller. Primitive Baptists, as noted in the last chapter, actively rejected missionary activity and evangelical denominations that had become the American mainstream. In doing so, wrote Waller, they "self-consciously perceived themselves as a separate community, independent from and diametrically opposed to an evangelical/commercial worldview."[47] The link between evangelical Christianity and the emergence of a national market economy and a middle class is important here, a link that has been made by Appalachian "old school" Baptists as well as American historians.[48] Primitive Baptists, understanding themselves as "in but not of" the world, condemned worldly gain—in matters material and social—as selfish and dangerous. Individual pursuit of profit and gain was sinful because it was an overvaluation of the worldly, but also because it threatened to disrupt social patterns of cooperation. It meant placing an illusory sense of value over real value, which was grounded in God's design. Hence Devil Anse's privileging of social and economic gain over community and family cooperation violated Primitive Baptist social ethics. It is worth considering, moreover, that in seeking to resolve conflicts that erupted as the result of his commercial activities by means of "outside" authorities, Anse bypassed and ignored local systems of social classification and authority that privileged the church and the social order that the church legitimated. Waller notes that his nickname, Devil, "if it did not originate in his commercial activities and aggressiveness, was sustained and reinforced by them." In fact, she cites Anse himself as saying, "I belong to no Church unless you say that I belong to the one great Church of the world. If you like, you can say it is the devil's Church that I belong to." Traditional mountain values, wrote Waller, "equated preoccupations with money, pride, and status as worldly, and worldly matters were not simply a separate category from religious ones—they were, by definition, indications of being in league with the devil."[49]

If Devil Anse Hatfield's story hints at the religious dimensions of socio-economic transformation in the context of logging, a second Devil of eastern Kentucky was directly tied to the development of the coal industry. His story shares similarities with Hatfield's, but also includes some interesting differences. Devil John Wright, also known as Bad John Wright, was born in Letcher County in 1844, the grandson of pioneer settlers of the county.[50] After a stint in the Confederate army during the Civil War, Wright joined the Robinson Circus where he performed as a trick rider and sharpshooter. He later served as sheriff of Wise County, Virginia, just over the border from his home county in Kentucky, and worked as a Pinkerton agent. Perhaps most famous as the real-life source of the character of Devil Judd Tolliver in John Fox, Jr.'s novel *The Trail of the Lonesome Pine,* Wright was known for his ability to track down and capture outlaws—and for the number of men he was said to have killed in that pursuit. Although late in his life he claimed to have killed only two men, legend had it that anywhere from twenty-seven to ninety men died at his hand.[51] In the mountains, legends mattered more than truth in establishing the image of this man called "Devil." He also was said to have fathered thirty-five children by several women. At the age of eighty-seven, Devil John underwent a conversion experience and was baptized in a river, thereby joining the Regular Baptist Church.[52] Devil Anse Hatfield also experienced conversion late in his life and was baptized by one of the "oldest and most respected hardshell preachers" in Logan County, West Virginia.[53]

Although the resources are lacking for the kind of close social historical analysis that Waller undertook in the case of the Hatfield feud, it is nevertheless tempting to apply some of her insights to the life of Devil John Wright. He, like Hatfield, was also known as a "feudist," and he found himself on both sides of the legal system. Wright's individualism and bravado put him outside of the law at times and certainly outside of respectability in many cases, but for the most part his activities were on behalf of legal authorities. His employment in the circus indicates that he was willing to take part in nontraditional forms of work for personal gain. And, most important, he eventually solved his financial difficulties by aligning himself with the forces of modernization. Not only did he willingly sell his Letcher County property to speculators who began surveying the region for coal in the 1870s, but he also joined up with a mineral speculation company, aiding investors and industrialists as they bought land and mineral

rights for tiny amounts of money from mountain residents. It was in this capacity, working in conjunction with the new structures of power and authority represented by commercial interests and a legal system that often protected them,
that Devil John's rough behavior rubbed against local social customs while im-
plementing new and foreign rules. As with Devil Anse, the name "Devil" might
not have originally derived from Wright's association with modernizing forces,
but it was "sustained and reinforced by them" and showed him to be in tension
with community values, even perceived as a threat to them. Also like Devil Anse,
his name itself indicated his social position as one straddling the forces of change,
aware of and implicated in older social values yet choosing, in the setting of a
transforming world, to play by different rules. Wright's predicament was representative of many rural Kentuckians at the close of the century, strapped between
a difficult way of life and the temptations offered by the emerging capitalist
economy. New opportunities to make money offered great rewards, but they also
threatened to tear the fabric of social life and its tightly related system of values.
To turn one's back on opportunity meant a life of struggle, but then again traditional religious and cultural patterns insisted that life was inherently a struggle
and that worldly gains that seemed to promise freedom from that struggle were
ultimately bound to fail. Worldly gains taken at the expense of others, or for selfish reasons, were indeed sinful.

The relevance of Devil John Wright's story becomes especially clear in the
particular context of Wright's relationship to the process of social and economic
change in the mountains: it was in large part due to Wright's efforts and those of
the investment company with which he worked that eastern Kentucky's coal
industry was able to assert the massive influence that it did in the decades that
followed.

The existence of large amounts of soft, bituminous coal under the eastern Kentucky and West Virginia ground was known early in the nineteenth century, but
these resources were not developed because of the problem of transporting minerals out of the hills.[54] Instead, the largest coal producing area of Kentucky in the
nineteenth century was western Kentucky's flatter lands. And, in fact, the majority of coal used by the steel and power plants that drove industrial America came
from the northern and western markets in Pennsylvania, Colorado, and Illinois.[55] Because of the complete lack of railroad infrastructure in the hills, coal

producers and railroad companies initially favored the construction of transportation lines between already-expanding centers of commerce over any plans to extract the central Appalachian mountains' minerals.

Nevertheless, as early as 1871, the governor of Kentucky established a Bureau of Immigration and developed a plan to recruit foreign labor and capital investors to the state in an effort to exploit its natural resources.[56] The problem of transportation was a real one, and mining in the mountains could not be a profitable business until railroads could be persuaded to enter the area. They would have to be enticed by the lucrative nature of the coal and timber markets themselves, since there seemed little other financial reason why they should expend energy and money on an endeavor into such a commercially undeveloped region. There was no doubt about the presence of coal under the hills, however, and in anticipation of eastern Kentucky's entrance into the national coal market with its "natural wealth" that lay free for the taking, private speculators began actively buying up land and mineral rights. Many of them were from out of state, such as Richard M. Boas of New York City, who purchased vast quantities of land in Pike and Letcher counties between 1887 and 1891. Some were even from overseas, such as the investment group from England who planned and built the "Magic City" of Middlesboro in 1889; by 1893 they went bankrupt. Others, though, were natives of the region who speculated on land themselves or who acted as brokers for out-of-state investors.[57] As the mountains became more and more connected with commercial interests outside the Appalachian region, especially from the North, the already existing social distinctions in the mountains grew wider. The upwardly mobile class of people, primarily located in the county seats—educated and connected to economic, social, and political networks in larger cities such as Lexington or Louisville—understood the potential of the coal industry and attached themselves to speculative or commercial interests that stood to gain from development.[58]

It was one of these men, John C. C. Mayo, to whom Devil John Wright sold his land and for whom he began to work in the 1890s.[59] A native of Pike County, Mayo graduated from Kentucky Wesleyan College, where he developed an interest in geology and minerals.[60] After college, working as a teacher in his home county, he spent his weekends exploring the Big Sandy Valley for coal deposits. Once he attained his law degree and was admitted to the Kentucky bar in 1886, he began to speculate in earnest, approaching farmers in the hills with the offer to buy the mineral rights to their land. His wife accompanied him on these trips, as legend has it, wearing a custom-made dress with hidden pockets holding gold pieces.[61] At the sight of the gold, many farmers immediately sold, most likely under the impression that they were getting the upper hand in this gamble over an industry that showed little or no signs of activity at the time. Plus, they understood that they were not selling the surface of their land but only the rights to the minerals below the ground. Between 1892 and 1907, Mayo, with Devil John Wright's help, acquired 700,000 acres in eastern Kentucky.[62] Some of this land was developed by mining corporations that Mayo helped to direct. Large amounts of it he eventually sold to companies like the Consolidated Coal Company, a business based in Maryland with holdings in Pennsylvania and West Virginia, which built the company town of Jenkins in the place where Wright had once lived. Mayo became eastern Kentucky's first millionaire.[63]

Mayo's story might strike some as startling, not the least because it announces that an Appalachian native was a millionaire who held such great power and wealth, cutting across popular images of mountain poverty and ignorance. At the same time, it would be too hasty to claim that he sold out his people, although some might rush to that judgment. The key to understanding his actions lies, beyond simple greed, in the overwhelming embrace of industrial and capitalist progress that was sweeping the United States, especially the middle classes, who stood to elevate their financial and social stature at the end of the nineteenth century. The rising professional class who occupied eastern Kentucky's county seats shared in the wider trend. It would not be off the mark to call this orientation to industrial progress a form of intoxication. These were the years of invention, when the Columbian Exposition in Chicago in 1893 mapped the history of humanity along an evolutionary trajectory from primitive to civilized, from nature's captive to ruler of the world through technology. The Exposition located America's progress at the pinnacle of this timeline and pushed forward toward the future as embodied in its most popular attraction, the "Electric City," with its eight-story-high Edison Tower of Light. Henry Adams wrote that "Chicago was the first expression of American thought as unity," and that unity expressed a collective representation of the nation's utopian possibilities as it envisioned them.[64] Electricity, of course, was fueled by coal. Against this backdrop, Mayo was able to understand his actions as bringing salvation in the form of economic progress to the people of his region. The untapped resources of the mountains were the very source of power that drove industry. Not only that, but according to the vision of progress he embraced, the industry that was required in order to excavate the coal from the hills would bring commerce and jobs to the region—and with commerce would come culture. For Mayo, the Appalachian region lacked any meaningful or valuable culture. He was not alone in this opinion; it was shared by writers and missionaries who had been producing images of Appalachia for the American public since the 1880s.[65] According to Mayo and other boosters of industrial progress, springing from the mountains along with the coal would come the liberation of the mountain people from their bondage to nature and its accompanying fatalism and superstitions.

A series of murals that hung on the wall of the mansion that Mayo built in Paintsville best expressed the mythological vision of industrial progress that he shared with other eastern Kentucky elites. A description of the murals written in 1921 portrayed them in language that reveals the power that they still had over the imagination of industrial progress a decade after they were painted and while the coal industry continued its expansion:

> Beginning with the picture of a young man seated upon a boulder, his eye steadfastly on the ground, the artist portrayed a shadowy scene beneath the surface, in which appeared the outlines of a massive and muscular giant, firmly chained by the seamless strata of stone and coal. Ages had passed during which no man had suspected the presence of the mighty being whose thews [sic] ached for the freedom of action, until the youth in the picture, gazing into the secret places below, caught a dreamer's vision of hidden power.
>
> Having sensed the presence of forces unsuspected by many generations of men, contented to till the soil and plow the hillsides above, the dreamer was seeking for a key which would unlock the treasure house beneath.
>
> Not many would enter with him into the vision of the things to come, when the corded muscles would be unlocked and the giant bidden to take his stride along the banks of the placid stream.
>
> In other pictures on the same wall, the story was told of his huge success. For when the slumbering Goliath of the hills at last awoke, he trod the line with transforming power; and from the Ohio to the Breaks of Sandy, the record of his prowess was told in brick and stone. Cities arose as if by magic. Imposing business houses soon stood beside more ornate temples of Divine Worship. Hundreds of dwellings of happy, contented people appeared.[66]

The sense of progress depicted in the murals celebrated the triumph of human will over nature's forces. Unchained, they magically (and naturally) led the mountains toward the values and institutions of America's industrial capitalist marketplace: cities, businesses, and ornate (as opposed to the mountain's plain) churches.

It was clear from statements given at Mayo's funeral in 1914—held at the Mayo Memorial Chapel, a Methodist church that he helped to build near his mansion in Paintsville—that others shared his vision. They also revealed the company that he kept. Honorary pallbearers included the Kentucky governor and an ex-governor, senators and other politicians, and elite from the region. They compared Mayo to "Columbus and other great captains and leaders in the history of the world" in his sense of purpose and persistence toward "the realization of the possibilities of wealth located in the hills and valleys of his beloved mountain section," despite all obstacles that had deterred others.[67] But more than seeing him as a farsighted investor, Mayo's eulogists saw his deeds paralleling those of colonists in other parts of the world. "Founding a new empire in Africa," the Louisville *Evening Post* wrote, "Cecil Rhodes, in his dying delirium murmured a line from [Alfred Lord] Tennyson: 'So much to do; so little done.' In Eastern Kentucky a like drama on a smaller and less conspicuous stage is passing, and one of the chief actors has been John C. Calhoun Mayo."

This was the world and worldview with which Devil John Wright became associated. By joining in Mayo's vision and actions, Devil John moved away from traditional patterns of life. Focusing on wealth and worldly progress was, as in the case of Devil Anse Hatfield, alien to traditional values. Although Mayo understood his actions to be helpful to eastern Kentucky society, they were nevertheless disruptive of that society and entailed a different set of values, a different sense of duty and obligation, and a different idea of community. Moreover, they were built upon ideas of work and authority that were decidedly removed from the household localism of the subsistence farm in rural mountain society.

It is telling that Mayo was also an active member of the Methodist church, which by that time was not "indigenous" to rural eastern Kentucky.[68] Although Methodism helped to shape the religious culture of the mountains in the early nineteenth century, by the 1840s eastern Kentucky was predominantly made up of independent Baptist churches. By the end of the nineteenth century, Methodism had become associated in the minds of many rural Appalachians with missionaries and the "foreign" religion—locally called "railroad religion"—that they brought with them to the mountains when Appalachia became a heavily trod missionary field for nationally organized Protestant denominations.[69] Decidedly nonlocal and aligned with the "foreign" denominational forms that mountain churches had actively rejected throughout the nineteenth century, railroad religion was connected historically to the process of modernization and development. The mountains, which had been ignored as an isolated backwoods region for much of the nineteenth century as the United States expanded westward and engaged in North-South conflicts, was suddenly "rediscovered" in the 1880s as both a mineral field and a missionary field.[70] In the words of Olive Dame Campbell, who extensively traveled through and studied Appalachian culture with her missionary husband, John C. Campbell, from 1908 until 1912 before founding the John C. Campbell Folk School in North Carolina in 1925, two types of people headed to the region at that time: "those who saw the natural resources and sought them regardless of the interests of the natural owners; and those who with missionary zeal rushed in to educate and reform."[71] The simultaneous arrival of industrialists and missionaries, both ushering in tremendous social, cultural, and economic change, could not help but appear connected in the perception of mountain residents.

Actual institutional connection between "railroad religions" and industrial interests was complicated.[72] They sometimes worked in tandem, but more often the relationship was cultural. In a study of the development of the industrial mining city of Middlesboro, Kentucky, sociologist John Gaventa suggested that religious institutions played a strong role in instilling the "ideological apparatus" that was part and parcel of industrial capitalism. According to this model, missionaries and preachers helped to change the values and behaviors of mountain residents, urging them away from their traditional rural orientation and toward "modern" habits and perspectives that internalized capitalist structures of authority.[73] Reports from missionaries who were involved in what was called "mountain white work" from the 1880s onward underscored the point that nationally organized denominations saw Appalachians as materially poor and linked their material conditions to religious and cultural causes. They saw Appalachian culture's acceptance of God's design and the human place in it as "fatalism" that could be overcome with education. Indeed, visitors to the region during this period commented continually on the fatalistic attitudes that led mountain natives to think that they could not change their conditions. Much as in the scenes portrayed in Mayo's murals, missionaries and social workers alike saw themselves as bringing aid to a "retarded frontier" that had been left out of the flow of progress and civilization.[74]

In truth, missionaries and settlement workers held ambivalent attitudes toward the residents of Appalachia and their ways of life. On the one hand, they were drawn to what they saw as a simple way of life that was quickly vanishing in modern industrial America. Charmed by mountain folkways, crafts, and localism, they saw in the rural mountains a counter to the fragmentation and alienation that they criticized modernity for fostering. On the other hand, reformers were thoroughly modern themselves. Mountain white workers, whether supported by religious or secular organizations (and the line between these was blurry), were primarily women from the northeastern states who reported in diaries, letters, and publications that they were put off by the lack of manners, education, and hygiene that they found upon arriving in the mountains. It was these aspects of mountain life that they sought to change, while trying to maintain the simplicity and authenticity that they found valuable.[75] As "foreign" observers struggled to express what they valued and what they did not in mountain culture, religion and "superstition" came under special criticism.[76] Religious affiliation became one important way that mountain natives like Mayo, who resided in developed towns, aligned themselves with industry and progress, and differentiated themselves from Appalachian stereotypes and rural residents.[77]

In this setting, rural eastern Kentucky natives perceived a connection between the industrial and religious forces that were simultaneously transforming their cultural, economic, and natural landscape. Many recognized that railroad religion's orientation to the world ran counter to their own, placing human industry and will above God's design.[78] What mountain natives saw as the acceptance of limitation and divine plan, missionaries saw as fatalism. What missionaries saw as progress and improvement, mountain natives saw as a religion too focused on the world and not open to the power of the Holy Spirit. As one astute observer wrote in 1933,

> An almost insurmountable barrier between missionaries of all denominations and the people they have come to assist, lies in differences regarding basic conceptions as to the nature of religion. . . . Holding such divergent views, both the Highlanders and the missionaries find it almost impossible to recognize the validity of the religious experiences of the other party. The missionary tends to minimize the religious values possessed by the Highlander, characterizing them, in the words of one such minister, as "intense and strange spiritual vagaries." The Highlander, for his part, tends to believe that the "brought on religion" with its coldness and its heretical doctrines is not religion at all.[79]

Presbyterians, Methodists, Congregationalists, Episcopalians, Southern Baptists, and others expended a considerable amount of time and resources on their mountain white work, transforming the religious landscape of central Appalachia but at the same time driving an even deeper wedge between nationally organized denominations and mountain churches that increasingly perceived "railroad religion" as a threat to their very understanding of the nature of human beings and the world. As the industrial economy in eastern Kentucky grew into the first decades of the twentieth century and towns and county seats grew into cities and commercial centers, their downtown areas resembled most other growing American towns religiously. The stone or brick churches that were most visible, most powerful, and most integrated with the civic, political, and economic institutions were those of the large national denominations. Methodists and Southern Baptists prevailed, as they did elsewhere in the South. Old Regular Baptists, independent Holiness, and other "mountain" churches remained in the rural areas or on the outskirts of towns.

John C. C. Mayo's story is just one, a dramatic one, of the tremendous economic activity that was transforming eastern Kentucky from a rural area oriented toward farming to a principal site of production for the nation's industrial coal concerns. Mayo's particular vision and investments did not reach full development until around the time of his death. Over the course of the first two decades of the twentieth century, the economy, demography, and landscape took a new shape, defined by coal operations and driven by their needs. Mines sprang up wherever railroad lines and coal deposits merged, and around many mines coal companies developed towns, or "camps," to house their workers.[80] Ironically, the value and obligation that eastern Kentucky rural culture placed on work was largely responsible for leading farmers to take up "public work" building these towns, laying railroad tracks, and mining coal. While Devil John Wright joined forces with the highest powers of development, most of his neighbors entered on a scale that was less grand. Driven by the complex interplay of material needs, available opportunities, and new desires, eastern Kentucky residents forged new lives that were built around the work of mining coal.

THREE

COAL TOWN LIFE

Only during the last decade has eastern Kentucky become a coal field of national importance. It is now a far-flung battleground of old traditions and new ideas. The old-time, quiet, picturesque mountain and hill land regions are rapidly becoming more and more restricted in area. Everywhere may be noted the advance of new railroad grades, the construction of new coal mining operations, and the growth of new industrial cities.

—WILLARD ROUSE JILLSON,
The Coal Industry in Kentucky, 1924

A mountain man becomes a miner. He moves his family and a few household goods from the picturesque cabin in the cove or on the ridge to a desolate shack in the sordid village that has sprung up around the mine. He had not realized that he would have to buy all his food. . . . He has to pay even for water to drink. The life of nature, of which he was a part, has been torn from him, and, stripped naked of all he has been accustomed to, he might as well be in a dungeon. The vices of our industrial progress fasten their tentacles upon him and soon suck out his life. His children are surrounded by ugliness instead of beauty, their time is spent in idleness instead of the healthy-minded recreations of the woods and the educative family chores incident to tilling the soil.

—JAMES WATT RAINE, *The Land of the Saddle-Bags:
A Study of the Mountain People of Appalachia,* 1924

WHEN ASKED WHY SHE THOUGHT people traded farming for mining, one miner's wife who lived both on a farm and in a coal camp replied that "there was no money in farming. Farmers in eastern Kentucky . . . raised what they needed for themselves, not for market. The farms were small."[1] With the increasing penetration of a cash economy into the mountains, owing to the timber and mining industries, accompanied by population growth and the declining availability of tillable or affordable land, "public work" became even more of a necessity. Mining offered this opportunity. "They made money and they could buy things with money," the same woman continued. "That's why they went to the coal mines." So work brought men and their families to the coal mines, but the meaning and place of work in everyday life was changing dramatically. Mining families found older patterns of life disrupted and familiar values challenged. Still, mining families worked with and sometimes transformed familiar cultural resources, including religious idioms, as they navigated new forms of power and oriented themselves to their new world.

At first, mining functioned like other additive labor in the mountains. Farmers would find work with coal companies, usually in the winter when there was less farmwork, as a monetary supplement to their other forms of production.[2] As the demand for coal grew during and following World War I, however, and the number and size of coal companies increased, the relationship between farming and mining was gradually inverted. The transitional period, lasting through the 1920s, involved more than an economic shift; it was also a profound cultural and social transformation. Kentucky writer James Still captured some of the tensions involved during this process in his novel *River of Earth*. The story is set in the early 1920s as Brack Baldridge, trying to provide for his wife and family, is lured time and again to the work of mining. The work is sporadic, however, driven by the market and labor supply. His wife, Alpha, tired of moving from camp to camp to find work, longs for the life of farming where the family could settle down and stay in one place. "Forever I've wanted to set us down in a lone spot, a place certain and enduring, with room to swing arm and elbow, a garden-piece for fresh victuals, and a cow to furnish milk for the baby," she cries. "So many places we've lived—the far side one mine camp and next the slag pile of another. Hardburly. Lizzyblue. Tribbey. I'm longing to set me down shorely and raise my chaps proper." For Alpha, the world of farming is already slipping into the realm of nostalgic desire, patterns of life that are no longer an everyday reality. Brock, however, has a different perspective. "It was never meant for a body to be full content on the face of this earth," he replies angrily to Alpha, banishing even the idea of a contented life as a false hope—or a sin. Life is meant to be hard work and struggle, he seems to be suggesting, and it was necessary for him to mine coal to fulfill his manly duty of providing food for his family. "Against my wont it is to be treading the camps, but it's bread I'm hunting, regular bread with a mite of grease on it. To make and provide, it's the only trade I know, and I work willing."[3] In the novel, and in reality, that work profoundly impacted and shaped the contours and textures of life in eastern Kentucky.

By the height of the coal boom in the 1920s, most men in Bell, Harlan, Perry, Letcher, Floyd, and Pike counties were mining coal as their main means of employment, and the U.S. Coal Commission determined that 64.4 percent of miners in eastern Kentucky lived in coal towns. As the Baldridges' story suggests, eastern Kentucky miners could be a mobile lot, either by choice or necessity, migrating from farm to coal camp and back, or from company to company and mine to mine in search of better wages and conditions. It is difficult to determine the real numbers of steady coal town inhabitants, since people were often coming and going. Meanwhile, the number of farms in eastern Kentucky rose only slightly or declined between 1900 and 1930; in Harlan County, to cite one example, the number decreased every decade during that time, despite a rapidly increasing population due to births and the influx of people coming to work in the mines. Most miners and their families, therefore, were intimately familiar with coal town life.[4]

The extent of the coal industry's transformation of the landscape of eastern Kentucky, and of the patterns of movement and exchange within it, are mind-boggling. A string of coal mines and their affiliated towns quickly sprang up, one after another, paralleling the state's border with Virginia for over 100 miles. They effectively reoriented the environment around industrial landmarks instead of natural ones, with the result that people came to locate themselves in space with reference to mines and camps.[5] In Harlan County alone, over twenty-five coal towns were built between 1912 and 1928.[6] By 1927 there were thirty-three new towns in Letcher County, thirty-seven in Perry County, and forty in Pike County. One of the most profound examples of the area's transformation remains today in the names of towns and geographic locations that were created or renamed as mines came into existence. Where once places had been named for settlers, landmarks, local events, or biblical characters and sites, the

industrial landscape was made up of places named for coal companies and sometimes their officials. Hardburly, for instance, was the name of a town founded by
the Hardy Burlington Mining Company. The coal town of Van Lear was named
for Van Lear Black, director of Consolidated Coal Company (known as Consol),
who with John C. C. Mayo was instrumental in acquiring the land and mineral
rights owned by that company. Jenkins, likewise, took its name from George C.
Jenkins, another Consol director. Other examples abound. The men for whom
these towns were named were not natives of the region—they typically resided
in the northern states where the coal companies were also headquartered. Other
towns, or camps, were simply known by the mine portal number that they were
built around: "mine number one" or "camp two."

Coal camps were entirely owned and operated by the coal companies that
built them to house workers and, often, their families. The location of coal mining operations, combined with settlement and transportation patterns in the
mountains, made it necessary for companies to provide housing if they were going to bring together and hold a regular workforce. Boardinghouses were fine for
single working men, but as mining became a regular line of work, entire families
required a place to live near the job site. Company towns, then, were as regular a
feature of coal mining operations as the mines themselves during the first half
of the twentieth century. Although their popular image is a bleak one, coal towns
varied widely in their conditions and amenities. It is hard to generalize about
their cleanliness or state of repair. Some were haphazardly thrown up, usually
in the beginning stages of a mining development or around mines where companies expected that the supply of coal would be depleted quickly.[7] Many camps
never advanced past the basics for a variety of reasons: the companies that owned
them may have cared little for the welfare of their workers, or they were smaller
companies that had little capital available for town development. Such minimal
camps have become familiar images, made up of bleak-looking box frame houses
all of the same style lining a narrow valley, perhaps with railroad tracks running
down the middle or behind the houses.

Others coal towns, however, presented a counter image. These, fewer in
number but larger in size, were well planned and elaborately constructed, owned
by huge conglomerates that in some cases were able to use the coal mined in Kentucky for their own steel refining plants elsewhere, thereby retaining higher
profits. The "model towns" of Lynch, Benham, and Jenkins are examples: Jenkins, in Letcher County, was owned and built by the Consolidation Coal Com-

No. 203 Mine Camp, Jenkins, Ky., 1913. Item 137, The Jenkins, Kentucky Photographic Collection, 1911–1930, 2001AV01, University of Kentucky Archives. Used by permission.

pany of Maryland. It was known as a "5 by 5 town, five miles long and five yards wide," but it was actually over eight miles along a mountain valley and was composed of a number of smaller towns (Jenkins, McRoberts, Dunham, Burdine, and others) incorporated into one large one.[8] Benham and Lynch, located two miles from each other, were two of eastern Kentucky's largest operations, the former owned by the Wisconsin Steel Company and the latter by United States Coal and Coke, both of which were affiliated with International Harvester of Chicago. Benham's first train car of coal shipped in September 1911, while Lynch, built quickly in anticipation of demand created by World War I, shipped its first load in 1917. Lynch boasted the largest coal tipple in the world at the time as well as a modern electrical plant that supplied power to Benham and surrounding towns.[9] Jenkins's plant generated electricity for surrounding towns, too. "Model towns" like these were constructed around theories of urban planning and workplace design that emerged from studies of the successes and failures of America's increasingly dense and industrialized cities. Progressive urban planners saw in coal towns the opportunity to design industrial villages and cities from the "ground up" in the undeveloped Appalachian hills, as compared to the more frustrating challenge of working with previously existing structures in already developed cities.[10] To retain a productive and reliable workforce, these nicer towns were built with the idea of supplying miners, their families, and company officials with all the amenities that they might desire, including stores, movie theaters, schools, sports teams, hotels, auditoriums, churches, and banks. The paternalistic goal was contented workers and a setting designed to attract both miners and officials.[11]

Although most coal towns were not so elaborate as Jenkins or Lynch, they still could hold out the promise of a life that was unattainable through farming. Many of those people who moved themselves or their families to the camps were there out of economic necessity, but it would be a mistake to imagine that coal mining was purely and simply a desperate act born out of impending poverty. Coal towns were complex places, disrupting patterns of life that had dominated the mountains for a century, but they also instilled new desires and ambitions. Coal towns had much to offer people who were accustomed to subsistence farming. For some, the convenience of a local store stocked with items that were difficult to obtain on rural farms was a boon. One wife of a coal miner, asked later in her life what she had liked best about living in a coal town, noted the availability of fresh meat and vegetables. On the farm where she grew up her family had to preserve and can their foods to last out of season, and the closest store was a two- or three-mile walk away.[12] In comparison, coal camps could ignite in some rural residents fantasies of an easier life where the world was at one's fingertips. Marvin Gullett, who lived in the Blue Diamond camp in Perry County in the 1920s and 1930s, recalled that "most people felt they was going to paradise when they moved to the mining camps. It was a way of life that they liked. The wages was so low on the farm you couldn't make more than a dollar a day, or fifty cents a day. [In the mines] they would make seven, eight, or ten dollars a day." That was during the boom years when demand for coal was high and mining provided wages that were unheard of elsewhere in that part of the country. Yet, again, the move to mining was also a move away from familiar values and structures of living, and Gullet pointed out that "some people wouldn't be satisfied with it, though most people settled down to that way of life for economical reasons. They could make better money around the mining country, is why some followed mining, not that they liked it too good."[13] Clearly, the transition to mining as a primary occupation was full of ambivalence and carried the potential for both moral and aesthetic dilemmas.

Whatever their reasons for moving, miners and their families encountered and created a new world in coal towns. It was in many ways a hybrid world, a mixture of rural and urban, as the variety of amenities already noted suggests. Despite the Appalachian location of eastern Kentucky, which was still being represented in the nation's popular media as a backwards, rural area out of step with the times, coal towns were directly linked to the material and social concerns of urban America. Coal drove industrial furnaces and locomotives; it fueled the electrical plants that powered the lights of the cities; coke, a derivative of coal created by baking it at high temperatures, was a necessary component of the production of both iron and steel. In other words, the physical labor exerted by coal miners literally powered America's industrial and increasingly urban development. Coal towns were not only the roots of the industrial production process, but thanks to the industrial design and ideology that lay behind many of them—and the fact that company officials also lived in them—they were strongly shaped by the market-driven ideologies of urban life. This combination of urban patterns in an out-of-the-way place, transforming the region within the span of less than one generation, aroused both anxieties and a sense of possibility, much as urban areas did elsewhere in the country. As miners and their families navigated these new spaces, they drew upon their familiar patterns of life. In coal towns, however, they discovered that nature—or God's design—was no longer the dominant force dictating life's rhythms. Industry enveloped people in new "nature" where economic forces were just as powerful and often more determining of the dynamics of daily life.

One place where the industrial nature of coal towns revealed itself most plainly and directly was in the houses in which miners and their families lived. The structures themselves were both an indication and a source of new patterns of life that mining introduced, materializing the tension between hope and limitation that characterized the coal industry and the company town in particular. Houses in company towns were typically wood framed with a porch and two to four rooms, as distinct from the log house structures that were common to the Kentucky hills before the arrival of the coal industry. Coal town houses were heated by a centrally located coal-burning stove. Electricity was

relatively common, but running water was not, except in model towns; elsewhere, most houses had outhouses or "privies" nearby. The number of designs
or floor plans was limited, and houses were built close together in rows, creating a visual appearance of regularity. In some cases duplex houses brought two
or more families under one roof in coal towns, forcing people to associate daily
with nonfamily members in a way that they never had on their farms. While
houses may have been painted, often all the same color, in most camps the
paint competed with soot from railroad engines and coal dust that rained
down on structures built anywhere near coal tipples or train tracks. The dust
was ubiquitous in coal camps, a common frame of reference shared by everyone who had experienced mining. Some companies, especially those that
owned model towns, tried harder than others to keep their towns clean and
houses in shape. Most were not so well cared for. One miner who worked at
Consol on Smoot Creek in Letcher County recalled that "the living conditions
was terrible. Now I want to tell you, it was terrible. It was filthy, in other words.
Sanitation was out. . . . It'd been pretty hard to tell, actually, how people existed, but they did."[14] Sanitation was always a problem in coal camps throughout the 1920s. They shared with other urban areas the sanitation problems that
came with population density, which were only exacerbated by the lack of running water in most houses.[15]

Because they retained ownership of their houses and drew rent from miners' pay, companies exerted an immense amount of control over who lived in
their towns and what kinds of behaviors they would accept. Coal towns were
not democratic civic spaces, regardless of the amount of paternalistic care a
company might profess. Rental practices could also be the source of questionable financial gain for coal companies, even when a miner did not live in a coal
town. Gabe Newsome reported this arrangement at Dorton where he lived and
mined for the Wright Elkhorn Coal Company starting in 1927. "You had to pay
house rent if you got a job and the house a-sitting there empty," he said. "If you
had your own farm [within] a mile of it, you had to pay house rent or you don't
get a job."[16] Men told stories about having to pay rent on company houses
whether they lived in them or not. According to one story from the town of
Henry Clay, several miners checked their pay stubs one day and found that a
portion of their wages had been withheld for rent. Comparing pay stubs, they
discovered that they all were paying rent on the same house.[17] Conversely,
since only those who worked for a company could live in that company's
houses, miners who were released from work for whatever reason were also

required to evacuate their homes. Company control over housing was especially important as a powerful mechanism of extortion during periods of union activism in the 1930s.

Houses were one way that coal companies directly impacted the home and family life of miners. The company store was another. The store, usually standing in a centralized location in the town, was the primary—and often the only—place to purchase necessities. It carried food, clothing, and other personal items, and it sold the tools required for mining that the miner had to purchase himself—his head light, dynamite, tamping rod, and so forth. Most companies had their own form of currency, called "scrip," that was redeemable only for goods at the company-owned store. This way the company cut out competition from independent merchants who might keep stores near coal towns. The company store, moreover, often accepted *only* scrip (not cash). The result, at least potentially, was a closed economy in which a single company's unique coinage was used for wages and store purchases. Both scrip and company stores have become legendary for the way that they tied miners and their families to a coal company through debt. In some cases miners found themselves in debt to the company from the start, with their required rent and the cost of their equipment deducted from their paycheck. Paid by the ton of coal they loaded, miners never knew how large their paycheck would be until payday. When they went to draw their pay, they might find that after debts were taken out they had very little left.[18] One miner recalled that his brother "went down here below Pikeville at the Polley Mine Company and got him a job and went to work. And paid a dollar a day for board and got into debt for his board and had to stay twelve months before he'd quit. He stayed twelve months and drawed six dollars and come home and never did go back."[19]

Such stories recall the image of the company store popularized by Tennessee Ernie Ford's recording of Merle Travis's song "Sixteen Tons," in which loading sixteen tons of coal only made a miner older and deeper in debt. The company store even owned his soul. Historian Crandall Shifflett claims that the actual number of cases of "debt peonage" to companies was slight, but the oral history of coal towns reveals the company store as the source of many worries.[20] Indeed, as Travis's song might suggest, the store became a potent symbol in the coal fields at the time and through subsequent history as the setting or subject of stories that were commentaries on the inequalities and difficulties of the life of coal mining. As the interface between worker and company, the place where a person's work was translated into pay or purchases, the store was the primary site of industrial capitalist power as manifested in these exchanges. It was the concrete sign, therefore,

Garden and Meat Market, Jenkins, Ky., 1916. Item 52, The Jenkins, Kentucky Photographic Collection, 1911–1930, 2001AV01, University of Kentucky Archives. Used by permission.

of labor's commodification, where human labor was "redeemed"—often for less than it was worth, according to the stories that circulated among miners and entered coal mining folklore.

In spite of its potential for abuse, the company store was also in many ways the center of coal town social life and its intersection with the wider world. The store was a place where townspeople could pick up news from near and far, from around the town and from neighboring towns, and even from the wider nation outside the mountains. It was the place where mail came and went and a favorite site for exchanging gossip and visiting with other town residents.[21] Frances Turner, who lived in several camps as the daughter of a mining executive, described visiting the store at Weeksbury as "probably the social event of the day," which was probably true in other coal camps as well. "Where modern women might go to a discussion club, or to an afternoon bridge game, or to a matinee, or to an art museum," Turner said, "these women got 'cleaned up,' I remember they called it, and they went to the store. They managed to spend quite a bit of time there. They saw people from all over the coal camp in different parts of the store and it was a social occasion as well as a business affair."[22] Perhaps because the store was a space of sociality for women while men were down in the mines, and because women's labor was not translated into money at the store, women seem to have had a different relationship to the company store than men did. It appears in women's recollections as more of a social place than a source of stories of injustice. It was also the place where new products were displayed. In addition to all of its practical supplies for work and home, the store promoted the desire for nonessential consumer items like dresses and hats and entertainment like radios and phonographs. Nearly everybody passed through it each day, so life could almost be imagined as radiating outward from the store. The fact that it was *this* location, the center of commodification, consumption, and consumer desire, that stood at center stage in social interaction is significant, since coal towns owed their existence to commerce—and in complex ways they cultivated the consumer desires that were prevalent in developed urban areas. The store served as a hub, drawing people into the orbit of commercial life and connecting them through networks of trade, transportation, and news to other towns and beyond, even as it stood as a sign of a new relationship between work and subsistence. Replacing the church and "workings" as a primary locus of community interaction and exchange outside of the family unit, the store ironically embodied continuities of rural farming social patterns in the context of new, nonlocal networks that underlay the structures of social interaction in the industrial capitalist marketplace.

The store and attendant commercial outlets that were often connected to the store in more developed camps—places like soda fountains, grills, barber shops, and movie theaters—carried with them a way of life decidedly different from that known prior to the coal industry's existence. Along with the commodification of labor and the ready availability of consumer items, then, coal towns also introduced new patterns of leisure time that larger company towns tried to structure through organized, often commodified, forms of entertainment. Some of the nicer towns maintained baseball teams that competed against other companies' teams and sometimes against professional athletes. Star players were sought after, even recruited, by coal companies, and they were given more desirable jobs.[23]

Many camps had theaters that featured movies, vaudeville acts, traveling theatrical productions, and other events. The theater was the center of commercial cultural life and was attended by all classes of people.[24] "There was always in every camp I ever lived a movie house," according to Frances Turner.[25] For children, women, and men alike, movies were a popular leisure pastime, as were the other events that were presented in theaters. Wary of the potential for "immoral" or "improper" topics or behaviors in films or performances, some commercial centers like Harlan, in the midst of the coal fields, created censorship boards in order to police what was shown. Theaters in the rougher camps, where such cultural policing did not exist, may have been more apt to show racier material. Through films and performances, the cultures or cultural representations of the entire world came through eastern Kentucky's coal towns and must have contributed to new visions of the world and its possibilities.

During the 1920s, many miners also listened to radios and phonographs.[26] The incredibly creative developments of central Appalachian musical styles during that time period—including religious music—reveal the impact of these influences.[27] All of these things, said Frances Turner, "spread a new kind of culture to eastern Kentucky. I'm not saying it's a better kind of culture, I'm only saying a new kind of culture."[28] As her reservation begins to suggest, with the cultural variety of the mini-metropolis came also the anxieties and ambivalences that affected people in urban areas all over America at this time.

Working with Diversity

Adding to both the novelty and anxiety in coal camps was the everyday presence of people from places far from the mountains. A significant labor force was required to meet the high demand for coal during the 1920s, one that exceeded the capacity of the local population to fill. Coal companies therefore recruited employees from far-reaching locales. George McCoy of Jenkins described how companies would bring people from outside the mountains to work in the mines. "Do you know what transportation is?" he began.

> Well, they would send a man off, a labor agency say to Cleveland, Ohio, when they wanted miners. People would go to the labor agency looking for jobs. The labor agency would buy them a ticket and send them to Jenkins. They would live here

and if they had a family, they would set up housekeeping. Consol gave them a house furnished, on a lease, of course. They give them enough groceries to last them about a week, until they could get something in the office to draw scrip.[29]

Once they got to eastern Kentucky, many miners who came into the coal fields "on transportation" found it difficult to leave, since they were expected to pay the company back for the expenses of transporting them.[30] These people were not easy to locate in the traditional mental maps that eastern Kentucky natives used to place people in their familiar social networks. They were not kin, nor kin of known neighbors; they were not always from familiar or recognizable places; they had no local connections of social obligation. Their presence made the social fabric of the coal fields more complicated and dense, requiring new strategies of social exchange and "placing."

Transportation added still further to the increasingly complex texture of coal town habitation by bringing European immigrants and African Americans to the coal fields during the boom years between 1915 and the mid-1920s. Neither of these groups was widely represented in the mountains prior to industrial development, but in their need for workers coal companies brought African Americans from the deeper South and immigrants from all over Europe. An employee of Elkhorn Coal Company recalled going to Huntington, West Virginia, to attract black laborers to the coal town of Wheelwright in Floyd County, Kentucky, soon after it was incorporated in 1917. By the 1920s, he said, blacks were coming by train on their own from as far away as Alabama and Louisiana.[31] Northern destinations like Chicago, Detroit, and Harlem often overshadow the central Appalachian coal fields in studies of the Great Migration, but many African Americans also headed to the mines for work during the 1920s.[32] Likewise, it is commonplace to think of northern cities when one thinks of European immigration in the early twentieth century, but the coal fields attracted their share, promoting jobs in the North and abroad. One historian's breakdown of ethnic groups in Harlan County alone in 1920 gives an indication of the multicultural environment that coal mining produced: 320 Hungarians, 233 Italians, 145 Yugoslavians, 100 Poles, 98 Mexicans, 92 Russians, 69 Austrians, 70 Czechoslovakians, 19 Germans, 14 English, 14 Greeks, 13 Syrians, 8 Canadians, 8 Irish, 7 French, 7 Rumanians, 5 Scots, 4 Welsh, 3 Swedes, 3 Swiss, 1 Dutch, and 47 others of unknown nationality. Over time these numbers changed, as Italians replaced Hungarians as the largest group between 1920 and 1927, and after 1927 the overall percentage of immigrants in the area declined considerably.[33] The Johnson-Reid

Act of 1924 was in part behind these demographic shifts, as it limited immigration through quotas and drastically lowered the number of foreign workers who could enter the United States. Also, many immigrants who had come for the available work but found themselves in debt left as soon as they were able, returning to Europe or moving to northern cities when the coal market declined.

Neither African American nor immigrant labor ever made up even one quarter of the total labor force in eastern Kentucky's coal industry, but both contributed to the diversity and population density of coal camps and created an environment conducive to cultural innovation.[34] Among the more influential creations that emerged from the interactions of customs in this setting was the blending of white Appalachian and southern black musical styles that shaped the development of mountain and country music. The flip side to the potential for new and hybrid cultural forms, of course, was a pronounced apprehension of the unknown and perhaps threatening "other." The noticeable yet limited size of the African American and immigrant populations probably exacerbated a sense among white native miners that these were "outsiders" who were out of place in the mountains. Such anxieties lay behind very real limitations on the free interaction of cultural difference when it came to everyday social life and living situations. Coal towns, as microcosms of the social fabric of America during this period, were highly segregated places. Social distinctions were materialized in the built environment of towns so as to reveal a moral mapping and create a sense of controlled order out of the perceived chaos of racial, ethnic, and class differences. Most camps had special areas named after the ethnic group that lived there, like "Hunk Town" for the Hungarians and Polish and "Yellow Flats" for the Italians.[35] Companies in many cases built separate camps for African Americans. Referring to black miners, one resident of the town of Wheelwright said, "They didn't want them in the center of town, let me put it like that. For some reason the company didn't want them, Elkhorn didn't want them to go into town, so they just picked these two hollers out and stuck 'em up in here."[36] This resident also said that wages were the same for both white and black miners, and on the job all miners worked together without trouble.[37] They only socialized and lived separately. Still, oral histories tell of definite racial tensions. At Henry Clay, for instance, when a black miner killed a white miner in a fight, the black man and his family were quickly run out of town by an angry white mob.[38] Blacks and whites went to separate churches, schools, and even theaters. When they did use the same facilities, commonly understood seating patterns kept black and white apart. While there were many coal field residents who claimed that ethnic and racial diversity was seldom a problem, one white native Kentucky miner expressed the power and importance that maintaining these boundaries held for many when he said that he was raised to think that "anything that was foreign was against [our] way of life somehow." He continued, "I never even associated with these colored people; to me they was just as foreign as could be. We was taught from early times that because they had caused the great Civil War over slavery a Nigger was unworthy to be free, wasn't even worth [associating] with because he'd been sold into slavery."[39] He recalled many instances when American-born whites used violence to respond to trouble, or in many cases rumors of trouble, caused by African Americans or immigrants. Rumors and stories about these "others" shaped white miners' perceptions, but they should also be recognized as attempts by white mountain natives to name the unknown, to gain some sense of order and control by signifying the "otherness" of these other people and the anxieties that they provoked.

Segregated facilities and residential areas were created by the coal companies' policies, but in some cases white eastern Kentucky natives added their own religiously based inflection to the classification of different types of persons they were now living among. Just as Appalachian Protestant traditions claimed a biblical basis for gender differences, subordinating women to men's authority, these same traditions also provided reasoning through which to classify other peoples with reference to ideals of human conduct or divine design. As native whites confronted the potential chaos of differences in coal camps, they called upon *work* as one of the important resources that they used to navigate and order. They extended the concept, which bore so much weight in mountain culture's understanding of human purpose and value, to envelop and classify entire groups of people as inferior. African Americans, according to this logic, were inferior because they had been slaves, because they worked as cheap labor and took jobs from white workers, and because "whatever the boss puts on them they take it and won't open their mouth."[40]

Another group of people who were distrusted and disliked because of their rumored relationship to work was Jews. Some camps had independently owned stores nearby, competing with the company store for business. In some cases these stores were run by Jews, though in many cases they were not. Nevertheless, in some areas such independent stores were known as "Jew stores."[41] According to one miner, "The Jews were very much hated people." The reason was straightforward: "They peddled goods and mountain people thought anybody [who] wouldn't get out and work by the sweat of his brow and breath was terrible."[42] Other European immigrants, on the other hand, had the reputation of being extremely hard physical laborers. They escaped being categorized in terms of their ability or willingness to work, but white native miners found them suspect for another reason: many of the European miners were Catholic, and that was enough. One priest who served the immigrant mining population noted of native whites that "it is their firm conviction that the Catholics believe neither in Christ nor in the Bible, that they worship the Virgin and adore pictures, that they are a mixture of Mormons, Jews and Mohammedans, and that it is safer not to fool with them."[43]

Race and ethnicity were only two categories of social distinction, both heavily inflected with religious significance as they were articulated in the mountain white imagination. But the system of classification that subsumed all other distinctions of groups in the industrial setting, *class,* was indicative of a new order of the world that measured people and value in very different terms. Class had something vaguely to do with work, but the industrial world measured the value and reward of work through the logic of the marketplace. Class difference, like distinctions of race and ethnicity, was visibly inscribed in the material culture of coal towns. Frances Turner recalled that company officials' houses were bigger and nicer than the houses in which laborers lived, and they were often set up on a hill above the miners' homes. According to Mae Prater, the bosses "had bigger houses, and some of 'em had baths in 'em. None of the people that just rented, you know, when working the mines, they didn't have baths in 'em." Working families bathed in a washtub with water from the well, or miners used the communal bathhouse outside the mine entrance to scrub the coal dust off their bodies before returning home from work. The nicer towns such as Weeksbury also built clubs and hotels that only company officials could use. Turner described three levels of housing in Van Lear, which were typical of many towns: first were those structures belonging to top officials, which were the largest and nicest. The house that Turner and her family lived in was "probably seventy-five feet long." It included an attic ballroom, six bedrooms, three bathrooms, and a conservatory. The basement had six additional rooms, and the whole thing was heated by steam radiators. Next in line were the houses inhabited by bookkeepers, accountants, and doctors. The area where these houses were located was called "Silk Stocking Row," a name that appeared in other towns as well. As a younger and more socially inclined crowd, Turner said, these employees would meet for parties, picnics, and card games. Silk Stocking Row was the social center of the elite. Finally, there were the laborers' houses. These were assigned "on the basis of the man's efficiency; what he was worth to the company.... As he showed that he was a desirable worker he was promoted, maybe not money-wise, but he was moved into a better house in a better part of the camp." The center of camp was most desired, according to Turner, because it was where most of the social activity went on.[44]

Clearly, the social logic of the company town measured and displayed status in a highly discernible way. Although preindustrial eastern Kentucky was not the classless egalitarian society that some have pictured, in coal towns social and economic differences were compressed and inescapable, a proximate and visible material part of the landscape that miners lived in and moved through every day. Coal companies rewarded the commercial value of labor, weighing work in terms of the value a worker added to the company through production and efficiency. And the reward was material: a nicer house, in a nicer location, and perhaps a raise in pay or other perks. Work's value itself differed considerably between the preindustrial hills and this market-driven setting where the coal company, rather than nature, mediated labor's fruits. It promoted the perception of a marked disjuncture between work and reward that might have been partly responsible for the prevalence of gambling in many coal towns in the 1920s as miners tried their luck at striking it big and often lost what little they had. It is likely that the demand for money that the industrial economy intensified led to feverish competition, exacerbated by growing desires for commodities and the evident class differences clearly displayed on the landscape and made more pronounced by the growing wealth of commercial town centers.

Coal towns shared with other growing urban centers in the United States a distinct moral ambivalence. On the one hand, their density, diversity, and yearnings could cause stresses that overflowed into violent outbursts. Close living quarters combined with the loose sociality of worker mobility and the speeded-up rhythms of daily life to produce an atmosphere in which fights and even killings were not uncommon. Martha Clark, who lived in McRoberts during that time, painted a picture of the potentially tense atmosphere of coal town life: "It was, when we first came here, it was so many people here till they had these houses divided up, and they had steps to go down from the outside, so that different families wouldn't bother each other.... They were working in the mines, fighting and killing every Saturday, nearly every Sunday morning somebody was dead in the camp." Paydays were especially eventful times when gambling and drinking ran high, often leading to the aggression that Clark described.[45]

Miners' housing in a company town, ca. 1930s. Item 27, Herndon J. Evans Collection, 1929–1982, 82M1, University of Kentucky Libraries. Used by permission.

Yet, on the other hand, the sheer density of population, closeness of habitation, and shared occupation brought people together. "Once they was in close proximity to one another they become like a tribe," said one miner about life in the Blue Diamond coal camp. "They loved one another and got along pretty good." In fact, the new setting of work and living had the potential to create a new kind of kinship: "Everybody felt a common kinship," the same man continued, "because they all had to work and fare together the same way. There was even a commonship between the mine operators and the men at one time, before the Great Depression."[46] His use of the words *tribe* and *kinship* was telling. Kinship had always been the backbone of mountain life, structuring identity and relations at home and in the wider community.[47] As they oriented themselves to the unfamiliar world of coal camps, miners and their families refashioned an older idiom to articulate their new social world. Kin are familiars, individuals with relationships of obligation to one another. Mae Prater expressed the reciprocity practiced in coal camp kinship when she said that she "had some awfully good neighbors that lived right close by me. We were almost like sisters. We'd make quilts through the winter. . . . We'd quilt for each other, you know?"[48]

Home and Family

For the majority Appalachian native mining population, perhaps the largest adjustments, and certainly the most personal, were in the domestic sphere. Families found themselves in somewhat paradoxical situations. Living in a coal town was a means of fulfilling a man's obligation to work and to provide for family and kin. However, coal towns were decidedly male worlds, owing their existence to the single purpose of mining coal—a job restricted to men by gender roles, economic custom, and superstition. Men dominated the population, and their work shaped the towns' environment. Women's lives, therefore, were intensely transformed in this setting, both positively and negatively. Camps offered some women employment opportunities that were not viable in the rural mountain environment. For instance, most camps had boardinghouses for single men. These were usually run by women whose husbands were miners or, in some cases, company officials. Some women who lived near mines, like Florence Ramey, ran boardinghouses to supplement farm income. On some occasions Ramey would have as many as thirty-five miners boarding in her seven-room house.[49] Other women, if they had attained enough education, may have found jobs as teachers in the schools that the state and counties developed in towns and camps in conjunction with the industrialization of the region. Most women, however, continued the roles that they had traditionally held in their families, taking care of the home and raising children. But in coal towns these same duties took on new weight.

Women's time was not structured by farm chores but by their husbands' shifts in the mines. Men started their shifts before the sun came up, and women rose with them to prepare the lunches that men would carry with them into the mines. When her husband returned home, usually after dark, a wife was expected to have dinner prepared. Children (particularly girls, as boys were given more independence) might help with chores, but they were often in school. Throughout the day mothers looked after the children, went to the store, sewed, and cooked. There had always been a gendered division of labor on mountain farms, but in the camps it was transformed and intensified. Men brought in the money that was essential for life, but their labor did not produce any material products directly related to the home or family. Women, on the other hand, were suddenly responsible for all things domestic. "Mother was the mainstay at home," reminisced Marvin Gullett, who grew up in coal camps. "She made everything go as far as it could. We always made a little garden of stuff in the mining camps;

it was company land, and we let our stock run out in the woods. [We] didn't have to buy much out of the store, maybe a sack of feed every now and then, but there was great comfort [in having] this store." A good deal of women's time, however, was spent keeping their houses and clothes clean. In most camps coal dust settled over everything. Coal dust would "seep through the windows, it was on everything. A woman would work from dawn 'til night and never keep it too clean because you just couldn't get rid of all that dust."[50]

If work was never complete on the farm, it was certainly no easier in coal camps, for women or for men. The relentless dust never let anyone in a coal camp forget where they were or why the town existed. The smells and textures of the dust-filled atmosphere pervaded the experience of everyday life and had a particular impact on the activities of women. One man who grew up in coal camps described a particularly unpleasant scene:

> These processing plants were usually close to where the miners lived. There was dust in the air all the time and if it wasn't dust it was smoke from these old garbage piles that was burning. People had to contend with the scent of it and it's an awful sickening scent. It's sulphur. Just chokes you up.... [A woman] had it [rougher] than a man. The man, when he was at his job he was away from home. The woman had it to contend with day and night.[51]

The omnipresence of coal dust compelled some companies to initiate contests to determine which residents kept the cleanest houses, yards, and gardens. The idea was to encourage order, hygiene, and general middle-class property aesthetics, and many women took to this with enthusiasm.[52] It should be noted that the towns that promoted cleanliness were those with the resources and desire to maintain appealing residential areas. Many camps did not have such resources or desires.

Despite all of their cleaning, shopping, cooking, and raising children, women did find time to visit with other women. One remembered that quilting was a popular activity, carrying on a mountain tradition during which women would also talk about their families and their lives "and talk about how we managed to live and what we was gonna do."[53] This last topic was an important one. A woman's livelihood, and that of her children, depended upon her husband's paycheck and relation to the coal company. He was the primary, if not the only, source of income, and without his job the family would be evicted from their company-owned housing. Depending upon the camp and the company, women were sometimes able to raise gardens that supplemented their food supply and gave them a slight buffer during more difficult times in the coal market. But there was also the constant danger that was an inherent part of coal mining. Accidents happened regularly, and death was not uncommon. If a miner died, his wife suddenly had to find a way to support her family. Sometimes other mining families would pitch in money to help her for a while, but such charity could not last forever. Otherwise, a widowed mother might keep a boardinghouse, work as a maid in the houses of company officials or the company hotel if the town had one, find employment at a store, theater, restaurant, or other company venue, move to a commercial town to try to find work, or remarry. If she married another miner, she likely lived with the fear that he, too, might be injured or even killed.

Marriages felt the strain of the mining life.[54] It was difficult for some couples to survive the tensions that came with it. Anxieties about money, the dangers of mining, violence in camps, crowded living conditions, and all that coal dust would put stress on anybody; the long hours that husbands were away from their families while working in the mines just exacerbated the issue. "Many a time my husband got out at four o'clock in the morning and never come in till six o'clock in the night," noted Flora Rife. "Why, it used to be he never got to see his children except on Sundays."[55] Absent husbands and fathers were common when the mines were in full operation during the coal boom of the 1920s. Compared to today's busy working families, the hours might not seem unreasonable. Compared with farm life, however, the absence was cause for concern. A story that has entered the arena of folklore from that time period underscores the point. It tells of a miner who spanked one of his children one Sunday morning. The child ran crying to his mother to tell her that the man who comes around the house on Sunday mornings spanked him.[56] Fathers were surely not quite that unfamiliar to their children, but the story was widely transmitted because it said something about the perception that the division of labor that took men away from the home for long hours was threatening to the family structure.

Marriages were threatened in other ways by men's absence. Husbands were away from home enough during their long shifts in the mines that they often did not know what their wives were up to. Speculation could run wild and provoke jealousy and distrust. Rumors about sexual promiscuity or unfaithfulness caused trouble even when no overt transgressions existed. "People gather and talk through boredom and get some tale started and cause a fight between husbands," recalled Marvin Gullett.[57] One miner spoke of the questionable sexual morality in the towns in which he lived. "I knowed two men there," he said, "that swapped wives just like swapping horses. One of them had three kids and the other had six, I believe."[58] Whether or not he actually had firsthand knowledge of this behavior as he claimed is unknowable, but his report mimics the circulation of rumors and stories that charged the coal camps with ambiguity and worry. Like the dust constantly falling, stories swirled through the camps arousing desires, provoking anxieties, brandishing hopes, and sometimes compelling violence. They intensified the atmosphere as mining families sought to find, or make, order out of uncertainty. Yet paradoxically it was the attempt to feel out order, to find patterns and signs in the midst of chaos, that was responsible for the transmission of rumors in the first place.

In this setting, parents had reasons to question whether coal towns were appropriate places to raise children. One mother, who otherwise liked the conveniences of the company store and the community she was able to develop with other women in town, nevertheless felt that life was safer back on the farm where she grew up. She said that she would rather raise children on a farm than in a coal camp where she would have to worry about them too much.[59] Although schools were available in many towns, children still found time and energy to get into trouble. Marvin Gullet grew up in a coal town himself. He remembered kids called "outlaws" who would cause trouble and steal from the company store. Children also found the workings of mining machinery tempting to explore and play around. Gullett said that there were always lots of other kids around to play with in the camps. He and his friends used to "climb all over the old tipples." They used to use the tipple's chute as a slide, and discovered that if you removed the ball bearings from mining machines they made great marbles. What to a child, especially a male child, was a massive playground was for his parents a cause for constant concern. Sometimes a child would get badly hurt, or even killed, playing around the tipples and machinery.[60] But this play tended to be gendered: while boys ran around playing, girls had a different set of experiences in the camps. They were watched more closely and expected to stay around the house helping their mothers with housekeeping chores. "If they did anything they'd get out and jump rope or hopscotch, that's about it," said James C. Ward.[61]

Some parents worried that children raised in coal camps were not learning the importance of work, that they were in danger of becoming lazy. On the farm children had chores to do that taught them the value of hard work and showed them how they fit into the structure of their family, their community, and their world. Chores and children were an integral part of the household economy. The lack of the farm's work structure was only exacerbated by the commercial

Schoolchildren at play in Jenkins, Ky., ca. 1920s. Item 54, The Jenkins, Kentucky Photographic Collection, 1911–1930, 2001AV01, University of Kentucky Archives. Used by permission.

entertainments that were available in many camps or within reach of others by foot, train, or—as time went on—automobile. Children may have been more apt to attend school, usually up to grade eight, if they lived in coal towns than if they lived on farms, but they also had distractions like movie theaters, soda fountains, and sports that put a premium on leisure time over work time. More significantly, coal towns immersed children in the modern American world in which food and other items of subsistence were most familiar as commodities that were purchased at the store, not produced by one's own labor. One miner, speaking with hindsight in the 1970s about his life in coal camps, voiced this concern succinctly:

That's the difference between a child that's brought up on the farm and a child that's brought up in a coal camp: they didn't know the responsibility of life, of providing for theirself. I'd have to say that, honestly. Those children that was brought up in the coal camp, they didn't know anything about gardening—or the majority of them didn't—or how to provide, to make food for their own selves. The difference between them and a child that's brought up on a farm, that child was brought up on a farm, he had to perform when he got of an age and an ability to begin to work. He was trained and taught to do odd jobs, and he fell right into the same way of life; he picked right up where the other one left off. And they all worked together, more so as you'd call it a team, just like the old standard, "if you don't work, you don't eat." And that's about the way the old people was taught, their children was taught that, "if we don't work we'll have nothing to eat."[62]

His words suggest a certain nostalgia for the farm, illustrating one of the ways that mining families navigated the tensions of coal town life by holding it up for comparison to a life that had been left behind. The rural life of the preindustrial mountains became the imagined "other" of the coal town, transformed from an everyday reality to a symbol of desire, itself already a religiously charged idiomatic rendering of heavenly desire as it appeared in songs and images of heavenly reunion. Separation from a life imagined as more grounded, more integrated, and more self-sufficient was a theme echoed by many. It was a binary opposition that served well to express the anxieties that the coal mining life generated, and it hinted that solutions to those anxieties might be available by recovering the patterns of the past. Among the most significant resources that mining families carried with them into the industrial setting were the importance of *kinship* as a concept of obligation and reciprocity, and the place of *work* as a symbolic and embodied source of individual, social, and transcendent value. The commodified nature of industrial labor threatened the traditional, religiously charged meaning of both in critical ways. The mining life put pressure on marriages and reorganized domestic patterns. Yet people attempted to articulate their new social relations through the idiom of kinship. Mining also disconnected work from the direct production of subsistence, inserting the mediation of money and company. Yet work remained a measure of human value and character, and in spite of anxieties about whether or not children were learning to appreciate work and its deeper significance, many young boys started early to work in the coal mines.

Coal Town Churches

Many of the same pressures that shaped the larger industrial environment also shaped the topography of coal town churches. It is dangerous to generalize about the "typical" coal town's religious landscape, other than to note that many towns had churches (though not all of them did).[63] In some cases, there was only one "union" or "community church" that was shared by all denominations. Churches, like every other aspect of coal towns, were racially segregated, so the shared space would be used at different times by black and white worshipers. Sometimes companies had two community churches, one for "whites" and one for "coloreds." When there were several churches of different denominations, as was the case in larger towns and, of course, in model towns, they often exhibited an unexpected diversity (within the confines of the Christian tradition). Among those towns with several churches, it is possible to make the further generalization that Methodist, Freewill Baptist, Missionary Baptist, and Holiness-Pentecostal churches were the most prevalent.[64] Finally, one last generalization calls attention to transformations in the religious landscape in the wake of industrialization: although Old Regular Baptist churches were the most common churches in rural eastern Kentucky at the turn of the century, they did not appear in coal towns. There were many reasons for this fact, including most obviously that men and women in coal camps who preferred to attend Old Regular Baptist (or other independent mountain) churches attended churches that were located outside of the camps. There is a good chance that they continued to attend the churches that they or their family had attended prior to moving to camps or churches that were established near camps. Mountain churches were closely linked to kinship and community, so there is reason to believe that miners and their families would return to churches associated with their family and community even if that meant that they attended infrequently. But there were other factors that influenced the new landscape of organized religion in coal towns. Most important was the fact that the camps were company owned and run. Any churches within their boundaries, therefore, stood on company-owned property and required company approval.

Churches came into being in a variety of ways. In Dunham, a camp that was part of Jenkins, Consol built a community church in 1912 for use by all denominations. By 1931 it was deeded to Freewill Baptists, suggesting that they were dominant by this time.[65] In Louellen, the company built a frame building for use

Methodist Episcopal Church in Jenkins, Ky. Item 72, The Jenkins, Kentucky Photo-graphic Collection, 1911–1930, 2001AV01, University of Kentucky Archives. Used by permission.

as a community church in 1919.[66] It was located next to the school that the company also built on one end of Main Camp, and its Sunday school room served as a classroom during the week. The existence of a Sunday school room hints that the building was designed for religious education as well as worship, a relatively "modern" conceit in the mountains that more traditional churches shunned but one that appears to have been a regular element of coal town churches of all de-nominations. The Lynch Community Church was built between 1918 and 1920 on land donated by the company. The United States Coal and Coke Company also paid half the costs of the building's construction, a common practice in nicer company towns.[67] Although intended to serve all of the (white) Protestant denominations of the town, the church was managed under the auspices of the Methodist Church, South. Indeed, Methodist churches were among the first to appear in the nicer coal towns, and their physical structures were the most elaborate. Their members tended to be company managers and officials. The Lynch church was representative in its offering of Sunday school classes, Bible classes, a band and choir, and a Ladies Aid Society.[68] For several years it was the only church available for the white population of Lynch. Meanwhile, the First Baptist Missionary Church and the Good Temple AME Zion Church appeared in 1919, both black churches constructed with support from the company. Apparently there was no Baptist church for whites in Lynch until 1929, a situation that was atypical. By 1930 there were seven churches in Lynch, according to the *Tri-City News,* a newspaper covering the coal towns of Lynch and Benham and the independent city of Cumberland. Five of them were for whites, two for blacks.[69] They included, in addition to those already mentioned, the Church of God (Cleveland, Tennessee), a Roman Catholic church, and a Greek Orthodox church. A Hungarian Protestant church also existed between 1924 and 1929.[70]

Although white natives to the region made up the majority of miners in eastern Kentucky, their religious history has received no more documentation, and perhaps less, than that of immigrant coal miners.[71] The Greek Orthodox church in Lynch stands as material testimony to the spiritual life of Greeks, Russians, and others once upon a time in this overwhelmingly Protestant region. Information about Orthodox worship is scarce, but the building itself reveals that it was important enough to the company and its Greek Orthodox workers that resources and space were devoted to its construction in Camp One. The church's changing use also tells a story about the transformations of the religious demographics of the eastern Kentucky coal fields: the structure was bought by a Southern Baptist affiliated congregation in 1928 after the immigrant population rapidly decreased following the end of the coal market boom.[72]

Even more common were Roman Catholics. The Catholic churches in Lynch, Jenkins, and Benham remain as witnesses to this history, and diocesan archives contain records and letters between priests and bishops that help to fill in the gaps.[73] In Jenkins, the Catholic population was largely made up of Italians who built the town's stone buildings and carved its elaborate stonework. Visiting priests from Alabama oversaw this community from 1912 until 1913, when a resident priest was assigned to the area. He also presided over Catholics in Pike, Letcher, Knott, and Perry counties, and he traveled monthly to Hazard. By 1914

the church in Jenkins was completed.[74] Mountain natives were curious and un-
sure what to make of unfamiliar Catholic religious practices in their midst. Relations were at times tense but do not appear to have been overly so, considering
the history of anti-Catholicism elsewhere in the country. Still, the diversity that
came with the coal industry included unfamiliar religious ideas and practices
that added a dimension of spiritual anxiety to the already complicated social
mix. Native Protestant miners tried to identify and contain that anxiety to some
degree by classifying Catholics in the category of identifiable but falsely guided
"religious others," but they could not avoid the fact that they had no control over
the presence of such foreign religions.

Companies that owned the nicer towns were motivated to build churches as
part of their programs to advance worker contentment (including both officials
and miners), and they often saw churches as civic organizations that were necessary for town growth and moral improvement. The churches that appeared in
both coal towns and the growing commercial towns in the coal fields were models of this civic understanding of religion, tied closely to schools and associated
with promoting the economic progress that industry brought to the mountains.
The Methodist church in Jenkins, for instance, established through company aid
along with the Baptist and Catholic churches in the early years of the town, also
started the town's first kindergarten.[75]

Many of the Southern Baptist Convention affiliated churches—including
some of the Missionary Baptist churches—began at the instigation of preachers
or missionaries who came to the coal fields driven by the goal of bringing
religion to a mountain population whom, they imagined, lacked proper religious instruction or institutions.[76] The difficulties that these missionaries had in
overcoming indigenous religious attitudes—which opposed missionaries, paid
preachers, and seminary training, insisted that humans could not save themselves, appeared to be fatalistic, and believed in visions, dreams, and omens as
authentic sources of religious knowledge—became a common theme in missionary reports.[77] Among the preachers participating in this transformation of the
region's religious ideas and practices were eastern Kentucky natives who had
distanced themselves from mountain traditions and attended missionary-run
schools, earned their preaching credentials in seminaries, and otherwise connected themselves to the new culture that was forming amidst the growth of
commerce and industry.

The received wisdom about religion in coal towns suggests that class was an
important factor in church attendance. For instance, E. V. Tadlock, superinten-

dent for mountain work for the Presbyterian Church, U.S.A., described the religious situation of coal towns in a 1929 article published in *Mountain Life and Work,* the primary magazine for missionaries to Appalachia. He observed that in the mountain churches that many miners had known in their rural communities, "probably few were members, but they attended the monthly services and owned allegiance to the denomination. They expected some time to ally themselves with the church, in the Lord's own time. Though they may not have belonged to the church, the church belonged to them, and it had a place of influence in their lives." But in coal towns, he claimed, organized worship appeared in a new light. Here, "they find that the church is allied in some way with the industrial setting. The pastor is not of their choosing or way of doing." Class differences provoked "a spirit of real hostility toward the church as an institution," according to Tadlock, and consequentially most mine camp residents did not attend.[78] Reports from coal camps elsewhere in Appalachia, and in earlier years, echoed this assessment.[79] Elizabeth Hooker's oft-cited study of mountain religion, published in 1933, also noted a "social gulf between company officials and white-collar employees with their families, on the one hand, and the miners with their families on the other; so that neither group readily joins the church or Sunday school started by the other."[80]

Yet it is important to recognize that class distinctions were not simply about money and economic power. Class was articulated throughout the mountains in specifically religious ways that were formed over a relatively long duration of time. In particular, the historical connection between the arrival of the coal industry and the arrival of missionaries who carried the denominations that prevailed in the coal towns was a key factor in this process. Rural eastern Kentucky churches had long opposed the theological, doctrinal, and practical aspects of the churches that were now springing up throughout the coal fields. These new churches not only served the growing commercial class but also rubbed against the church traditions of the rural mountains—and this might also provide a clue into the reason why many native miners did not attend company churches. As an example, take the church at McRoberts. It was a Missionary Baptist church established in 1918, and in a procedure that was not unusual among coal towns, it employed a pastor whose wages were provided by funds pooled by the community.[81] Its Missionary Baptist designation already aligned the church with changes in eastern Kentucky's religious landscape. The name does not make clear, however, whether the church was in the rural mountain tradition or not; it may have been associated with the Southern Baptist Convention, or it may not have been.

But the fact that the pastor was paid is an important signal. Churches in the mountain Protestant tradition in general were opposed to the notion of a preacher being paid for his work, for reasons as theological as they were social. One miner recalled of mountain churches that "if a preacher had a-come around to one of the churches and a-wanted money for his preachin', they woulda led him to the door and shoved him out into the yard. There was no such a thing as preachers at that time in this country receiving money for their preaching. They believed in the old time ways. The Bible says 'freely you receive, freely give.' That's the kind of church we were brought up in, in the Protestant faith."[82] According to this way of thinking, the church at McRoberts, although ostensibly belonging to the community, may have alienated native miners at a fundamental level. At the very least, the paid preachers would have caused controversy among religious miners who had grown up in the rural tradition feeling that preaching was a calling, not a primary livelihood. Pastoring as a form of wage labor was a sign of the reach of the money economy into areas of life it had previously not touched, and it threatened to remove the preacher from the experiences of daily work and life that the community shared.

In another example of religious articulations of class, the modern churches that were associated with commercial progress in burgeoning town centers openly disparaged mountain sacramental worship practices. On one occasion the *Tri-City News* published "A Message from Dr. R. F. Jasper, Pastor of the Cumberland Baptist Church, on the Subject of 'Foot Washing.' "[83] His reading of this tradition took an approach typical of "modernist" churches at the time. He argued that foot washing was important in biblical times as a practical matter in the context of dusty roads and bare feet. However, he wrote, Jesus never intended it to be an ordinance, and there was no reason for churches to keep it up. Of course, foot washing was a central element of the sacrament service at many mountain churches. Doing away with it was a sign of the distancing of modern Baptists from closely heeding to their physical body, and the bodies of others in the community, as rich sources of religious experience. The Cumberland Methodist Church similarly challenged tradition when it installed a baptizing pool in its basement, thus eliminating the need for a river or stream. Was its purpose to replace outdoor baptisms or simply to make baptisms more comfortable in the winter? The answer is lost to time, but in either case it was a movement away from mountain worship's immersion in nature.

Nevertheless, these and other churches hosted revivals that were well attended, and miners were likely among the participants even if they never joined a church.[84] The episodic patterns of religious behavior continued in the world that mining created. And the religious landscape of coal camps, while different from that of the rural mountains, was active; churches did exist in camps, some of them led by preachers who were also miners, and somebody was attending them (even if many others were not). Flora Rife's story is revealing in this regard, saying something about the transformation of religion in the industrial setting. Rife was born in 1904 on her family's farm in Floyd County, but they moved to Jenkins soon after the mines opened. "My mother was a member of the Old Regular Baptist Church from the time she was eighteen years old until she died," she said. "My father wasn't no member of the church but he went to church." They apparently had a choice between Freewill Baptist, Church of God, and Old Regular Baptist, and they chose the last. But things were different among the younger generation in the camps. "In the mining camps," she said, "the majority went to the Freewills. But out in the country, the majority went to the Old Regulars. . . . In Jenkins went to the Freewills, majority. . . . All the younger people went there [Freewills], and I enjoyed it there." Rife explained why she and others in camps preferred the Freewill churches: her parents "let us choose the church of our choice. Anyone we wanted to go to. And they teach Sunday school in the Freewills and the Old Regular Baptist don't teach Sunday school."[85] And so, as education and Sunday School became desirable along with the new values of the industrial setting, religious demography began to change. But the Freewill Baptist churches managed to blend more traditional mountain religious practices, idioms, and gestures with these new organizational developments, retaining the familiar while also incorporating the new.

Although coal town churches were the most visible evidence of religious practice among mining families, it is important not to let church buildings or attendance blind us to other locations or forms of religious practice. For instance, organized worship took place in people's homes and outdoors as well as in churches, and for the most part this type of activity cannot be recovered. There are glimpses, however. Nora Figger worshiped and had Sunday school with neighbors in their homes on Number Two Hill in Burdine in 1927.[86] The Mount Sinai Baptist Church in Lynch began in the home of a coal miner in 1917 before it moved to a dedicated building. Holiness and Pentecostal congregations also met in homes, outdoors, or in churches elsewhere when they did not have a church building in the camp.[87] But it should be clear that religion took forms other than organized worship, and the majority of rural eastern Kentucky natives had never been church members. While nonmembers may have attended churches for social and community reasons in rural areas, the camp environment offered many other temptations and substitutes for the little free time that miners and their families had in their new work arrangements. The division of time into *work* and *leisure* in the industrial capitalist setting meant that commercial activities like movies, baseball games, boxing, theater shows, radio, and phonographs competed with church for time on Sundays. Perhaps, too, people might leave town to visit family who lived elsewhere in the hills. During those visits they might attend a mountain church, or clean a family cemetery, or attend a funeral or a homecoming. Or they might not. Or they might visit with friends and neighbors in their own towns, perhaps playing music that might or might not have religious significance. In any event, church attendance was not a priority for many, just as it had not been before industrialization. Indeed, historian Crandall A. Shifflett found that "the institutional church, not to say Christianity itself, seems to have had surprisingly small influence upon mining families in coal towns. Nevertheless, nonchurchgoing miners still might describe themselves as religious and express their belief in God." As an example, he cites Mae Prater, a miner's wife, who said that although she rarely attended church,

> I always tried to make myself satisfied and felt like I had a lot to be thankful for anywhere I lived. . . . We get down, you know, low, then I'll think about our homes and our families and everything and I'll think we got a lot. We've got a *lot* to be thankful for, and we need to live just as close as we can live to the Lord, because sometime or another we're going to leave here and we're going somewhere, going for eternity, eternity, it says forever and ever.[88]

In so saying, Prater exhibited a personal expression of religion that said a lot in its simplicity about the way that religious orientation persisted in people's daily lives. When recovering the religious history of coal mining families in the 1910s and 1920s, Prater's words suggest, it is worth considering that attendance at coal town churches is not a good indicator of religiosity. Whether they attended church or not, many eastern Kentuckians still lived in a world patterned by an overarching sense of order, power, and mystery that had roots in both the Bible and their daily routines and experiences. These ideas continued in coal towns, and surveys of religion in mining camps therefore overlooked important ways that religion may have factored into people's lives. For example, in coal camps midwives continued to "catch" babies, and many women sought their services as well as the services of herbalists and faith healers. Each of these "gifts" carried religious significance in mountain culture. People in the camps called upon such practitioners, often preferring them to the doctors who increasingly asserted the authority of medical knowledge.[89] While the health of mining families and others in the hills benefited immensely from the arrival of medically trained doctors, many distrusted them long into the twentieth century.[90] In cases when doctors did not seem to be able to heal a malady, people often turned to other types of healers whose authority they trusted because it was said to come from God or from knowledge of nature's patterns and powers. Midwives and other traditional healers also tended not to charge money for their services, or they charged very little, and they related to their patients as neighbors with whom they shared obligations of exchange and care that money did not respect. Just as some eastern Kentuckians objected to the commodification and professionalization of religious authority, so they also resisted the same tendencies in healing. Attitudes toward both likely were related to the idea that these practices were freely given by God as gifts and should therefore be freely given in turn. Other religious practices and idioms persisted in coal towns as well, including the belief in the importance of work, kin, and nature as orienting concepts, and a sacramentalism that read the world for signs and omens. Traditions continued, even as they were transformed through the structures and experiences of industrial coal mining.

Life in coal camps was hard. The struggles themselves became part of what it meant to be a coal miner. Miners and their families forged community out of shared patterns of life and shared difficulties, and their new lives found some of the traditions and values of the farm continuing. They transformed other aspects of life to meet their new setting, and they created new ways of inhabiting the world. Coal towns were places of extremes. Perhaps the most obvious, and the most difficult, was the distance between the desire for a better life and the obligations that one had to care for family and community through hard work and, on the other hand, the disruptions in family and community life that grew out of industrial coal mining. Even the landscape of organized religion in the coal towns challenged rural traditions. But in the complex and difficult context of coal towns, miners and their families actively transitioned from farms to mines in ways religious and spiritual as well as material. And in the mines, the physical work of coal mining itself informed, provoked, and challenged religious expression.

FOUR

"IT'S ABOUT AS DANGEROUS A THING AS EXISTS"

The hard-working miners, their dangers are great,
And many while working have met their sad fate.
They are doing their duty, as all miners do,
Shut out from the daylight and darling ones too.

The miner is gone, we see him no more;
God be with the miner wherever he may roam;
And may he be ready Thy calls to obey,
Looking to Jesus, the only true way.

—"THE HARD WORKING MINER,"
recorded in Harlan County, Kentucky

COAL MINES IN EASTERN KENTUCKY were of the drift mine type. That is, they bored into the sides of mountains horizontally, as opposed to mines that drilled vertically into the ground. The mine was a dynamic structure, growing larger each day. As they dug out the coal, miners created the space in which they worked, called "rooms." As the tunnel grew deeper, more and more rooms branched off of one or more "hallways." As one miner, Monroe Quillen, described it, "A big coal mine is similar to walking into a hotel. You're on a certain floor, you go down the main corridor for a ways and then you'd turn off on a wing. Well, that's what we call 'sections' in the mines. Then when you turned little places off there, that's your 'rooms.' You're assigned a room just like if you go to a hotel and register you're assigned to a room. You go in there and you go to sleep. A coal miner goes in there and he loaded him sixteen ton of coal in that room."[1]

Mines could extend for miles inside of mountains, and in some mines during the 1920s miners rode to work on the electric cars that were used to haul the coal out of the mines to the tipple, where it was sorted. "They had electric motors and they had plenty of bank cars and they'd take eight or ten or maybe twelve of them bank cars and couple them all together and we'd call that a mantrip," one miner explained. "We'd get in them bank cars and ride in. And some places it'd be a mile and a half ride to get to work, to where the work would be." Not all mines had electric cars, however, and mules often pulled the cars loaded with coal. The size of a room could vary from 15 to over 100 feet wide, but the ceiling was often too low to allow a miner to stand upright. In those cases, kneepads were a necessity as miners did their work kneeling all day. The work of coal mining basically consisted of four steps: cutting, drilling, shooting, and cleaning up. First, the miner would cut into the face of the coal seam down low by the floor, creating an "undercut." In the earliest years of mining, cutting was done by hand, but by the 1920s, many mines had cutting machines that did the job faster. Once the miner had made a good undercut, the next step was to drill holes into the coal face above the cut. This was usually done by hand using a breast auger, although drilling also became mechanized later on. Most eastern Kentucky miners in the 1920s drilled by hand. The strategically placed holes, usually three of them, would hold the explosive black powder used to shoot the coal. Miners carried the powder into the mines along with their carbide lamps and their lunch pails, transporting it in safety jugs designed to insulate it from sparks or other sources of ignition.[2] Powder in place and tamped, the miner stepped away a safe distance from the face and yelled, "Fire in the hole!"— a signal to other miners that he was about to ignite it. The explosion blew the coal down from the seam to the depth that he had undercut it. The last step was to clean up the shot—that is, to load the coal into the awaiting car for transportation to the weigh station and the tipple. Up into the 1940s, eastern Kentucky miners loaded coal by hand using shovels. They separated the desirable coal from the other rock, either slate or limestone, that also came down with the shot. When they were finished cleaning up a shot,

Miners working with a cutting machine, No. 204 Mine, Jenkins, Ky., 1916.
Item 109, The Jenkins, Kentucky Photographic Collection, 1911–1930,
2001AV01, University of Kentucky Archives. Used by permission.

they repeated the process, advancing deeper into the mountain. Autie Stiltner recalled the regularity of the process: "Clean up a big cut of coal and a cut of rock. Load it in cars. All day long. Load in cars and sent it outside. Had to clean up, have a big cut of rock and a big cut of coal and you have to get them both in one day before they let you come out.... You just had to work till you cleaned up. Wadn't no hours to it. Take you eight or nine hours, you had to do it. That's the way it was."[3]

Miners for the most part worked alone, responsible for their own cuts and cleanup. They were paid by the ton of coal rather than by the hour. Their work rhythms, therefore, were not like those of industrial workers in factories and mills, who were closely supervised and regulated by the clock.[4] Miners had a degree of independence at the face of the coal seam, although there were definite limits to that freedom. Whatever they shot down, they had to clean up before they were able to finish their shifts, and the weight of their loads was measured by a supervisor or weighman who, in some cases, was less than honest. If the load had too much unusable rock mixed in with the coal, the miner might be docked some pay.

Mines were dusty, dark places, and the work was extraordinarily difficult. But miners grew to appreciate their underground environment and in some cases developed something of a mine aesthetic. A miner might express distaste for a particular company or one of its mines: "It's too low. It's low coal. Scratch your back . . . the seam was low. Well, you'd get in little old places, you'd have to go under something that high, that tall, about like going under this table."[5] In one case, Teamus Bartley, a miner at Edgewater Coal Company in the Elkhorn fields, grew quite attached to the particular seam and room that he was working. "I worked the last day in Number Two that it ever run," he recalled. "And the boss come told me, said, 'When you get this car loaded, put your tools in it; we're quitting this seam.' And I said, 'Where we going to now?' And he said, 'We're going to the bottom seam.' I had the best place to work I thought I ever had in my life. I hated to quit. I had the prettiest place to work in I ever had in my life. I told him, I said, 'I hate to quit this place worst ever was.'"[6]

In this way miners made the mines their own, a familiar habitat in which they belonged. At times the reality of being under the ground, burrowing deeper and deeper into a mountain, could cause a miner to reflect about where he was, locating him in a mysterious part of the world that was, in a real way, untouched by human hands. Monroe Quillen poetically described the mine as a place of hard work, but also of beauty and discovery:

> It's just like being in a cave, only the cave doesn't run smooth like a seam of coal. That seam of coal is absolutely smooth. I enjoy working in the mine, myself. I was never afraid in there. It's not a place to take a vacation or loaf—it's made to work in.
>
> I thought to myself lots of times: 'I've been somewhere today nobody ever went before.' In the mountains I've scooted myself up under rocks to stay dry [and] I've wondered a lot of times there, too, if anybody had been there before. There's a possibility of that, but not when you clean up a cut of coal in a coal seam. No man has ever been that far before.[7]

The mine even had its own seasons, Quillen noted. The temperature was steady all year, standing at about seventy degrees, but July, August, and September were the "sweaty months" when moisture settled in the mines. So mining placed men in a direct relationship with the earth in a way unavailable in other environments. They learned to listen to its sounds to determine if the roof was steady or if it needed extra support from timbers. Solid rock sounded differently, when knocked, than loose or weak rock did. The mine would sometimes make sounds on its own as the earth settled and shifted to accommodate the spaces and pressures that digging created. Some of the sounds were familiar; others warned of danger.

Mining was, and remains, an inherently dangerous occupation. To be a miner was to face toil and danger every day, deep beneath the ground in places that most human beings never ventured. Miners, therefore, shared a common bond, built out of their work experiences, that separated them from nonminers. Down in the mines, it was said, all men were equal, regardless of race, ethnicity, or religious background: "We treated a black one just like we did a white one, 'cause in there a few minutes, you was all black anyhow."[8] Usually more than one miner worked a room, and conversation would develop as they loaded coal. During breaks in their work, waiting for a new car to load once the one they had been filling was taken away, miners talked with each other about their lives. "Miners is about the closest people to each other that you'll ever find," miner Melvin Profitt said in reference to the camaraderie they developed in their workplace. "They know what each other has been through." He felt much more in common with his miner friends than he did with anybody else. "It's an unknowing question, actually, to say why, but they'll just about go to the limit."[9] To become a miner, then, was also to be initiated into a community.

For boys, becoming a miner was a rite of initiation into maturity and manhood. The mine was a resolutely gendered space, and mining was a masculine labor. This social fact was also upheld supernaturally by a belief that many miners in central Appalachia shared with others in places as diverse as Bolivia and Wales: that a woman's presence in a mine would bring bad luck.[10] To be a miner in eastern Kentucky, therefore, was to be a man. Men who grew up in coal mining remember wanting to be like their miner fathers. Their fathers left the house before the sun came up and returned home late at night. But their sons knew that during the day they were under the ground, an exciting prospect for boys. Not only that, but they were working with the machinery and equipment that young boys found so intriguing. Melvin Profitt first went down into the mines when he was only six years old. "My dad was a miner. I would go in there and this coal was tall enough 'til I could chase around in there, hand him a file to file his auger with, or a pick, or something he needed from the outside. I could stand up and run from one place to another where he would had to run on his knees. I guess I was a quite a bit of help to him and I really enjoyed it."[11] And so fathers and sons developed new types of bonds around the work of mining, bonds that were

Man at the coal face of a room in No. 205 Mine, Jenkins, Ky., 1912. Item 113,
The Jenkins, Kentucky Photographic Collection, 1911–1930, 2001AV01,
University of Kentucky Archives. Used by permission.

highly gendered given the nature of their work, and bonds that helped to build
mining from a job into an identity. When a boy officially started to work in the
mines as an employee, it signified his status as a man. It meant that he was now a
hard worker, that he could provide for his family, and that he could face the dangers of the mine without fear.

Many miners began working in the mines as soon as they were able, at age
sixteen. They often began work as trappers, opening and closing the doors that let
cars, mules, and ponies through as they pulled carloads of coal. Trappers were an
important part of the mining operation, because the doors that they controlled
also directed air circulation within the mine. If they were not operated correctly,
gas and dust could build up in the mine and create the potential for an explosion.

Autie Stiltner began working in the Elkhorn coal fields as a trapper when he was sixteen. The job signaled his coming of age by giving him responsibility for safety in the mine and by allowing him to fulfill his manly duty of working to make money for his family.[12] In the context of capitalism, the ability to make money was an indication of transition to adult status. And the desire for money and all that it signaled pulled many people into the mines. "See, at that time, things were pretty hard and people [who] had a boy that's old enough to go in the mines, and sixteen was as early as you could go, why they always put them in the mines," according to Paris Goble, who started mining in 1917. "I didn't have to go, I guess, but, yeah, I wanted to go. I wanted to make some money."[13] Another miner who started working at an early age spoke to the symbolic importance of becoming a miner by saying that "the men were the breadwinners in the mining camp, and when [a man's] son got big enough to work he followed in his father's footsteps. Back in those days nobody thought of being anything but a miner when he was a young man."[14]

Whether a boy or a man, new miners were put through initiation rites by other miners. Their transformation into their new status involved learning a new language and new skills, while also confronting the tight-knit existing work community and the constant threat of danger. It has been suggested that the famed "sixteen tons" that miners claimed they loaded each day was an overstatement—that they averaged closer to ten tons—but that loading the larger amount of coal did serve as an initiation ritual. Older miners would slack off on their work enough to let a newcomer "make sixteen" his first day as a sign of his manhood.[15] Other initiation rites took the form of joking behavior, highlighting the gap between the in-group of miners and the initiate who was not yet familiar with his new underground world and its ways. A miner described matters this way:

> Well, a new miner was, everybody tried to take care of him. But of course, they'd have him down to things that was impossible to do, like hunting rib shears, roof jacks, and things like that and they wasn't no such things like that. You take a new man in, some smart alec would send him out of one place over to another to get a roof jack, to jack the roof up a little higher or something while the mines, they wasn't no such thing as a roof jack. He didn't know the difference, pulling pranks on each other and things like that. They all tried to take care of him. Of course, sending him out after a roof jack or rib shear or something like that was unnecessary, but they wanted to have a little fun. And that's what they would do. Tell them big scary tales. They was scared to death, riding the mantrip. Everybody else was sitting up straight. He was laying down in the mantrip, afraid he was gonna run into the top, everybody kidding him.[16]

Behind the joking, however, lay a real sense of the dangers of mine work. As this passage reveals, one aspect of becoming a miner was overcoming fear. Joking is often a response to fear and uncertainty, and this same miner said that a lot of joking went on between miners as they worked. "That's all there are, hard work and joke, foolishness," he said. "Hard work and joke. Yeah, there's a lot of joke in the mines. You hardly knowed anybody was serious about anything." Joking allowed miners to push aside their fears, giving the appearance of control and familiarity with the dangers that were an inherent part of their work. Mining fostered a bravado that equated manliness with the lack of fear, and the initiation into manliness entailed confronting and overcoming the fear of the mine. Without courage and the ability to face danger with a laugh, mining would be unbearable. But this insistence upon bravery was only valuable up to a point. This miner continued, "When I first started to work, it was pretty scary. And then I got so I wasn't a safe miner, because I got so I wasn't afraid of nothing." There was something to fear, and a healthy fear kept miners alert to real dangers. "It's plenty dangerous," he added. "It's about as dangerous a thing as exists. About as dangerous a job as you can work at."

When folklorist George Korson enumerated the dangers of coal mining in *Coal Dust on the Fiddle*, his collection of mining stories and songs, he articulated the primeval, archetypal world of forces that made up the mine environment deep under the ground by dividing his chapter into four sections relating to the four elements: earth, air, fire, and water.[17] Each of these posed a threat to the well-being of miners who worked so closely with nature inside of the mountains. Cave-ins and slate falls—rocks falling from the roof—were the earth's danger. The air, too, could be hazardous. As already noted, trapper boys kept the air circulating so that gas and dust did not accumulate. It was impossible to avoid breathing coal dust, however. "We didn't know that it was dangerous," said Charlie Campbell. "We'd just eat it and go on."[18] According to Frank Fugate, "We was under the impression that breathing that coal dust, [the] mineral in it would be good for us instead of an injury. Many a time I go in and you couldn't see nothing. Your light would just . . . dim your light down, in that smoke and dust."[19] Unfortunately, the result of inhaling coal dust, day after day, was not better health but widespread black lung disease, not recognized until the 1960s. Coal dust was so much a fact of everyday life, both inside and outside the mines, that miners had names for different types of it. "Bug dust" was the fine coal from the cutting machine that accumulated on the mine floor and made a cushion that could act as a padding and actually save your life if a rock fell on you.[20] If gas or dust did accumulate, then fire was an imminent threat because it would set off an explosion. Some mines were known by miners throughout the coal fields as being particularly gaseous. Talk and rumors about these mines passed through the region's camps. Louellen's slope mine was one. "It really wasn't too awfully gassy, but they had to watch it [conditions in the mine] all of the time," remembered one miner who worked there from 1924 to the 1940s.[21] Finally, some mines were plagued with bad drainage, and water that seeped in from the ground accumulated. In those situations miners worked all day in damp or wet clothes. In some rooms they worked for hours lying on their backs in the water. All mines had moisture, however, especially in the "sweaty season," and if they had electrical equipment in them, as they often did, water elevated the risk of electrocution.

Between 1902 and 1927, over 2,400 men died in the Appalachian mountains as the result of mine explosions. That averages to over 90 men per year. Most deaths in coal mines were not from explosions, however, but from slate falls that accounted for over 71 percent of mine deaths in the United States between the years 1906 and 1935.[22] The numbers of injuries were even greater. In oral history recordings, miners described a litany of broken bodies as they told of their work experiences. "I had one of them kettle bottoms fall on me. . . . It skinned my back up. Just tore the hide off my back," said Autie Stiltner, laughing. "It never scared me. I just knew it'd fell on me is all."[23] Henry McIntosh, who mined in several places in eastern Kentucky in the 1920s and 1930s, recalled that he "never did have nobody get killed [near him]. I got a rock on me once pretty heavy, but it didn't injure me too bad."[24] The matter-of-fact tone of both of these men indicated the ordinariness of this danger. Others were not so lucky. "I knowed several men got killed," remembered Simon Swiney.[25] Motorized cars were another common hazard, causing the loss of fingers and limbs on many occasions: "They had a motorman and what they called a brakeman that coupled those cars and getting where lots of times they'd get fixed between cars and get crippled up, yeah, lots of 'em."[26]

Clearly, if a man was to work productively in coal mining, he had to overcome the fear of danger. Sometimes it took him some time to get up the courage to work underground. Usually, though, his initial trepidation was overcome by the desire to prove himself a man and by the reward of pay that was considerably higher than one could make doing other jobs around the coal town.[27] Over time, miners became used to the dangers in the mine. Mining got "in their blood."[28] It became part of their identity. One miner, after he had worked a lifetime in the mines, insisted that "when I started in, I wasn't gonna work except a couple or three months. It growed on me or something another, and I wound up 42 years and 6 months."[29] But even for the most hardened miner, coming face-to-face with mortality could cause second thoughts. Indeed, the confrontation with mortality and the limits of human existence was an essential element of the religious orientation that emerged from the work of mining. Miners were no strangers to the daily possibility of being crippled or maimed or even killed in the process of earning their bread. "Yeah, man, it was bad," recalled one. "You go in there to do a day's work, you went ahead and done a day's work, and if you got through all right, why, it was all right. If you didn't, you was hurting."[30] Death and danger were, for miners, everyday facts of life. In accepting them, miners were not being fatalistic, just realistic. They encountered daily the limits of human life.

There were many times when the brave shield that mining men wore cracked. Witnessing a fellow miner's death could cause deep anxiety, never more so than when the deceased's position and the witness's were perceived to be interchangeable. Such occasions acted as prophetic alarms, mirrors that reflected a potential reality in which the positions were reversed. It was impossible to keep fear at a distance in such situations. Teamus Bartley's experience illustrates that the effect of such incidents was tactile, immediate, and directly felt through the body.

> One evening I started in the mines. I had been to the powder house and got my powder and I come out to get the mantrip to go into the mines and the motor come out with one car hung to it and a dead man on it. And I walked up and look at the man and he was a Bartley. His name was James Bartley and the slate had fell on him and killed him. I studied pretty strong about just turning around and going back to the house. It hurt me pretty bad to have to go on in the mines after he had been hauled out dead. It made a bad feeling on me. I never was under no slate fall. Only a little bit. I had a little slate on me, not enough to break no bones or nothing. But I had pretty good luck.[31]

Other miners attributed their well-being to luck as well, a vague but important commodity that they were glad that they had, especially when their own lives were put into such stark perspective. "Luck" was a concept employed to name the sense that there was some kind of pattern or power behind the fact that some miners lived while others died, that some were injured while others escaped harm. Otherwise, these incidents would be mere statistics, meaningless and random. Luck offered the sense that there might be some significance to events, even if it could not be fully understood. Other miners were more direct in their attribution of meaning, giving credit to God who watched over them and kept them safe. Bartley himself, in fact, looking back on his life of mining, assessed that it was only "with the help of the blessed Lord" that he had made it through a life of hardship and "ups and downs." But it is also important to note that witnessing his kin's death did not just make Bartley have second thoughts about returning to the mine or that he credited God with keeping him safe. His experience also produced a *feeling* in his body. "It hurt me pretty bad" and "made a bad feeling on me," he said, voicing a commonly held sense that a person's body could be affected not only by the physical aspects of mining but also by the social aspects.

Accidents also produced prophetic stories of a different sort that were tinged with notions of divination. Just as eastern Kentucky folklife taught people to read certain signs and omens for what they might tell about future events, stories about mining accidents often contained similar elements. Melvin Profitt told such a story from his own experience, which spoke to the dangers of feeling too comfortable in the mines and the importance of intuition:

> I was supplying track one night and I went in this place and [the roof] sounded like it was ready to fall. A boy by the name of Fields, about sixteen years old, [was] cussing me when I got up in there to bring him some track. I said, "Son, I'll get it to you right away, but you don't need no track in here. What you need is timber and if you don't get some timbers, you're going to be dead."
>
> "By God!" he said. "I know as much about this rock as you do. I's raised in her."
>
> I said, "I don't dispute that now, but I tell you this is going to fall in." I went back out for some reason, I don't know why I done it. I looked at my watch as I went out and exactly fifteen minutes from the time I went out the motorman told me about that boy getting killed. That slate had fell on him. He's just mashed in a jelly. I couldn't hardly make my mind up to go back to work the next day. It's awful.
>
> I guess I passed up death several different times, or at least I felt like I have, in mines. I don't know how many times I've run out from under rocks and they'd fall in.[32]

Although miners learned to listen to the sounds of the mine, learning its language and reading its signs, an accident could happen at any time. "The worst thing about living in the mining camp," Marvin Gullett related, "one was always in constant *dread*. . . . You couldn't be confident about when the top was going to fall in. Only God above knew." He spoke from the experience of being both a miner and the son of a miner. "Many a time I'd go to bed and lay and worry whether Dad would come back alive or not," he said.[33] It was this uncertainty that led to the constant scanning for signs that would portend a disaster. Eastern Kentucky miners were not the only ones who participated in this practice. Miners from all areas knew stories about omens that preceded a cave-in or an explosion. They came in many forms, not only the sounds of the mine itself. Feelings, visions, and dreams were common portents of coming disasters. The belief even made its way into a song that became popular among miners and nonminers alike, starting its life as a commercial recording but entering oral tradition and the folklore of miners. There were many versions of "The Dream of the Miner's Child." One was printed in the *United Mine Workers' Journal* in 1911; others were recorded in the eastern Kentucky coal fields by folksong collectors in the 1920s and 1930s. Here is one of its variants:

> A miner was leaving his home for his work,
> He heard his little child scream,
> He went to the side of the little girl's bed—
> "Oh! Daddy, I've had such a dream."
>
> > Chorus:
> > "Oh! Daddy, don't work in the mines today,
> > For dreams have so often come true,
> > Oh! Daddy, my Daddy, please don't go away,
> > I never could live without you."
>
> "I dreamed that the mines were all seething with fire,
> The men all fought for their lives.
> Just then the scene changed, and the mouth of the mines
> Were [sic] covered with sweethearts and wives."
>
> > Chorus
>
> Her daddy, then smiling and stroking her face,
> Was turning away from her side.
> But throwing her small arms around Daddy's neck,
> She gave him a kiss and then cried:
> "Go down to the village and tell your dear friends,
> As sure as the bright stars do shine,
> There's something that's going to happen today,
> Oh! Daddy, don't go to the mine."[34]

Other versions include additional verses in which the father, heeding his daughter's warning, returns home at the last minute before entering the mine. Before the end of the day, the mine explodes. Once the song entered the oral tradition, people associated it with their local histories of mine disasters. One pastor in Wise, Virginia, for instance, claimed in the 1940s that it was a true story about a mining disaster in Coal Creek, Tennessee.[35] The song found a home in many mining communities, but its story fit especially well into the religious traditions of eastern Kentucky, where dreams had long been taken seriously as indications of future events. Against the background of coal mining, especially up into the 1930s when unions and federal laws forced stricter safety standards, stories and songs such as these were ways that miners could feel a level of control over powers both human and natural that were otherwise out of control. They were an innovative response to life's uncertainties, drawing upon everyday experience and traditional religious idioms, with the added innovation, in the case of "The Dream of the Miner's Child," of imported music from commercial recordings. Such tactics were ways to put disasters and mining deaths into a context that gave them significance beyond the merely contingent and accidental. Furthermore, they held out hope that the next disaster might be avoided, if only people were able to read the signs properly.

When disasters did happen, they often immediately provoked religiously charged responses. One straightforward way that they did this was by becoming occasions for instant conversion to Christian faith. The May 1902 explosion at the Fraterville Mine in Coal Creek, Tennessee (just south of the Kentucky border), was a powerful example. The explosion killed all 200 men who had just entered the mine to start their shift. However, many of them did not die instantly. In the few hours that they spent trapped below the earth, they wrote letters to the loved ones they were leaving behind. "I have found the Lord," wrote one. "Do change your way of living God be with you Good Bye." Another wrote, "Ellen, darling Good Bye for us both. Elbert said the Lord had saved him." And another: "My time is come to die. I trust in Jesus. Teach the children to trust in Jesus. May God bless you all is my prayer. Bless Jesus it is now 10 minutes till 10 and we are almost smothered. . . . I hope to meet you all in heaven. May God bless you all wife and children for Jesus sake good bye until we meet to part no more." Nearly all of the brief letters asked the survivors to put their trust in Jesus, for the writers wanted to be reunited with them in heaven.[36] The miners' heaven was imagined as a place where families would be reunited for eternity, where the fractures caused by death and worldly difficulty would not exist. Heaven held out hope beyond the constant threat of danger in the world of mining.

I know of no direct parallels to the Fraterville letters in eastern Kentucky, but it is likely that similar conversions and intense devotional moments accompanied accidents and disasters there, too, as they did elsewhere. In a mine explosion in Stuart, West Virginia, in 1907, a Polish miner's body was found "kneeling in prayer against the room rib. With his hand he had made the Sign of the Cross in the coal dust on the rib."[37] In a mine explosion in Layland, West Virginia, in 1915, forty-two men were trapped in a room for five days and were near giving up hope when one of them, overcome by gas fumes, had a vision of an angel leading them to safety. His vision inspired the men to renew their efforts to signal any possible rescue crews. They all walked out alive. But 115 others had died in the explosion.[38] When the Three Point Mine in Harlan County, Kentucky, exploded in 1943, the local newspaper reported that the twelve men trapped in the mine spent their time in prayer before they were rescued.[39]

One unusual case in eastern Kentucky illustrates that a life could be changed fundamentally by a cave-in and the conversion that accompanied it. Harrison Mayes was mining coal in Middlesboro, Kentucky, when a loaded coal car ran out of control and crushed him up against the mine wall. Mayes, near death, asked God to save him—and in return, he promised to devote his life to ministry. Mayes lived. His ministry, however, took a creative form that was decidedly modern and decidedly in keeping with the sacramental and independent religious style of mountain tradition. He did not belong to a particular church or denomination but instead took his message to the public in 1918 by making signs that he placed on roadsides. They displayed messages like "Get Right with God" and "Jesus Is Coming Soon," and occasionally they revealed a leaning toward Holiness and Pentecostal theology, such as "Regeneration, Sanctification, Holy Ghost Baptism." He painted his first signs but soon started molding them out of concrete. In the 1940s he began to put his enormous, heart- and cross-shaped concrete signs around the nation. By the time he died he had planted his signs in forty-four states and devised a plan to take his "Planetary Aviation Evangelism" into space by erecting his signs on other planets.[40] While his story is certainly unusual, it is significant that an Appalachian folk artist whose work dots the American landscape began his ministry in a sudden religious conversion in the midst of a mining accident.

Mules and Men

Outside of the actual physical dangers of their work, miners were also subject to the uncertainties of the economic system and the hierarchies of power that existed in the industrial setting. While their work bound them together into a community of shared experience, it also placed them at the mercy of an industry that had a tendency to treat them as little more than beasts of burden. As miners recalled the early decades of mining in oral history interviews, the days before federal labor regulations, they regularly described their work situation as slavery.[41] According to one, for miners the situation was "exactly like back in the 1800s when slavery was in. The working class people in this country were in bondage, they were nothing more than slaves up until the year 1936. There ain't no doubt about it."[42] Miners voiced this perception of the company's attitude toward them in various ways, providing a glimpse into how the developments that industrialists like John C. C. Mayo understood as progress appeared from the position of those whose bodies fueled the work. If mining transformed raw mineral into wealth for industrialists and the isolated mountains into modern cities, for miners it turned men into mules; in fact, they felt they were less than mules, according to one story that was told widely in the mine fields. Harry Moore, an Old Regular Baptist preacher and miner from Floyd County, remembered:

> They thought more of the mules and horses than they did the men that worked for 'em. The men had to make about fifty cents a day, but this mule and this horse that they worked in this coal mine, they'd work all day and they'd put him in the barn, they'd feed him a good meal, hay and grain; they didn't much care about whether this man who put [the coal] in the car had anything to eat or not.[43]

And again, Gabe Newsome from Jenkins:

> They all just throws you around like driving a mule. That's all there was to it. They said up at Jenkins one time, "You be careful with them horses and mules; we apt to get one of them killed and then we have to buy them." Just as good as said not to pay attention to the man. My grandpa said one time that the boss told the men right in the mines, "Boys, keep that mule out of that electric wire there. Them things cost money; they're not just like hired men." They just didn't care, buddy.[44]

Although the sheer widespread transmission of the story is a signal to its basis in oral tradition rather than empirical fact, its repetition calls not for dismissal but for scrutiny. Why did the story appear again and again from miners all over eastern Kentucky and beyond? What was it about the story that made it particularly compelling? The story of mules and men is obviously a story about unfair working conditions. But it is also a story of the perceived inversion of a natural order, and in this sense it is an assertion of inherent human worth. When miner Ken Vanderpool recited the story during an oral history interview, he also discussed driving mules on his grandfather's farm when he was younger.[45] It was clear in his telling that in the proper order of things, as represented by the farm, *men* drove *mules*. As a commentary on social relations and exchanges, the story of mules and men in the coal mines unveiled and criticized capitalism's structuring of value, which turned men into commodities at once similar to and less than mules. Mules are products of technology themselves, a combination of horse and donkey. In relating a story in which the company valued a mule more than a man, miners commented on a fundamental imbalance in the natural order of things that not only placed technology and artifice over the human but also replaced inherent or "natural" value with value created through the marketplace of commodities. But this critique was not carried out in economic terms or through rational argumentation. Instead, it was expressed by turning the system of exchange into a story of specific material transformation and violation of nature. Like a folktale, it transmitted important truths and social criticism in a relatively indirect form. Although it was clearly a story critical of coal companies, and reported as true, it said more than it appeared to say about proper human relations.

Both Moore's and Newsome's versions of the story ended with a moral about "care." What coal companies lacked, as revealed by stories told about their treatment of mules and of men, was care toward fellow human beings. This meant one, or both, of two things in the vernacular of mountain culture. First, the companies were immoral, sinful, because they did not live up to the biblical injunction to love and care for fellow human beings. Second, the companies evidently did not consider their workers to be human, placing them outside of obligations of care that encompassed human communities. In either case, the work environment of coal mining was in some ways inhuman and threatened human community and care. Men went into mining because it promised to pay them so that they could provide for themselves and their families better than they were able to do in any other form of work. The duty to work—required, the Bible said, in order to eat—brought them there. But as laborers in the mining industry, and increasingly when the coal boom ended in the later 1920s, they found that their work did not produce family, community, and social stability, as they might have anticipated it would, but instead produced discord.

The Tactility of Social Exchange

As with the story about mules and men, miners criticized the power that the company had over them, and the way that they were treated, in the form of stories about exchanges. The company store was the setting for many of these narratives. The store was the primary locus of the exchange of money and goods between miner and company. It was the place where miners received their pay, often in the form of scrip, and where they bought their necessities. It was the place where they paid rent and purchased the powder and tools for their work. And, in many cases, it was the place where they found that they had less pay coming to them than they had expected. It was thus the concrete manifestation of the abstractions of power that came between a man's work and his livelihood in the industrial setting. Miner Tom Hunter portrayed a miner's perception of these interactions with the company with reference to the biblical book of Revelation when he said that "having the stamps [scrip] was the same as marking your forehead. You had to be marked before you could get anything."[46] The company played the role of Satan, with the added horror that Satan controlled access to livelihood. This was not the normal natural world but Satan's world where men needed the mark to obtain the fruits of their labor. The company—and the company store—thus had a direct impact on physical well-being, too. Ben Foster, another miner, related a story from a Harlan County coal camp.

> One morning, I was over to the store, and a man comes in that had been working since eight o'clock the evening before. He says to the store manager, "Buddy, give me some aspirin. I'm achin' all over." He had been cutting coal all night long. Well, the manager says to him, "You ain't gettin' no aspirin until the bulletin comes in." I turned to him and gave him a dime. That's all aspirin was, ten cents a box. I've thought of that many, many a time. Wouldn't give the man even a box of aspirin even after he'd worked a twelve hour shift.[47]

Foster was moved to help by what he witnessed. The man's pain that the manager was unwilling to help relieve was a materialization of the failure of reciprocity between worker and company. An exchange such as this haunted Foster, and he "thought of that many, many a time." In other words, as this one event played and replayed in Foster's mind, it became a sign, or perhaps a cipher, that contained a message about the nature of things in this industrial world. It was an episode to which to return "many, many a time," because it revealed something significant about the company's mediation—through the store and the manager—between

Mine entrance, 1922. Item 106, The Jenkins, Kentucky Photographic
Collection, 1911–1930, 2001AV01, University of Kentucky Archives.
Used by permission.

work and its product. In this case, for the aching miner, the work produced
pain—and the company and its accounting methods seemed to mediate even the
miner's relationship to his own body. In a great many cases, stories of unbalanced
transactions between miners and company powers involved an element of bodily
pain. In Foster's case, the company caused pain but refused to take it away. Other
stories expressed how the power relations in social interactions and exchanges
themselves produced real tactile effects on the bodies of those involved or even on
those who were only witnesses. Indeed, in their telling, such stories seem designed
to record and transmit a visceral response, the significance of the event apparently

intensified and authenticated by the physical, embodied response it produced. In a manner similar to what Melvin Profitt and Teamus Bartley experienced on witnessing mine fatalities, exchanges that enacted power imbalances also elicited bodily reactions. Profitt told the following story that expressed the transformation of exchange into nervous tension and tactile strain.

> I come out one night, I guess it's at least nine o'clock, there was one of them little jack-legged bosses standing there and [he] looked over at me, said,
>
> "You cleaned up?"
>
> "Yeah, I cleaned up."
>
> He looked at [this] old, poor fellow, I was in sympathy with him. "No," he says, "I didn't."
>
> "How many cars do you lack?"
>
> He said, "I guess there's four more in there."
>
> "Well," he said, "you get the hell in there! If you can't get it out, let somebody in who can get it." He run that old man back in there. It's either go back or lose his job. My nerves run as high as a pine tree many times like that.[48]

As companies tried to get the maximum output from each worker, not cleaning up a cut of coal was, by the mid- to late 1920s, reason for being fired. And in the company town, to be fired meant to be evicted from your home. Therefore, in addition to the uncertainties of mine accidents, job layoffs, and the daily dangers of the camp environment, for those who lived in coal towns "their dwelling was uncertain" because "if the company got rid of a man or fired a man, or he lost his job, he had to move. Forthwith. There wasn't no fooling around about it. He had to go . . . regardless of how many children he had."[49] To Profitt, this "old man's" predicament and his treatment by the "jack-legged boss" produced a visceral effect, widening the parameters of the exchange to include the witness, physically, in its force. While the boss, from his own perspective, may have thought that his trouble was solely with the "old man" and had nothing to do with Profitt, from Profitt's perspective the exchange manifested the weight of a much larger pattern of power in which he was located alongside, or even in the same place as, the "old man." Miners often talked about sharing their fates with other miners. It was a fact of the underground work setting. If a mine caved in or exploded, all the men in it would likely die. It also meant that miners shared social and work experiences in a culture that was shaped by a single industry. It is therefore reasonable that Profitt could easily see himself in the place of the "old man." However, witnessing this imbalance of power resulted not in a reasoned response about power and capitalism but in an emotional bodily sensation called "nerves."

"Nerves" were a common complaint in the anxiety-producing setting of coal mining, and a variety of things could make them "run high." A study of complaints of "nerves" in eastern Kentucky found that "surprisingly, this seemingly ambiguous complaint possesses substantial social and medical communication value among its users. Family members and neighbors nod their heads knowingly and sympathetically when a patient indicates that the person is suffering from this socially acceptable malady."[50] Nerves have been interpreted as an embodied metaphor for the experience of class inequality and as "a lay idiom for emotional distress." A cross-cultural examination of symptoms of "nerves" and the contexts from which the complaint emerged suggests that nerves were associated with self/ society relations and reflected the subjective and existential experience of imbalances of power.[51] That analysis would fit Profitt's case. Anthropologist Nancy Scheper-Hughes has elaborated further on nerves, or *nervos,* in the context of a community of poor Brazilian sugar cane cutters, offering some interpretive insights that are applicable to eastern Kentucky coal miners. She explains that as a folk diagnosis of distress that localizes broad social forces in the individual body, nerves signals a particular way of inhabiting the body, a "body praxis," common to cultures of manual labor. In the physical work of mining coal, miners came to know and relate to the world through their bodies such that, as Scheper-Hughes notes concerning cane cutters, "theirs is a social class and culture that privilege the body and that instruct them in a close attention to the physical senses and symptoms."[52] The body, therefore, mediated both material and social forces and became a primary site of both knowledge and expression. Hunger, pain, disease, bad feelings, and nerves were all signs of a world out of balance, and in turn bodily symptoms took on allegorical significance.

What is important to notice here is that the bodies of miners mediated not only the physical labor of cutting, shooting, and loading coal but also the social dimensions of coal town life. For miners, the economy was not about abstract principles and profit margins; it was felt as somatic experience. Miners saw, and in fact *felt,* that the political economy classified human beings differently depending upon their location in the structure of production. Industrial power had profoundly existential and tactile dimensions, in other words. Commentaries on the physical effects of social interactions were at the same time commentaries on the connection between socioeconomic power and human value, feeling out human purpose. In the dust, dark, damp, and pains of the mines and camps, miners felt the forces of capital not as abstractions but as forces impinging upon their bodies. Their experiences, both in the mines and in social relations, told them that life was uncertain and fragile, despite the bravado and courage that they put forth in its face. They gave those experiences religious significance by turning them into moral commentary centered on the embodied effects of social interaction, raising in a concrete form critical questions about human value in the industrial coal mining context.

Yet it would be a mistake to think that this awareness necessarily led directly to an oppositional sense of class consciousness that pitted workers against their bosses. Class relations within coal towns were decidedly ambivalent before the Great Depression, and even then they varied from company to company and from town to town. Miners formed a sense of community and trust from their shared work experiences. They differentiated miners from nonminers, and mining was a basic part of their identity; it got "in their blood." Nevertheless, despite the intense feelings of discomfort that they so often said they experienced when encountering imbalances of power that were built into the social structure of industrial capitalism, miners had complicated relationships with their bosses. It appears that they were able to separate the animosity that they felt toward unfair plays of power from the individuals whom they knew as bosses and supervisors. In other words, there was a disjuncture between the abstraction of the company or system of power and the concreteness of individual company officials. Folklorist Alessandro Portelli has found that miners, in oral histories, displayed nuanced linguistic strategies that maintained this slippery separation. When citing unjust labor practices, they referred to the abstract notions of the company and capitalism as an anonymous "they." But when referring to the individual men and women whom they knew personally, even if those persons were in positions of power within the same company, miners used the more personal and concrete "he" or "she." Bosses who lived in the camps with miners were also neighbors, Portelli points out, and in the paternalistic mining industry the company—and its officials—positioned itself as caretaker of miners even as it also wielded power over them. The company town was, after all, owned by the company, and miners were its employees. According to traditional and widely held conceptions of employer-employee responsibility, employers were expected to look after their workforce. Kinship provided the basic model by which to understand the workplace relationship, drawing from the ideal of the family farm setting and perhaps conceptions of artisanlike master/apprentice relationships. Portelli noted that miners looked to mine officials for praise and reward.[53] They also compared their bosses and towns to worse places and felt a sense of pride and belonging that invested their choices and efforts with a defensive attitude. In other words, in spite of—or maybe because of—the difficulties of both work and social life in mining towns, miners could develop an allegiance to their own officials while directing their complaints elsewhere. They used their verbal strategies to negotiate the ambivalence of this relationship. In a sense, they considered their bosses to be at the mercy of the same market forces as themselves and looked to officials' paternalistic nature to protect them. At the same time, miners criticized the *sources* of their troubles by abstracting them from human agency into impersonal forces. Above all, they tracked the *impacts* and *effects* of unequal distributions of power, reading them and commenting on them as signs of the forces with which they had to contend. In this context, they developed tactics and strategies that gave their experiences significance materially, existentially, and spiritually.

Theology at the Limits

As the experiences of miners reveal, the life of coal mining was a theater of extremes. Mining offered the chance for a better life, an opportunity to fulfill the religiously sanctioned human obligation to work, and the possibility of making money to provide for one's family. This was an important matter in eastern Kentucky during the years of industrial development and the decreasing productivity of rural farming that accompanied it. On the other hand, the work of mining and life in coal towns brought a new set of anxieties and problems. Constant dread, danger, and social relations that made "nerves run high as a pine tree" were facts of everyday life, but so were new commercial desires, previously unavailable leisure activities, and the other benefits that industrial centers offered. Within these circumstances miners and their families developed a sense of community and made the life of mining their own, forging a new identity and culture of mining. But that culture and identity developed in relation to a particular "structure of feeling," in the words of cultural historian Raymond Williams. Less formal or institutionalized than a "worldview" or "ideology," the term *structure of feeling* is meant to designate the social experience shared in a particular community's specific material and historical setting. It is another way of talking about both the *feeling* of a place and time and the cultural *styles* that emerged from particular shared circumstances: "We are talking about characteristic elements of impulse, restraint, and tone; specifically affective elements of consciousness and relationships: not feeling against thought, but thought as felt and feeling as thought: practical consciousness of a present kind, in a living and interrelating continuity." These "*affective* elements of consciousness and relationships" are commonly identified as "subjective," but the label of subjectivity obscures the relationship between "social" and "personal" that makes up the experience of a particular time and place. To put it another way, the material and social setting of industrial coal mining in eastern Kentucky had a particular presence, a rhythm and texture that had an impact on the experience of life that was markedly different from the experience of subsistence farming or other modes of production that mining families had known elsewhere. It came through the work of mining, including the hours of work and the structure of pay. It came through housing styles and the layouts of towns. It came through the company store and its products. It came through the coal dust settling on everything. It came through the radio and music and foods. It came through the varieties of people who lived in coal towns and their shared and differing desires and outlooks. It came through the particular history that native miners shared and experienced in the industrial transformation of the hills. It came through all the everyday aspects of life that were shaped by the social and material dynamics of industrial coal mining. It was intimately tied to industrial structures of power. And although mining families were able to draw from existing cultural and religious idioms to orient themselves to their new world, those idioms had to be reworked to articulate the new structure of feeling of the mining camp accurately, in ways that continued to make sense in their new environment. In Williams's terms, "There is a frequent tension between the received interpretation and practical experience," for "practical consciousness is what is actually being lived, and not only what is thought is being lived."[54] Mining families struggled to find a language that would accurately speak to and from the personal and social experience of life in this place.

The stories of miners' experiences during the first decades of eastern Kentucky's industrial mining development record their attempts to articulate the sense and feeling of their new world and its significance—not as a fully formed ideology or worldview but by thinking *through* experience itself. Miners communicated the experience of their daily lives in stories that voiced those experiences as immanent, somatic commentaries about human value, exchange, responsibility, and mortality. In many cases, those narratives spoke indirectly (and sometimes directly) to religious concerns, drawing upon both existing and newly found symbols and metaphors—like mules or company stores—to articulate the *presence* of this new world's structure of feeling and

its impact on their lives. In the process, they revealed that the material setting of industrial mining was not only an economic or political concern for
miners but an existential and spiritual one, mediated primarily through the
body.

Some miners, especially those who felt the call to be preachers in addition to
working in the mines, were more inclined than others to translate the structure
of feeling of coal town life into explicitly theological terms. They are helpful
guides to recovering more fully the religious attitudes that emerged from this
environment. Miner Frank Fugate, an Old Regular Baptist preacher, was one of
these men. He spoke to the experiences of existing in a world where danger and
anxiety were everyday realities but where the promises of a better life were always
within sight, when he said that "you've got plenty of troubles nagging your natural existence here. You've got trouble on every side of you, trying to preserve your
natural existence. Well, the only safety we've got is God. If we can wholly trust
him and know him as we should, then that life is worth living. It lives and it enjoys freedom, liberty." And if they could trust him as they should, Fugate continued, God would take an active stand in seeing miners through their troubles.
"He'll guide us and he'll take care of us," he said.[55] The traditional religion of the
mountains, its forms of Protestant Christianity and its wider sense of order and
powers gained a new resonance in the context of coal mining. Indeed, another
miner revealed how tightly these theological statements were tied to the structure of feeling of everyday life when he described the dusty environment of the
coal camps with which he was so familiar, presenting in tactile images the everyday experience that was the material and social counterpart to his theological
orientation. "There was dust, coal dust, in the camps, in the houses; it was impossible to keep 'em out," he said.

> You'd see little children runnin' around, they'd be just about as black as their par-
> ents comin' in from work. They was right in this dust. There wasn't too much
> control of this dust and the filth that come from these mines. . . . You seen them
> ol' mothers and daughters out . . . with a washboard and a washtub scrubbing
> their clothes out, when they'd hang 'em out on the lines, why, then the usual thing
> was getting the dust right back on the clothes again. It was something you lived
> with day and night as long as you was in around the mines or the coal camp, either
> one. They were subject to dust.[56]

Recall the earlier statement concerning the relentlessness of coal dust's presence
in the camps: "A woman would work from dawn 'til night and never keep it too

clean because you just couldn't get rid of all that dust."[57] Out of control, unyielding to human power, the dust defied women's long labors against it. But there was no alternative: "you just couldn't get rid of all that dust," but you had to do what you could.

Like the "troubles nagging your natural existence," the dust was both material reality and metaphor, experienced and narrated and thereby becoming a means by which to express the total significance of life as it was lived in the eastern Kentucky coal camps. In a world "subject to dust," camp residents nevertheless kept cleaning and pushing on, even though the dust just kept falling around them. To give up in the face of difficulty and despair would simply be wrong, even sinful, according to the widespread understanding that human beings were creatures commanded by the creator to work in this world. Indeed, *not* to give up in the face of seemingly endless trials was a particularly important implication of this perspective. Ceasing to work, out of fear or resignation, would spell disaster. According to Fugate, "If you let that life of yours get in the clutches of fear and in the clutches of all the uprisings of this world, it's going to rob you of every freedom and liberty in your heart." What missionary observers of mountain culture had described as a resigned fatalism comes across rather differently in this context, revealing itself instead as a theological expression of hope and strength in the face of daily encounters with human limits in which, Fugate said, "I don't know why more people didn't get blowed up dead."[58]

In the coal fields, material experience and religious imagination wove through each other, through the constantly falling dust and dangers of the mining life, articulating a view of human existence as struggle and work. As writer Emma Bell Miles observed of Appalachian culture, "Courage seems to me the keynote of our whole system of religious thought."[59] Another miner-preacher, Talmadge Allen, illustrated her point when he said, "Hard times'll come, but the good'll always overcome the bad. It's gonna take a lot of beatin's, though, and a lot of hardness for you to come out on top. I've never seen it fail in my life." By reversing the valuation that one might expect, this miner-preacher gave a positive meaning to suffering that looked beyond the present situation to a later reward. The form that reward would take remained ambiguous, implying that it was not *only* otherworldly, as critics have often concluded; it might also come in a person's lifetime. In fact, according to this Old Regular Baptist preacher, suffering *added* to a person's worth. "A man never did suffer none never did nothin'. Ain't been nowhere unless he's had some things to overcome."[60] So, in a sense suffering was itself a kind of work, and it entered the discourse of work as an orientation to life. As James Still's character Brack Baldridge understood ("it was never meant for a body to be full content on the face of this earth"), hard work was a constitutive component of human existence.[61]

The hard life of mining—both the physical labor and the difficult world into which the work brought miners and their families—intensified a traditional orientation to the meaning of being human *and* was made bearable by understanding it through a familiar religious idiom. Aud Williamson, who worked in the mines in Van Lear, suggested the pervasiveness of this attitude even among "sinners" when he described praying aloud as he stood day after day in water working a twenty-six-inch coal face. "Lord, give me a shelter for my children," he prayed, seeking—or articulating—a significant meaning for his suffering. "I'd get so hot in there, a suffering and so hot, wet with sweat. You wouldn't believe how much a human body would sweat and live through it . . . your clothes . . . you had on . . . to protect your body, would be so wet. And I would pray. I prayed so many times, 'Lord, just give me shelter. . . .' I wasn't a Christian at the time. But I did, I prayed for shelter and a home. We lived in a coal company house. I always wanted a home for my children."[62] Was he praying for a home that was not controlled by the company? Or was he simply aware that in the company town his house would be taken away if he did not endure his suffering? In either case, responsibility for family made suffering meaningful, or so he prayed. The fact that he "wasn't a Christian at the time" indicates the reach of the idioms of prayer and suffering in mountain culture.

Beyond suffering, in the mines the physical body resounded with sacramental potential, pointing through and beyond itself to greater significance as experiences of death and injury bore witness to the limits of the human body and mortal life. Death and injury marked life's fragility at the same time that they compelled the imagination toward a more stable state of existence, one not fettered to the contingencies of the material world. Yet it was always the concrete, visceral body that served as a sign of the spiritual world beyond, through which this world was accessed and imagined. Miners' bodies were marked physically by the records of wounds suffered: scars, lost fingers, broken limbs, shortened breath, and hacking coughs. Injury was an everyday part of the work. Death, too, was not uncommon and was always within the realm of possibility for anyone who went under the ground each day. Such daily familiarity with the body's limits demanded religious articulation.

According to a commonly held—and likely comforting—view, the dead might be gone from the world, but they lived on in heaven. Many miners, in a continuity of mountain tradition, extended their community to include their deceased kin, and they looked forward to the time that family members would be reunited for eternity. Taking care of graveyards and memorializing the dead, then, were important social and religious practices that ritualized the maintenance of this extended kinship to which they were still obligated. Family and community reunions transcended the present, first by acknowledging those who had gone in the past, and second by looking ahead to meeting them in the future. The difficulties of the moment therefore had a larger context that helped to make them more manageable. If material existence was defined by its inescapable limitations—constant troubles, human suffering, hard labor, and death—heaven was the opposite—a place where labor ceased and kin were able to live together without the anxieties that wove through their earthly existence.[63]

Like so many aspects of coal mining life, however, attitudes toward death could be quite ambivalent. Death was simultaneously an end and a beginning, the conclusion of earthly life and the time of heavenly reward. It held an inherent conflict, evoking both sorrow and joy. The latter was clearly in evidence in the lyrics to "On Jordan's Stormy Banks," an eighteenth-century hymn that continues to be sung in Old Regular Baptist and other mountain churches today:

> On Jordan's stormy banks I stand
> And cast a wishful eye
> To Canaan's fair and happy land
> Where my possessions lie.
>
> There generous fruits, that never fail,
> On trees immortal grow—
> There rock and hill, and brook and vale,
> With milk and honey flow.[64]

Heaven is represented here as a beautiful place of abundance that is longed for even though death is the only means of travel over the river to Canaan. But another traditional song known in the eastern Kentucky coal fields at the time voiced a seemingly contrasting attitude. Dock Boggs, who popularized "Oh, Death" among a wider American audience during the folksong revival of the 1960s, learned the song in 1930. Boggs worked as a coal miner in Letcher County during the 1920s and 1930s, but during a brief break from mining between 1927 and 1929 he recorded several songs for commercial release.[65] The lyrics to "Oh, Death" showed a familiarity with death, figured anthropomorphically in conversation with the singer. But rather than welcoming his visitor, the singer begged death to give him more time. Here, death was a dominating figure who did not play favorites, and dying was identified with the physical body that would soon return to dust and worms. Visions of heavenly glory were starkly absent:

> What is this that I can't see
> With icy hands taking hold on me?
> I am death and none can excel,
> I'll open the doors to heaven and hell.
>
> Chorus:
> Oh, death, Oh, death,
> Can't you spare me over til another year?
> Oh, death, Oh, death,
> Please spare me over til another year.
>
> Oh, death, someone would pray,
> Couldn't you call some other day?
> Children prayed, the preachers preached,
> The time of mercy is out of your reach.
>
> I'll fix your feet so you can't walk
> I'll lock your jaw so you can't talk
> Close your eyes so you can't see,
> This very hour, come go with me.
>
> I'm death, I come to take the soul,
> Leave the body and leave it cold,
> To drop the flesh off of the frame,
> The earth and worms both have a claim.
>
> Chorus
>
> Mother, come to my bed,
> Place a cold towel upon my head.
> My head is warm, my feet is cold,
> Death is moving upon my soul.
>
> Oh, death, how you treating me,
> You close my eyes so I can't see.
> You hurt my body, you made me cold
> You ruined my life right out of my soul.

Chorus

Oh, death, consider my age,
Please don't take me at this stage,
My wealth is all at your command,
If you'll remove your icy hand.

The old, the young, the rich or poor,
All alike with me, you know;
No wealth, no land, no silver, no gold,
Nothing satisfies me but your soul.[66]

The attitudes expressed by each of these songs existed in the coal fields, and there is a good chance that a single miner would embrace each of them at various times in his life. They were both available options for expressing the significance of mortality as a defining aspect of life—and one that no earthly riches could overcome. One spoke of the spirit, the other of the body, two dimensions of human existence in mountain tradition that tugged in different directions and yet, of necessity, coexisted. The self lived between these extremes, and death both divided them and tied them together. In either case, death was the cessation of the constant flux of mortal life in which "dwelling was uncertain." Against the backdrop of mining, this phrase might be understood as both a description of coal town life and a religious idiom. It spoke to the power that company towns held over miners' housing, yet pointed beyond to a more fundamental significance that resonated with the coal camp's structure of feeling: no amount of wealth or power could keep death away. As a human limit situation, however, death was also a threshold. If the flux of life ceased, it opened the possibility of life at a standstill, eternal, outside of time and the contingencies of mortal history. Would that frozen moment turn out to be emptiness itself, or would it be the promised good that would overcome the bad once the price of suffering had been endured? Death was an occasion, then, for imagining life without the "troubles nagging your natural existence."

The physical body itself was tied to those troubles and contingencies. That connection, "Oh, Death" makes clear, did not end even with death as the body continued to go through the process of decay. But death could also be imagined as freeing the essential, spiritual self from a demanding physical body that had to work, confront illness and disease, and navigate ambiguous social forces. In the eastern Kentucky coal fields, the social and the physical were tightly interwoven in bodily experience, and social disruptions (manifest, for instance, in imbalances of power and unequal exchanges) were felt as bodily sensations. The body, then, was a source of limitation even as it was the source of imagining a mode of existence without limitation. For Christians, salvation through conversion was the significant difference between the mortal body and the eternal soul. Drawing attention to the mortal body and its limitations, then, could provide a powerful urge toward conversion.[67]

It is important to note that in Appalachia, somatic bodily sensations had long held special religious significance. The Bible was the central scriptural authority, but the body was the primary source of authentic religious knowledge concerning the state of the soul. Conviction of sin, the presence of the Holy Spirit, omens, visions, demonic temptations—all were known through feelings in the body. Healing, too, was a religious idiom, revealing the balance of the body, the state of the soul, and (in some cases) the presence of supernatural forces. When, in their talk, miners narrated their experiences of social interactions and exchanges into *felt* experiences—thinking through the body as they tried to articulate the structure of feeling of the place—they brought their situation into potential contact with the local religious vernacular. The experiences of hard labor, tensions at home, anxiety, and constantly falling dust, as well as economic and social inequality that resulted in nerves, bad feelings, hunger, or other somatic symptoms, could therefore lead directly to religious articulation and practice. The episodic, crisis-oriented structure of feeling of the coal camp likewise resonated with—and intensified—a common mountain religious mode of understanding. It is not surprising, then, that new, intensified social forms of religious performance emerged in the industrializing coal fields, drawing energy and religious power from the realities of mining life.

FIVE

POWER
IN THE
BLOOD

*There is power, power, wonder-working power
in the blood, in the blood of the lamb.*

— LEWIS E. JONES,
"There Is Power in the Blood," 1899

*In the Holiness-Pentecostal Church, you're
working your way into heaven.*

—VERNON WATSON,
in Troy D. Abell, *Better Felt than Said*, 118

THE STRUCTURE OF FEELING OF the coal miners' world—"subject to dust," full of broken bodies and heightened nerves produced by the work and environment of mining—found its clearest and most dramatic religious articulation in the Holiness-Pentecostal worship practices that grew throughout the coal fields during the period of industrialization. "Holiness," as this emergent style of expressive, tactile Christianity is called in the central Appalachian vernacular, built on widespread mountain religious traditions but transformed them, intensifying them and energizing them in the industrial setting.[1]

Whereas the felt presence of the Holy Spirit was a defining feature of worship in most mountain churches, it was heightened and elaborated in Holiness worship through often visceral manifestation of outward signs of the inner experience.[2] Holiness believers shouted, cried, jumped up and down, spoke in "unknown" tongues, and fell on the floor shaking and praying. Preachers shouted and ran around the room, sometimes breaking into song. The music that accompanied Holiness worship was energetic and loud, played on guitars and tambourines, sometimes banjoes and fiddles. Such spectacular physical behavior was frowned upon by those in more emotionally restrained churches—both denominational and of mountain origin—and it earned Holiness believers the demeaning title of "Holy Rollers." Nevertheless, many people of eastern Kentucky found Holiness worship to be profoundly significant. For some it was the promise of physical healing that made them take notice, or the emphasis on strict boundaries of morality and selfhood. For others it was a compelling revelation of the reality of the spiritual world or simply a religious style and performance that seemed appropriate to the everyday experiences of the life of coal mining. But Holiness religion was no less significant for those who did not accept its promises or premises and who saw it instead as a form of fanaticism or escapism. The controversial nature of Holiness signaled that this form of religious expression touched upon emergent concerns that were crucial to understanding the religious worlds of eastern Kentucky's coal miners

By 1931, when social worker Elizabeth Hooker conducted a survey of native churches and missionary activity in southern Appalachia for the Home Mission Society, she could not help but notice that Holiness religion was a prominent part of the landscape and dynamics of central Appalachia. Her description of their worship is worth reciting at length:

> Some attend out of curiosity and others because of the dearth of religious privileges. Biblical passages quoted freely by the speaker awaken the confidence of the hearers. A challenge to perfect Holiness of life arouses their consciences. Loud, emotional preaching, with encouragement to the physical expression of feeling through the clapping of hands, stamping, dancing and the like, rouses the audience to a high pitch of excitement. When this stage is reached, some shout, others fall down in a stupor, and others are affected by involuntary movements, such as twitching, bending the body rapidly up and down, jumping on the benches or desks, rolling on the floor, or pounding at the windows. These movements the preacher declares to be superinduced by the Holy Ghost.[3]

The "second blessing" by the Holy Ghost, said to be the cause of such "excitement," was understood by believers to be a higher level of purification and sanctification that followed the "first blessing" of conversion and baptism. The second blessing, according to Holiness believers, made its recipients free from sin and supposedly incapable of sinning in the future. Those who received it also gained the power to heal the sick and to be impervious to poisons.

While this sort of religious practice could be found throughout the Appalachian mountains, Hooker found an especially high degree of Holiness-related activity in the Northeastern Cumberland Plateau region—the home of the eastern Kentucky coal fields. "Holiness preaching is more common and Holiness phenomena are more intense" in this area, she wrote, than in any other area of Appalachia. Indeed, Holiness revivals were already a regular part of the coal field environment by the 1920s. Despite their ubiquity, Holiness activities were nearly invisible to census-takers and surveyors and therefore also to later historians. There was a good reason for this: like much of Appalachian religious culture, Holiness worship tended to be unorganized. It often took the form of revivals that drew crowds and attention but seldom congealed into an organized church or resulted in a large growth of membership in existing churches. Holiness preachers frequently maintained their independence by not belonging solely to one particular church, but instead preaching at a variety of existing churches (usually Baptist in eastern Kentucky) in continuity with long-standing mountain tradition. According to the 1926 Census of Religious Bodies, Holiness churches accounted for 3.8 percent of the total number of churches in the counties of the Northeastern Cumberland Plateau covered by Hooker's report. Yet Hooker noted that these organized churches were "few in comparison to unorganized groups holding meetings with more or less regularity."[4] When they did organize, mountain Holiness churches tended to follow the Appalachian pattern of independence and autonomy and therefore they fell through the cracks of ordinary survey techniques.[5] An accurate accounting of the numbers of such churches remains problematic today as it was in the past. Still, Deborah Vansau McCauley asserts that the independent, nondenominational church, often Baptist but more often Holiness-Pentecostal, "is perhaps the most common form of religious organization in . . . Central Appalachia. It is also the least visible and least considered in writings on mountain religious life."[6]

For many Americans, independent Holiness churches have become highly charged signifiers of Appalachia's uniqueness and, in many cases, its despair. Not only are Holiness churches a central facet of eastern Kentucky's religious landscape, they are also the face of coal mining religion in the American imagination.

Yet the history of Holiness religion in this region is exceptionally difficult to recover. Oral history has helped to form a picture of the transformation from subsistence farming to industrial coal mining, but it is less revealing of the meanings and functions of Holiness religion as it was actually experienced and practiced in the fabric of mining life. There are at least two reasons for this. First, the oral historians who conducted the interviews that make up the major collections of Appalachian oral history typically did not probe their subjects for descriptions of religious worship or insight into what particular religious practices or idioms meant to people at the time. They were more often concerned with collecting information about social life, labor conditions, and folkways than with recovering religious life. If religion was discussed, it was usually limited to naming the types of churches in a particular area or reciting how often people went (or did not go) to church. Second, ordinary people often have trouble articulating and elaborating the "meanings" or significance of religious practices in the first place. Religion works through idioms, gestures, and symbols that often communicate nondiscursively. They gain significance in the ways that they are able to connect to particular settings, experiences, feelings, or tensions that otherwise are difficult to put into words. Moreover, people are inclined to think of religion ahistorically, as if current religious practices have not undergone changes in meaning. This comes across clearly in many recorded oral histories in which subjects have little to say about historically situated worship practices other than surface descriptions if prompted. Such material clearly leaves a problem for the historian. How can the history of Holiness religion, which appears to have been an important part of the story of religion and industrialization, be recovered?

One possibility, which I have chosen to follow in this chapter, is the careful comparative use of studies of Holiness-Pentecostal religion from other times and places. There is some danger in this approach, since religions are never lived and practiced apart from the everyday dynamics and pressures of specific situated places. Pentecostal religion in one place does not carry the same layers of signification that it has in another place. Nevertheless, with a conception of the ideas and practices of Holiness-Pentecostal worship and a rich sense of the everyday lives of mining families, the significance of Holiness religion for those people in that time and place begins to open itself up to interpretation.

Following this approach, this chapter recovers and seeks to interpret the significance of Holiness religion in the context of early industrial coal mining. It begins with a general history of the Holiness-Pentecostal movement, followed by a discussion of the particular emergence of Holiness churches in Appalachia and eastern Kentucky. The remainder of the chapter explores the significance of Holiness religion against the background of the everyday life of industrial coal mining.

Holiness-Pentecostal Religion

The appearance of the first independent Holiness churches in eastern Kentucky and central Appalachia coincided with the arrival of mission activity and economic development in the mountains in the late nineteenth century.[7] Yet Holiness religion should not be viewed simply as a "railroad religion" that "foreigners" brought to the mountains, nor did it form independently in the hills apart from interactions with missionaries and industrialists. Rather, it was an innovation on both "mountain" and "foreign" religious forms in the context of the dynamic forces of power and resistance that created new religious, economic, and social patterns.

To understand the emergence of Holiness religion in eastern Kentucky, it is helpful first to review the development of the Holiness-Pentecostal movement in American religious history. "Holiness" in this context refers to an idea taught by John Wesley, the founder of Methodism, that by God's grace Christians could be freed entirely from sin and the temptation to sin. They could, in other words, attain a state of sinless perfection. Although Wesley held that Christian perfection was attained through a gradual process, he also taught that its realization was signaled by a singular experience of "sanctification," or a "second blessing" that followed the original conversion experience. Wesley traveled the English countryside in the mid- to late eighteenth century, bringing his new form and style of Christianity to a predominantly working-class audience who had been alienated by the intellectual, text-based Anglican churches. He preached to crowds in public spaces, often to the disapproval of the Anglican church. He also encouraged lay preachers to act similarly, spreading a message that emphasized the ability of God's grace to purify the converted from sin through the second blessing of sanctification. Across the Atlantic, Methodism proliferated rapidly throughout the American frontier during the Second Great Awakening and after, appealing to a diverse, often uneducated, and marginalized rural population who benefited from Methodism's emphasis on individual conversion, emotion, and itinerant lay preaching.[8]

By the 1830s, as the denomination became part of the cultural and social status quo of the American mainstream, American Methodists played down the doctrine of "entire sanctification" in favor of a more gradualist understanding of perfection. Indeed, by midcentury, Methodists and Baptists, churches that had once been upstarts, had become the largest denominations in the United States, and the experiential and transformative elements that had been so central to the revivalist atmosphere of Methodism's growth had become subdued.[9] But this shift in emphasis was not greeted with approval by all. Phoebe Palmer, in particular, responded by forming the Tuesday Meeting of the Promotion of Holiness in New York in the 1830s, which was designed to return the focus of worship to the personal experience of sanctification. Over the following decades, through meetings and publications produced by Palmer and her supporters, interest in Holiness grew; it was soon an interdenominational popular religious movement supported by parachurch networks. With the organization of the National Camp Meeting Association for the Promotion of Holiness in Vineland, New Jersey, in 1867, summer camp meetings became a regular feature of the movement—especially for middle-class adherents.

As the popularity of the Holiness movement grew beyond its Methodist roots, alternative theological positions on sanctification and perfectionism began to emerge, often in competition with one another. The Calvinist Keswick "Higher Life" view was an especially popular one, spread by revivalists like Dwight L. Moody. This Reformed position understood sanctification as a gradual process that occurred throughout a person's life following conversion, punctuated by a distinct work of grace through which the Holy Spirit granted an individual special power for Christian service. It therefore contrasted with the sometime Wesleyan understanding of sanctification as an instantaneous event.[10] Moody and his fellow revivalists also added then-current premillennial dispensationalist theories about the imminent return of Jesus to their message, supplying an important idiom to the developing popular religious milieu. Holiness and premillennialism supported each other, as the rapid spread of Holiness appeared to premillennialists to be a sign of the impending era of the Holy Spirit that would usher in the end of the world. The idea that the day of judgment was at hand compelled people to seek refuge in Holiness beliefs.

Even as Holiness was growing into an ever more independent and popular movement nationally at the end of the nineteenth century, Methodists and other mainline Protestant churches were becoming more focused on social reform and education, turning their energies toward the maintenance of the middle-class society of which they were now a part. Their Social Gospel emphasis on worldly reforms appeared to be incompatible with the pietistic concerns that Holiness leaders argued were the proper locus of Christian practice. In response, Holiness leaders amplified their call to a return to the experiential core that they felt the mainline denominations were neglecting—very much as Wesley himself had originally advocated in the earlier British Anglican context that gave rise to Methodism in the first place. Somewhat ironically, the Holiness movement was to Methodism in the nineteenth century what Methodism was to the Anglicanism and the established Protestant churches in the eighteenth century, calling for a "return" to the "true" meaning of Christianity, focused on individual salvation, that the established churches had forgotten.

By the last decades of the nineteenth century, Methodists and other mainline churches denounced the Holiness movement and detached themselves from it completely. One reason was the inability of the established denominations to maintain control over the decentralized movement. Another was the desire by mainline churches to distance themselves from both the emotionalism of Holiness worship, which turned off the middle- and upper-class members of more prestigious churches, and the opposition of Holiness teachers to worldly accommodations.[11] But the Holiness movement did not need the approval of mainline churches to survive. It existed on its own as a diverse, independent popular movement, in some cases organizing into new denominations. Its generally decentralized, popular form opened the door to a great variety of innovations, often driven by competition between Holiness leaders for authority. Different teachers and schools offered distinct theological and practical perspectives on Christian perfectionism, some extending the idea of the "second blessing" to third, fourth, or more blessings. Outward evidence of sinlessness and sanctification became increasingly important for Holiness believers as they sought for proof of both their own salvation and the truth of various doctrines and practices. Signs of holiness could be as mundane as unornamented styles of dress or refraining from smoking and drinking, but as the stakes grew higher the signs grew more dramatic. Faith healing was particularly significant in this context, and by the 1880s it was a central practice of the movement. "Faith homes" and their practitioners taught that sanctification produced the ability to heal both physically and spiritually. By the 1890s some Holiness believers were claiming additional outward signs of sanctification in the form of special powers and spiritual gifts, including prophecy and ecstatic speech in unknown languages.

The idea that speaking in tongues was evidence of sanctification by the Holy Spirit is said to have originated with Holiness preacher Charles Fox Parham and his students at the Bethel Bible College in Topeka, Kansas. There, according to Holiness-Pentecostal tradition, the Holy Spirit rained down in 1901, ushering in the new Apostolic Age. Parham took his preaching, teaching, and healing practices to the mining region at the intersection of Kansas, Missouri, and Oklahoma, holding revivals there in 1903 and establishing Apostolic Faith missions in those states. In 1905 he moved on to Houston, Texas, where he opened another Bible school that emphasized prophecy and speaking in tongues. Here William J. Seymour, an

African American Baptist Holiness preacher, witnessed the phenomenon of tongues speaking and embraced the belief that it was evidence of sanctification.

All of these threads came to a head in 1906 at a revival led by Seymour in a church on Azusa Street in Los Angeles. Seymour had moved to Los Angeles that year with Parham's blessing, carrying the Apostolic Faith teachings with him to the storefront church where he became associate pastor. While he was preaching one day, a number of people began speaking in unknown tongues. Their utterances, accompanied by jerking, shaking, and spinning, they claimed, were signs of baptism by the Holy Spirit. Pentecostalism was born. The evidence of spiritual gifts, these adherents believed, was more than just a sign of individual sanctification: this was the dawning of a new millennial age, which was at the same time the restoration of the past days of the Pentecost. The second coming of Jesus, they felt, was surely right around the corner, and in preparation the Holy Spirit was anointing his saints just as in the days of the original apostles. When a massive earthquake struck San Francisco days after the initial scene of the spiritual outbreak, it only increased the believers' sense of urgency that the end of the world was imminent.

Word soon spread and attracted visitors from near and far. The revival continued for three years and proliferated throughout the nation as pilgrims to Azusa Street returned home, to the South and Midwest especially, where they planted Pentecostal churches in places that had already been prepared by Holiness activities. Over the following decades individual churches organized into denominations which, though remaining peripheral and often oppositional to mainstream American religious life through much of the twentieth century, nonetheless embraced the denominational structure common to American religious institutions.[12]

The strong Pentecostal belief in active supernatural powers and their practices relating to gifts of the Spirit have long interested scholars of religion and culture who note that Pentecostalism in many ways bucked the trends of modernization and secularization. According to this view, Pentecostalism was a reactionary religion, an oppositional response to modernity or a compensation for social or economic disempowerment.[13] In what is perhaps the most influential study of the social history of the movement, *Vision of the Disinherited: The Making of American Pentecostalism*, Robert Mapes Anderson argued that Pentecostalism was a religion of the "disinherited" and the oppressed, those on the bottom end of the social and economic changes wrought by industry and urbanism at the turn of the century. Anderson's interpretation of Pentecostalism deserves comment here because of its importance in the general literature and because it fits the situation of eastern Kentucky's coal fields in some ways but misses it in others.

According to Anderson, early Pentecostals came from rural-agrarian backgrounds and either felt disoriented in urban areas or had difficulty adjusting to the decline of rural life. They also had generally low social status. Therefore, they "were ill-equipped to perceive their position in the social order or to alter it even if they had perceived it." Anderson found that the key difference between those working poor who became Pentecostals and those who did not was the nature of their religious orientation prior to encountering Pentecostalism. Those who came from religious traditions where the "heart" was emphasized—that is, emotional worship, focused on the Spirit and on miracles—were more likely to become Pentecostal than those who did not. Pentecostals came from Holiness, evangelical and revivalist traditions, and "the more crudely superstitious forms of Catholicism," according to Anderson. "There is no doubt," he claimed, "that material and social deprivation plus an animistic religious outlook combined to predispose most of the recruits to the early Pentecostal movement. . . . Pentecostals, old and new, have typically testified that before their conversion to Pentecostalism they felt empty and hungry for God or for something they could not articulate. In short, they felt deprived."[14]

Clearly, the first part of Anderson's description—concerning the religious backgrounds of Pentecostals—fits the case of native eastern Kentucky miners. Unfortunately, this tells us little because it was a background that was widely shared by those who became Pentecostal and those who did not. Moreover, Pentecostalism, or simply "Holiness" in the mountains, overlapped in significant ways with other independent church worship styles that were not called Holiness. Anderson's analysis is not so much wrong as it is overgeneralized in this case.[15]

The general history of Holiness-Pentecostal religion is necessary background for understanding that its appearance in eastern Kentucky was not an anomaly of an out-of-the-way region but related to national trends. But recovering the particular significance of Holiness in the coal fields requires notice of the social, religious, and economic dynamics taking place on the local level that shaped the context within which this specific area practiced and witnessed Holiness activity. Therefore, while it is uncertain precisely when the first independent Holiness churches appeared in Appalachia, it is important to note that McCauley argues persuasively that it was probably in the 1890s. Their emergence therefore coincided not only with the national growth of the Holiness movement but also with the renewed interest in the Appalachian mountains by both missionaries and industrialists. Recall that by the 1890s Appalachia was already a fast-growing mission field, with missionaries of national denominations and parachurch organizations making their presence known throughout the mountains. At the same time, the mountain economy was beginning to shift away from subsistence farming, and with that transformation came associated realignments of the social fabric. In broad terms, eastern Kentucky's religious landscape was at that time becoming polarized between traditional mountain churches and religious culture on one side and "modern" national denominations on the other. Against this background, Holiness churches first emerged in this area as a strategic intervention by native residents into the rapidly transforming religious landscape. Holiness, in other words, appeared as something new-yet-traditional, a distinction that emerged in the space between "railroad religions" and Old Time Baptists, that spoke *to* and *from* new realities as experienced by mountain natives. McCauley has suggested that the earliest independent Holiness churches in central Appalachia were formed when independent mountain Baptist churches, or ex-members of such churches who struck out on their own, attached the appellation "Holiness" to their name in the 1890s in an effort to differentiate themselves, on the one hand, from existing conservative Old Time Baptist churches like the Old Regulars and, on the other hand, from the worship practices and polity of the "modern" so-called "railroad religion" that came into the region with missionaries and industrial development.[16]

"Holiness" as perfection—rebirth—through the experience of the Holy Spirit was not a new concept in the mountains. Nor were the emotional or tactile worship practices that were at the core of the Holiness-Pentecostal movement. The incorporation of this label by independent mountain churches therefore suggested a distinction of something new as well as a recognition that this new distinction shared a continuity with tradition in opposition to the modern trends and foreign styles of "railroad religion."

Whereas the terms *Holiness* and *Pentecostal* designate meaningful denominational, doctrinal, and theological differences to many Americans, in central Appalachia "Holiness" is usually a more generic term that encompasses the entire Holiness-Pentecostal spectrum. This is most evident in the practice of speaking in tongues, which is generally considered to be a marker of Pentecostalism. As Deborah Vansau McCauley explains, "When asked if they are Pentecostal, people who worship in mountain Holiness churches will often say yes, but they refer to themselves almost universally as Holiness."[17] In keeping with the local vernacular, I have chosen to use the term *Holiness* when referring to Holiness-Pentecostal religious beliefs and practices.

The pattern of movement from Baptist to Holiness was exemplified by Josiah Saylor, an early convert to Holiness religion in eastern Kentucky, as related by historian David L. Kimbrough in *Taking Up Serpents*. Saylor's family had belonged to mountain Baptist churches since before Josiah was born in Forrester's Creek in Harlan County in 1830. Josiah experienced conversion, joined the Baptist tradition of his family, and remained a Baptist long after his father died in 1870. Yet in 1900 he left the Baptists, bringing his whole family with him to join a Holiness church in which he remained until his death in 1929. Why did he become a Holiness believer? According to Kimbrough, the impact of "railroad religion" on the mountains threatened to destroy the emotionalism and mountain worship practices that were familiar to Saylor. Saylor watched as churches that called themselves Baptist reduced the role of the Holy Ghost in their worship practices and hired seminary-trained preachers. At the same time, Holiness evangelists traveling through the mountains asserted the importance and centrality of just those aspects of worship that people like Saylor felt the newcomer churches were dismissing. Saylor, in essence, simply followed the Holy Ghost where it led—which was toward Holiness, away from churches that seemed to be abandoning a focus on the experience of conversion and emotional worship of divine presence. In this way, the newly arrived "outsider" ideas and practices of Holiness and Pentecostal missionaries were readily interpreted as variations and continuities of existing mountain traditions. Thus Holiness took new dynamics and ideas into account while maintaining continuity with local tradition. Adding credence to this interpretation, Kimbrough has noted that Holiness "practices and beliefs represented an intensification and elaboration of traditional norms, not a drastic aberration from them."[18] I will return to this point later.

As McCauley suggests, mountain Holiness churches emerged as a form of religious innovation in response—and resistance—to the changes that came over the mountains at the turn of the century. In addition to affirming the experiential centrality of the presence of the Holy Spirit in worship, an important aspect of this resistance was the continued assertion of congregational autonomy as exhibited by the proliferation of independent churches. But Holiness worship also, and more often, took the form of another familiar aspect of Appalachian religious culture by holding meetings and revivals that existed completely apart from organized churches. In fact, it seems that the majority of Holiness meetings tended to be more or less spontaneous and episodic events. They appeared to their participants to be more the eruptions of the Spirit than the productions of human institutions. According to Elizabeth Hooker's 1931 field research, a "typical" Holiness meeting began with the arrival of an uneducated itinerant "Holy Roller" preacher who would announce his intention to hold a service or a revival in any available space, whether it was outdoors in a field or inside a building. If a community church was available, it might be used; schoolhouses were common alternatives. The preacher would hold a series of lively meetings lasting several days or even weeks that would draw increasingly larger crowds. Eventually interest would dwindle and the meetings would draw to a close, usually without developing into any enduring organizational or institutional form because, Hooker said, many Holiness sects did not believe in "man-made" churches. "Holiness meetings are usually not held long at any one point," Hooker wrote. "But when the excitement dies down at one point it flares up in another."[19]

Unfortunately, there are no sources available documenting the numbers of people, let alone coal miners, who participated in Holiness churches, meetings, or revivals. It is evident, however, that Holiness grew dramatically in the eastern Kentucky coal fields during the 1920s. According to Reverend Alfred Carrier, a local Pentecostal historian who visited preachers around the region tracking the history of this form of worship in the area, Holiness activity—which Carrier defined as the physical expressions of baptism by the Holy Spirit, such as divine healing, falling on the floor, and speaking in tongues—increased dramatically in the early to mid-1910s. Carrier's journey through southeastern Kentucky revealed that Holiness began to spread rapidly in the region in the 1910s and grew throughout the 1920s in all of the coal mining areas that he visited. The picture he paints of the origins of the movement is one of sporadic and intensive flare-ups of the Spirit throughout the coal fields. For example, at Jesse's Creek a Baptist preacher held protracted meetings several times a year between 1908 and 1910, in which people were moved by the Spirit to fall on the floor and speak in tongues. According to Carrier's report, these people were not yet familiar with glossolalia as a regular element of worship, and it caused them "confusion" because they did not know how to interpret it. It may not have been until 1910 that two itinerant Holiness preachers, Z. B. and Dan Brock, taught that glossolalia was a necessary sign of sanctification, thus spreading throughout eastern Kentucky the standard Pentecostal interpretation that is said to have originated with Charles Parham in his Kansas Bible school.[20] Carrier found that Holiness believers held series of meetings in schoolhouses in Harlan County between 1910 and 1912, and throughout the 1910s and 1920s Holiness preachers preached on the streets and held meetings in homes. As the word spread about Holiness meetings, the demand—or the curiosity—grew. People traveled from the far side of Pine Mountain to get to a meeting in Wallins Creek in 1912, and the Creech Coal Company let participants ride mining machinery up and down the mountain to make the journey easier. Carrier reported Holiness believers on Straight Creek in 1913 and Holiness meetings in Pineville in Bell County in the mid-1910s. His accounts of Holiness activity in Bell, Harlan, Knox, and other eastern Kentucky counties continued into the 1930s.[21] In other words, the eastern Kentucky coal fields were on fire with Holiness religion throughout the period of industrialization.

Healing

There were probably a number of things that drew people to Holiness meetings and revivals, not the least of which was the spectacle of believers' physical expressiveness and the liveliness of Holiness music and preaching. Chief among the draws, whether considered authentic or fraudulent, were claims of extraordinary healing. Rumors spread throughout the coal fields of inspired preachers who had healed people of disease and, in some cases, even raised individuals from the dead. David L. Kimbrough relates that one of the most renowned incidents of healing in the coal field of Harlan County was attributed to preacher Sherman Lawson. In 1912 he went to the woods to pray when he felt the Spirit come over him. In prayer he felt that God was calling him to go to Wallins Creek in Harlan County, about fourteen miles away. There, God directed him to walk along the railroad tracks, past the coal mines and to a house where a young girl who had recently died was laid out for burial. With the girl's mother's permission, Lawson took the child's hand and prayed over her. She soon came back to life. The story of Lawson's miracle traveled throughout the county. Lawson was not raised in the Holiness tradition but began speaking in tongues in the 1920s when he went to the mountains to pray as he often did. In 1932 Lawson was credited with another case of raising someone from the dead.[22]

The circulation of stories such as these reveals the climate of miraculous expectation accompanying Holiness meetings. Resurrection of the dead was a rare act, but physical healing was a regular element of Holiness religion. Alfred Carrier cited several examples of Holiness preachers healing the sick in eastern Kentucky during this period. Lewis York, for example, one of the first to preach about the biblical basis for the signs of Holiness as found in Mark 16, drew large crowds to his meetings where he performed many acts of healing. He started several churches in eastern Kentucky's coal fields. With Johnny Roberts, another preacher, York was credited with restoring the sight of a blind girl.[23]

Although Holiness-Pentecostal believers strongly promoted a sense that the world was coming to an end and that judgment day was imminent, preachers such as these, Carrier noted, stressed spiritual activity rather than doctrine. "Sanctification came by repentance, confession, and faith in the atoning blood of Jesus," they claimed. "Also, that the healing for the physical body was provided for, in the atonement."[24] The day of judgment was near, according to Holiness preachers and believers, and worldly events were signs that confirmed this prophecy. But the practical effect of millennial urgency was a powerful focus on the event of sanctification (or the "baptism of the Holy Ghost") and its embodied signs. Healing was an especially powerful example, and it served as an immediate illustration of the power of the Holy Ghost over the limitations of the physical world.

Miraculous healing episodes were not unique to eastern Kentucky or to Appalachia. Grant Wacker, a historian of early Pentecostalism, has pointed out that the common focus on tongues-speaking as the primary sign or expression of Pentecostalism "represents a certain loss of historical memory, for an overview of the early literature leaves little doubt that in the beginning divine healing was, if not equally distinctive, at least equally important."[25] His statement is instructive for two reasons. First, the suggestion that healing was as important, if perhaps not as "distinctive," as glossolalia underscores Holiness's continuity with existing mountain religious practices. Focusing on speaking in tongues encourages the idea that Holiness was something new and foreign to mountain traditions. However, most aspects of mountain Holiness worship were familiar to mountain natives, even if they appeared here in intensified form. Noting that healing was just as important as tongues returns Holiness to a connection with the local religious vernacular, in which divine healing was an idiom inherited from the German Pietist and Anabaptist traditions. Indeed, Sherman Lawson's wife was herself a midwife who was known to heal with her hands.[26] Second, by calling attention to the place of healing in the Holiness-Pentecostal tradition, Wacker's statement directs attention to the significance of a religious form that focused so intently on the body and healing in a setting in which broken bodies and heightened nerves were so much a part of everyday life. In the coal fields men, women, and children experienced the fragility of life daily, and they were constantly aware of the effects of the play of power—social, economic, and spiritual—on their bodies. Holiness worship's popularity emerged from and resonated with the life experiences of this place, drawing much of its energy and urgency from the structure of feeling of mining life.

As might be expected, stories circulated throughout the coal fields that told of believers successfully healing bodies that were broken by the work of mining. For example, the *Church of God Evangel* printed the report of a miner who was wounded in a Lynch mine when "a solid piece of rock twelve feet long, eight feet wide, and nine inches thick fell on him." He was able to leave the hospital in five days after believers prayed for him.[27]

But industrial mining's wounds reached beyond the specific dangers of the work of mining itself, impacting the health of women and children who were bound up in its economic and social structures. Elma Davis's story is a good example of the effectiveness of Holiness's ability to address these everyday crises of mining life. Davis was the wife of a coal miner. She was born around the turn of the century and married at age fourteen. She lost one child to hepatitis and carried the burden of keeping her other five children healthy while her husband worked long hours in the mines. Like many wives of miners trying to make ends meet, Davis did what she could to help her family financially. "I took in washing and washed on a rub board for years," she said. "I've washed bankers' clothes on my rub board—because them women was too lazy to do it. Then I've sat up many a night sewing on my treadle sewing machine until midnight—sewing for other people. You have to learn to manage; it's a talent." Indeed, learning "to manage" was an important talent to develop in this setting in which traditional patterns of household management were disrupted and new forms were not yet habitualized in local knowledge. Clearly, mining impacted more than just the men who dug out coal. During the 1920s, before labor unions pressured coal companies to improve the conditions of mine workers, Davis said, "We was slaves, that's all—slaves." It was a sentiment common to many mining families. Davis's use of the plural pronoun says much about the reach of mining's effects into the household and daily life.[28]

Sometime during the 1920s Davis's daughter became very sick with "the pellagra," a disease caused by lack of niacin and tryptophan that is common in places where people consume large quantities of corn as their primary food source and lack milk or other foods that help the body to process corn. Corn, of course, was a staple of the mining family diet, cheap and readily available in the mountains. "It was a kinda a dreadful disease," Davis recalled. "She was just four years old. Her bowels ran all the time; she had a rash around her neck and lower arms and legs. Her skin was cracked. Her bowels never ran natural from February to August." When nothing seemed to be able to heal her—the company doctor said she was too young to take shots—a Holiness sister invited Davis and her daughter to church. "We'll take that baby, believing God'll heal her," Davis remembered the woman saying.

The church was a distance from her home and Davis had to stay overnight at a member's house. At worship, the Holiness believers prayed over her sick daughter. Healing did not come immediately, but they kept at it. "They prayed three times before they got victory," she recalled. "That red rash just left. They were shouting so, I'd put my head to her heart, to hear if she's alive. In three days you couldn't tell she'd ever had it. I knew there had to be something to that." Indeed, her daughter's healing had a profound effect on Davis's own faith: two weeks after witnessing what she understood as the power of the Holy Ghost to heal, she felt that power come over herself and move her body to dance as she was transformed. "I'd seen these holiness people dance, and I couldn't stand it. When I was baptized, I danced the feet out of my cotton stockings in that creek."[29]

Individuals like Davis remembered and recounted such dramatic healing events as elemental aspects of their conversion testimonies. Others told of similar episodes, witnessed or rumored, as evidence of the power, or claims of power, of the Holy Ghost, adding to the climate of expectation in a rapidly changing world where the cultural practice of scanning for signs of supernatural powers and an order beyond the world's order was already commonplace. And such episodes of healing were not restricted to special occasions or extraordinary circumstances. Holiness believers regularly prayed for healing, for themselves and for others, as a feature of worship and revival. In other words, illness, wounds, shattered bones, nerves, and getting "cripped up" could be religiously productive. Holiness believers, their sympathizers, and sometimes even curious onlookers took up the broken body as a medium for encountering and engaging with divine, supernatural power, that is, as a sacrament. In the words of Jonathan R. Baer, a historian of Pentecostalism, "as healing functioned sacramentally, it helped identify the body as a site of divine grace and power. Incipient Pentecostalism was characterized in part by its tangibility and physicality. Various ecstatic behaviors and manifestations located religious assurance in the physical expressions of the body."[30] In the coal fields of eastern Kentucky the natural resources for this particular sacrament were readily available. In Holiness religion, as Davis's case illustrates, the power of the Holy Ghost interacted directly with the power of industrial capitalism, mediated through the bodies of miners and their family members.

To suggest that material conditions influenced the development of religious practice and belief is not to reduce religion to a "superstructural" reflection of a material "base," as some formulations might have it, nor to explain it away as a secondary effect of a more "real" cause. Rather, it is to take seriously the dynamic interaction between people and the changing worlds they live in. Religion does not exist in a static, ahistorical vacuum. It is a constantly emerging practice. *Homo religiosus,* as historian of religion Jonathan Z. Smith has pointed out, is "preeminently *homo faber*"—human beings engaged in religious work as they orient and reorient themselves in the world.[31] In this case, Holiness religion in eastern Kentucky appears not simply as a local expression of a national trend, but more concretely and specifically as an example of an ongoing process of religious work in a place. It was a process that drew from existing religious cultural practices and newer arrivals in the particular context of a world shaped by rapidly changing forces and structures of sociality and exchange that had deep material, social, and existential impacts. These forces, as already noted, settled most concretely on individual bodies in tactile ways; Holiness offered an embodied mode of engagement that met these forces tangibly where they were most solidly experienced. It took up the nervous structure of feeling of the coal fields and read it through the lens of familiar religious idioms, "making something of things," as they say in the mountains, by scanning for signs of an other, supernatural, order.[32]

In transforming the pains and tactile impacts of everyday life into a source of sacramental rite, Holiness engaged in a profoundly creative act of religious work. "Meaning is always *produced*," Raymond Williams reminds us. "It is never simply expressed."[33] The work of producing meaning takes place in a specific cultural and material context, bringing together particular individual and social circumstances with available idioms, languages, structures, and gestures. It reproduces cultural forms at the same time that it "makes something of things," taking up and working with existing cultural forms in a context-specific manner that is informed by a place's and time's structure of feeling. In eastern Kentucky's coal fields, the broken body—and the power of the Holy Ghost to heal it—was an especially potent image and reality, filled with interpretive potential that was vividly played out in performances of Holiness healing events. The event of healing, first of all, made the power of the Holy Ghost concrete and present to witnesses and the person healed. Along with speaking in tongues and other physical manifestations of the Spirit, at the center of Holiness religion was a somatic form of knowledge of the material reality of divine power and its ability to transform the world physically. Not invisible or abstracted in symbols or words, the Holy Ghost instead made a material appearance. "When I can feel him coming into my body," one believer said, "I know God is real."[34] Second, healing mimetically represented Jesus's death and resurrection, a dramatic performance that literally reembodied the central episode of the Christian story and personalized it by placing the healed individual in a relation of identity with Jesus himself. Third, the manifest healing event served as an allegory of the eternal life that all human beings were said to be able to achieve through God's grace and the power of the Holy Ghost. As the Holy Ghost had the power to overcome the limitations of illness or injury, it said, so Christian salvation had the power to overcome death itself.

Heightening the raw sense of the presence of the Holy Spirit and its corporal impact, and underlining the transvaluation of pain and ruin into hope and salvation, was the centrality of blood as sign and symbol in Holiness worship. "There is power, power, wonder-working power in the blood, in the blood of the lamb," a popular Holiness-Pentecostal hymn declared, referring to the blood sacrifice of Jesus on the cross as the originating source of salvation, redemption, and healing. It was a visceral image, one that did not shy away from a focus on pain and suffering as productive forces of transformation and one that promoted an internalization of the reality of supernatural power.

The use of the physical body's finitude and limitations for sacramental purposes was presented in perhaps its most dramatic form in the practice of serpent handling. The handling of poisonous snakes during worship was, and remains, the most controversial of Holiness practices, adopted by a very small minority of Holiness people. Despite its relative rarity, for many nonbelievers, the Holy Rollers and the practice of snake handling were synonymous. Indeed, serpent handling has captured a disproportionate amount of the attention paid to religion in southern Appalachia, reproducing stereotypes of mountain culture as radically and irrationally "other" than mainstream America. However, although the handling of serpents was a limited and contested practice, it shared an underlying understanding of power and presence with more popular forms of Holiness worship that, in turn, shared a similar understanding with the wider Appalachian religious culture. In many respects the differences were primarily in degree of intensity.[35] Rather than an anomaly, therefore, serpent handling existed on a continuum with more common—and more widely accepted—forms of worship and with wider cultural conceptions of signs and powers. Seen in this context the practice provides a valuable window into the religious world of coal miners. Although serpent handling was certainly a marginal practice, in its marginality it displayed in bold terms the underlying dramatic structure that was present in only slightly less sensational form in other Holiness churches.[36] In its intensification of elements common to regional religious life, serpent handling again highlighted the centrality of the body as a potent sign and vehicle for knowing, feeling, imagining, and working with power in the coal fields.

It is hard to say when snakes were first handled in worship in eastern Kentucky. David L. Kimbrough, whose study of the practice in Harlan County is the most thorough history of serpent handling to date, claims that it was 1932. It is certain that in 1932 there were a number of occasions when snakes were brought out during worship at Holiness meetings and revivals in the coal fields of Harlan and Bell counties. As the next chapter will explore in more detail, this was an especially difficult time in eastern Kentucky, particularly for coal mining families. If miners described the 1920s as nerve-racking, the Depression years were still worse. Not only did mines shut down and miners lose both their pay and their jobs, but violent clashes between miners and armed company guards brought an atmosphere already charged with danger to another level. During this time George Hensley, the apparent originator of the practice of serpent handling, moved to Bell County. He worked mining coal for a while and preached at Holiness churches and meetings.[37] On these occasions he often brought the sacramental drama to new levels by playing literally with the boundary between life and death, introducing venomous snakes, poison, and fire into the worship service.

Hensley was illiterate, his knowledge of the Bible coming primarily from his wife, Amanda, who read it to the family each night and, most likely, from the oral tradition through which many an illiterate Appalachian came to know the Bible. As the story goes, in 1910 Hensley walked up White Oak Mountain in Grasshopper Valley, Tennessee, thinking about the instructions of Mark 16:17–18: "And these signs shall follow them that believe; in my name shall they cast out devils; they shall speak with new tongues; they shall take up serpents; and if they drink any deadly thing, it shall not hurt them; they shall lay hands on the sick and they shall recover." Hensley prayed for a sign, then soon spotted a rattlesnake which he put in a sack and brought home. A few days later he took the snake out at a revival meeting and, citing the biblical text, preached that the ability to handle it without injury was a sign of salvation.[38]

In 1912 Hensley became a minister in the young Cleveland, Tennessee-based Church of God. During the previous two years he had acted as an independent Holiness preacher, developing a following of people who came to his meetings to see him pick up snakes and drink poison as signs that he was saved by the Holy Spirit. Hensley traveled widely in the area, and his practices spread quickly. The Church of God embraced serpent-handling and defended the practice against charges that it was excessive, fanatical, and a misreading of scripture. The church's leaders argued that taking up serpents was a sign of Christian perfection, proof that the Bible was God's infallible word, and a sign that the salvation preached by other churches was inauthentic.[39] Hensley remained in the church for two years, citing "trouble at home" as his reason for leaving it in 1914. By 1923 he had "returned to his sinful ways," making and selling moonshine whiskey.[40] He was soon arrested and indicted on charges of selling liquor, and between 1923 and 1932 he lived in Cleveland, Ohio, where he had gone after escaping from a chain gang. In Ohio he started preaching again in tent meetings and revivals. By this time he was an independent preacher, no longer with the Church of God, which meanwhile had shifted its position on serpent handling.[41] Hensley moved to Pineville, Kentucky, in 1932, where he briefly worked in a coal mine and apparently introduced serpent handling to eastern Kentucky's coal fields.[42] Independent Holiness churches and preachers, many of whom could trace their introduction to the practice back to Hensley himself or those inspired by him, carried serpent handling throughout the mountains, but it primarily settled in coal mining areas in central Appalachia.

Mary Lee Daugherty, a scholar of Appalachian religion, has persuasively argued that serpent handling should be seen as an authentic sacramental practice, rather than being written off as the misguided following of instructions by biblical literalists. "It is my observation and hypothesis that the ritual of serpent-handling is their way of celebrating life, death, and resurrection," Daugherty writes. "Time and again they prove to themselves that Jesus has the power to deliver them from death here and now."[43] Understood in this light, the serpents appear as vehicles, taken up from the natural surroundings of the mountains, through which the dangers of life were given concrete form in a ritual setting. Playing with the boundaries between life and death, taking up danger as a productive source of religious experience, practitioners harnessed the power of blood and suffering to gain, if not control over their environment, at least a meaningful relationship with it on their own terms. And this is a vital aspect of the work of Holiness-Pentecostal religion. In submitting to the power of the Holy Ghost, practitioners not only aligned themselves with a power that they understood as greater than those of the world; they also produced the terms in and through which they would engage the forces that impacted their bodies and lives.

Holiness revivals can be understood, at least in part, as a form of ritual theater, making concrete and present the reality of the Holy Spirit and the potential for both physical and spiritual transformation. Built around the dramatic structure of crisis and release that was common to the wider religious culture of the mountains, it was a performance that many native miners could understand and empathize with, even if they did not become converts or church members. In difficult circumstances, especially, in which life was shaped and influenced by unseen but sharply felt forces, it may have offered a particularly commanding sense of rootedness, connecting people to a familiar conception and discourse of power that subordinated the troubles of the world to the superior and eternal promise of Christian salvation. As a public performance it afforded participants and witnesses a possible model for cultivating and sustaining, through innovation and adaptation, the sensory conditions of traditional religious practices in a new, industrial context. For converts, however, the power of Holiness went well beyond the drama and experiences of the worship service. As it transformed believers, making of them new, "reborn" selves who oriented themselves in relation to the presence of the Holy Ghost, Holiness remapped their world according to the powers of sin and salvation. Again taking up and "making something" of the given situation at hand, believers produced a sense of order from the complexities of diversity and desire wrought by industrial and commercial forces.

In theory, if not always in practice, believers inhabited this new order by transforming their everyday behaviors. On the one hand, there was a sense that a sanctified person would naturally turn away from any sinful activity. But on the other hand, and more pragmatically, Holiness believers in eastern Kentucky were aware of the constant threat of "backsliding," or falling back into a sinful life. The episodic movement from saved to sinner and back again, as illustrated by George Hensley's life, was a common biographical storyline in the mountains, regardless of denominational affiliation or theological orientation. Believers therefore often said that sinlessness and salvation required hard work, lest one give in to the ever-present forces of evil and worldliness. As one believer put it, "In the Holiness-Pentecostal Church, you're working your way into heaven."[44]

In the coal fields the threat of falling into sin was greater than ever before because the promotion of desire, rewritten as temptation, was everywhere a part
of the industrial and commercial landscape. So as both a sign of salvation *and*
a protective stance against backsliding, Holiness believers observed a series of
taboos that Grant Wacker has categorized as "pertaining to the mouth, eyes,
ears, body, and genitals."[45] Nationally, denominations differed in specifics, and
the particular behavioral proscriptions practiced by various eastern Kentucky
Holiness believers varied. But examples of mouth taboos, which included both
what went into the mouth and what came out of it, likely included abstinence
from alcohol or tobacco and prohibitions on swearing, lying, or gossip. Likewise with the eyes and ears: particular types of music, especially secular commercial music, were often forbidden, as were movies. Clothing was typically
modest, with restrictions on ornamentation, cosmetics, and clothes that would
arouse desire or express pride. In many cases these practices maintained strict
"traditional" gender boundaries: women were not to cut their hair, while men
were to keep their hair short.[46] Women were not to wear pants. Finally, sex was
an especially charged subject, forbidden outside of marriage and often restricted within it.

In a practical sense, then, Holiness religion met real social and personal
disruptions with pragmatic, if conservative, solutions.[47] Gambling and drinking were prevalent dangers, both physical and economic, in coal towns. Conversion meant giving these up. Commercially constructed desires for new fashions
and commodities, which led to a sense of constant material need and ate into
money that would otherwise be used for food, were proscribed. Movies, vehicles
of desire, fantasy, and temptation, were also prohibited. Finally, Holiness religion taught that true value ultimately lay in salvation, not in worldly goods. As
Elma Davis put it, "I believe we'd fare better if we just put God first. I mean me.
I've got plenty of room to get closer and move up. 'Seek ye first the kingdom of
God.' He didn't tell us to seek: new furniture, a better home, look better."[48] So
Holiness met many aspects of industrial, commercial culture directly with an
alternative and oppositional sense of value and purpose. Even the location of
their meetings illustrated this theme. Grant Wacker noted that Pentecostals
"particularly liked to take over the devil's warehouses—vacant saloons and
dance halls ranked high on the list—and turn them into houses of worship. Few
of these were accidental. Converts were affirming their ability to transform dis-
ordered zones into ordered zones."[49] In eastern Kentucky, meetings took place

in storefronts and school buildings in addition to homes, fields, and churches. In a poetic labor that highlighted the point that the Spirit could emerge from the ruins of what the world claimed as progress, Holiness believers in East Pineville built a church out of materials from an old mine camp that was being torn down.[50]

Yet, pragmatically, Holiness believers also incorporated and internalized some of the elements of the commercial world that they seemingly disdained, transforming those elements into vehicles for their own messages and practices. Holiness music, in particular, absorbed the emerging rhythms and styles of commercial music. The Victor Talking Machine Company's recording sessions in Bristol, Tennessee, in 1927 and 1928, which were among the earliest commercial recordings made in the Appalachian mountains and included Jimmie Rodgers and the Carter Family, captured the sounds of Ernest Phipps and his Holiness congregation from Corbin Kentucky. Phipps was a coal miner, a coal truck driver, and a Holiness preacher whose music illustrates further the engagement of Holiness with commercial forms introduced to the mountains with the coming of the coal industry. Recordings of Phipps's songs such as "If the Light Has Gone Out of Your Soul," "Shine on Me," or "A Little Talk with Jesus" reveal the use of fiddle, guitar, banjo, and syncopated clapping. Compare this to Old Regular Baptist worship that did not allow any instrumentation. Holiness music from this era had more in common stylistically with the early gospel and country music that was also recorded at the Bristol sessions, while still displaying the congregational participation, through singing and clapping, that was so evident in Holiness revivals and worship.[51]

Holiness, emerging at the intersection of tradition and change, produced powerful affective models for inhabiting the industrial world with familiar, if transformed, sensibilities and religious idioms. For believers, it took up a rapidly changing world and "made something of it" by transforming individuals and their relationship to their surroundings, confronting industrial capitalism's power with "Holy Ghost power." It was especially suited to the coal towns' structures of feeling with its emphasis on healing, in particular, and its general focus on the affective body. And sources suggest that many more who did not convert or join Holiness churches nevertheless participated in or witnessed revivals and meetings, perhaps seeing in them a continuation of the revival tradition with an intensification of both message and behavior appropriate to the rhythms and conditions of industrial coal mining.

Conflict and Resistance

Despite the innovative ways that they engaged the experiences and contradictions of mining life, Holiness believers in the coal fields were not free from conflict. Indeed, Holiness itself was a highly contentious form of religion, premised on an oppositional stance toward the world and its authorities in favor of what believers considered to be greater powers. Holiness practitioners themselves regularly faced harassment that sometimes became violent, including anything from aggressive speech or vocal challenges, to theological denunciations, to rock-throwing and gunfire.[52] Some of this came from fellow believers, with rivalries between Holiness preachers sometimes rising to the level of intimidation, according to Elizabeth Hooker.[53] But nonbelievers also mocked preachers and sometimes tried to interrupt meetings. In part, some of the discord over Holiness had to do with the threat that this new popular religious form posed to the long-standing Baptist hegemony in eastern Kentucky.[54] Old Regular Baptists had been the primary church of mountain residents, and it was from those old Baptist churches that Holiness preachers were drawing worshipers. But Holiness claims about the ability to harness supernatural power also aroused suspicion and ire among disbelievers. This was especially evident once serpent handling entered the picture and highlighted such claims in concrete spectacles. Onlookers often accused preachers who took up snakes of being frauds and charlatans. David L. Kimbrough reports that when George Hensley moved to Kentucky he preached and handled snakes in the yard of the Pineville courthouse, a common place for preachers of all backgrounds to preach in public on Saturday mornings. There Hensley saw other men handling snakes, but they "had ran yellow copper wire through the snakes' mouths so they could only stuck their tongues out, but not bite. They made a mockery of God."[55] Such instances suggest that questions of authenticity and legitimacy were significant factors shaping the religious landscape at the time. Knowing this provides a key to thinking further about structures of feeling and the relationship of religion to the coal town setting, for it indicates that there were competing models emerging for engaging the rapidly changing material, social, and religious environment of industrialization.

A glimpse at some of the conflicts involving Holiness people in eastern Kentucky reveals a gap between two contrasting orientations to history and human agency, one held by Holiness believers and the other linked to the forces of social and economic change. For instance, in 1927 a miner's wife complained in the *Church of God Evangel* that she and her husband were forced to leave the Blue

Diamond coal camp when he refused a diphtheria medication that the company required all of its workers to take.[56] The miner and his wife instead wanted "the saints to come pray for us," but the company did not recognize this form of health care as a legitimate one for its employees and laid off those who would not accept modern medical authority. Indeed, modern medicine accompanied industrialization—and missionaries—into the mountains, and the nicer coal towns included excellent hospitals. Professional academic medicine vastly improved the health of many mountain families during this period, but it is important to note that it also displaced and disparaged traditional healing practices that, as earlier noted, were intimately tied to ideas about God, nature, and the order of the world.[57] Social workers and missionaries representing national denominations were instrumental in promoting modern medicine in place of faith healing and folk remedies. One might imagine, then, that from a Holiness perspective both missionaries and industrial forces aligned with forms of healing that displaced the power of the Holy Ghost with human knowledge and authority. Indeed, Holiness practitioner Elma Davis recalled that "when I first got saved" in the 1920s, "we never thought of going to doctors. I ain't got much faith in them." Forty years later, at the time of her interview, she noted that she had since used doctors, "but I want to get out of that. Back then, nearly everyone got healed."[58]

In another illuminating case, Elizabeth Hooker recorded a school superintendent's comments on the use of schoolhouses for Holiness worship. "'The Holy Rollers are harder on school property than all the drunks in the county. They break the desks, tear up the seats and rock the windows. One building was so badly treated again and again that the school was consolidated with the one nearest it.'"[59] He went on to explain that Holiness people were opposed to schools, associating them with worldly knowledge and intrusive cultural change. We need to read these comments with a critical eye. The school official might well have held negative views of Holiness religion, and he likely exaggerated the damage in keeping with stereotypes of overactive and out-of-control Holy Roller worship. However, if schools were linked in Holiness perception with worldliness and, at the same time, with the changes that the region was going through, then the transformation of their utilitarian function by using them as places of worship might fairly be interpreted, following Wacker, as signifying the assertion of divine power over worldly value and historical change.[60] If the buildings were damaged in the process, it only served to underscore the point. Complicating matters, education in the region, like medicine, was also closely linked to missionary and social workers who helped to set up schools. Places like the Pine Mountain Settlement

School were designed to train mountain children in skills and behaviors that would help them to improve their opportunities in the modern world. However, the general attitude of missionaries and settlement workers toward mountain religious ideas and practices, including both Holiness and Baptist forms, was negative. Missionaries regularly represented mountain religion and culture as fatalistic, ignorant, and standing in the way of real progress.[61]

Missionaries and settlement schools were not always on friendly terms with industrial interests, and they were often critical of the excesses of capitalism, yet their sympathy for mountain residents was shaped by progressive ideals that often ran counter to mountain religious and cultural traditions.[62] Even as they condemned industry for its greed or its disregard for the plight of mountain communities and workers, progressives shared with industrialists a conception of value and improvement that was measured in the "worldly" terms of social, material, and educational progress.[63] One response, a conservative one embodied by Holiness preachers among others, was to reject education, medicine, and the religious authority of missionaries and national denominations because they displaced the power of the Holy Spirit with more worldly conceptions of progress and value. The problem of the industrialization of the eastern Kentucky coal fields, in this framework, was not simply one of economic or social disempowerment, marginalization, or exploitation; it was also a religious crisis concerning the subordination of extraordinary or supernatural powers to worldly ones. It was potentially also a sign of the fulfillment of premillennialist historical expectations that predicted increased worldliness as the end-times approached. But the religious crisis and the social crisis were intimately bound together, such that religious protest was itself a socially engaged form of resistance. Refusals of medicine, destruction of school property, and preaching against consumer temptations were all simultaneously acts of religious work and acts of resistance to the worldly authority represented by agents of social and economic change.[64]

Recall the murals in John C. C. Mayo's Pineville home on the eve of industrialization: they depicted the march of civilization as the extraction of coal brought with it the growth of cities, schools, and churches. This was clearly a vision of progress unleashed by human ingenuity and labor, and it was depicted as beneficial. In contrast, the premillennial perspective of Holiness believers saw a world running down, growing more and more sinful, as society moved away from a God-centered orientation toward a secular, or even materialist, view of things. The examples cited above illustrate cases in which these orientations came into conflict and clashed. But between these two defining poles lay a continuum of possibility for conceiving and engaging the industrial world. If religions are, to use David Chidester's definition, experiments in being human, then the coal fields of eastern Kentucky during the early twentieth century were creative laboratories where people were able to draw on and embody a variety of possible models of humanity.[65] For some, the Holiness proposition went too far in the direction of privileging supernatural power over human agency. For others, industrial capitalism's impact on every aspect of life signaled a world where market value had overrun human value, a world that rejected the reality of supernatural power outright.[66] Many miners and their families likely fell somewhere in between, as suggested by both their curiosity and interest in Holiness revivals, on the one hand, and their concerns about the authenticity of such practices as divine healing and serpent handling, on the other hand. Indeed, the ambivalence and, in some cases, open hostility that Holiness religion provoked points to the emergent nature of conceptions and articulations of the industrial environment as miners drew from their religious and cultural inheritance, innovating with available idioms, to forge new and appropriate ways of being in the world. These were not just abstract theological problems but related directly to everyday life as mining families navigated forces that impacted their health, well-being, and ability to care for their communities.

The conflict that played out in the religious activities of the coal fields was bigger than Appalachia; it was part of a larger struggle for understanding the nature of power and value in modern America and in modernity itself.[67] It underlay what has been called the "modernist/fundamentalist" debate of the early twentieth century, although that conceptualization of the issue abstracts from the particular stakes of the problem in specific settings of everyday life, glossing over the contextualized relations of power that shaped conceptions of difference. But this larger framework, as we have noted, informed the perceptions of missionaries and settlement workers who sought to understand mountain culture. It also informed the scholarship of historians and sociologists of religion. Indeed, it was this very conflict that led Robert Mapes Anderson, in his consideration of Pentecostalism in general, to assert that the movement was an inconsequential protest against the forces of capitalism and modernization. Anderson argued that Pentecostalism's form of resistance ultimately transformed social discontent into "social passivity, ecstatic escape, and, finally, a most conservative conformity." Believers, he wrote, "found in Pentecostalism a religious resolution that was almost wholly other-worldly, symbolic, and psychotherapeutic," that acted as a catharsis for their grievances. [68]

However, the voices of miners and their families suggest that the hardness of everyday life could not be escaped so easily into an "otherworldly" fantasy. Concrete reality kept asserting itself in daily experience. The dust kept falling. Indeed, as already noted, Holiness believers worked hard to counter the threat of backsliding and constantly navigated the temptations and dangers of the industrial setting. What is remarkable is not the "escapism" of Holiness believers, but rather their engagement with material and social conditions—giving religious significance to their everyday challenges, creating a map and orientation to the moral complexities of their surroundings, and producing bodily technologies and habits for navigating them. Rather than an escape, religion, for Holiness believers, was a form of *work*—work necessary to gain and keep their salvation in the midst of the world into which "public" work brought them, where the labor required for economic survival was at the same time destructive of life and community.

In this regard, it is instructive to consider the case of the Church of God (Cleveland, Tennessee)'s changing policies toward organized labor in the first decades of the twentieth century. Anderson noted that in 1912 the denomination forbade members from joining labor unions and barred union members from joining the church.[69] The church soon softened its position to accept those whose jobs required them to pay union dues but who did not otherwise take part in union meetings or activities. Anderson did not report, however, that the church ceased enforcing this resolution in 1928 and remained ambivalent on the subject into the 1930s—because church members continued to join unions despite official church policy.

The Church of God's opposition to organized labor grew out of a policy barring members from belonging to lodges, based upon a variety of biblical injunctions forbidding the swearing of oaths (Matthew 5:34–37 and James 5:12) and prohibiting Christians from consorting with unbelievers and those who deny God's power (2 Corinthians 6:14–17; Ephesians 5:4–7, 11, 12; 2 Timothy 3:4, 5). A. J. Tomlinson, the General Overseer of the church from 1909 to 1923, considered labor unions to be "too much like the mark of the beast for Church members to become entangled with them."[70] As the day of judgment drew nearer, in accordance with the premillennial beliefs of the church, it was important to draw church members together, not separate them. According to Tomlinson, labor unions promoted division within communities, sometimes between church members.[71] So what led the church to alter its stance? By 1926, when the church began changing its position on unions, not only had Tomlinson left the leadership of the church, but the church's membership had grown tremendously in the central

Appalachian coal fields. In 1926, 78 percent of the denomination's churches in Kentucky were in coal mining areas, as were 80 percent of their West Virginia churches. On the ground, in the coal fields, church members were acting in ways that contradicted the "official" teaching of their church, to the point that the church eventually reconsidered its policy. Holiness-Pentecostal believers thus appear to have been more engaged with the world than one might assume, suggesting that on the local level the experiences and actions of miners were dynamically shaping religious attitudes toward the relationship between industrial power and workers.[72] If Church of God members were actively confronting their material contexts in ways that included organized protest, despite the church's stance on such activity, we might surmise that members of local independent Holiness churches, wholly embedded in the industrial mining landscape, were similarly engaged, as likely were more transient participants in Holiness activities.[73]

In fact, as the 1920s drew to a close, miners who were made aware daily that they were "subject to dust" displayed a complex and at times ambivalent attitude toward the relationship between their spiritual striving and their material setting. The Depression would bring these issues to a head, and many coal miners, even Holiness believers, would come to find a religious significance in organized labor.

SIX

SUFFERING AND
REDEMPTION

*And so there was this Harlan, Kentucky, situation. The
eyes of the whole country had become focused on that
little spot. It had become a little ugly running sore,
workers being beaten, women thrown in jail, American
citizens being terrorized, newspaper men trying to investigate, being shot and terrorized. When you have got
a disease inside the body it has a nasty little trick of
breaking out in little sores of that sort.*

—SHERWOOD ANDERSON,
"I Want to Be Counted," 1932

THE EMERGENT EXPRESSIONS OF COAL miners' experiences discussed in the
last two chapters can be considered as examples of what political scientist James C.
Scott has called "hidden transcripts."[1] Without taking the form of organized protest
in the political or economic arena, they nevertheless enacted (sometimes subtle)
forms of resistance to industrial domination. At times, that resistance was discursive: stories that circulated about coal companies treating mules better than men, for
instance, expressed criticism of power relations in nonconfrontational form that allowed miners to voice their dissatisfaction without incurring direct material repercussions from their employers. Narratives about unequal exchanges and their tactile
effects on the bodies of both participants and witnesses were moral tales that

concretely illustrated how power differentials had real physical effects. And when miners, confronted with danger and death, placed themselves in the position of the injured or deceased, they felt and expressed the shared experiences that potentially linked all miners in a common bond. At those times they also gave significance to their suffering and mortality by placing both in a wider framework that pushed beyond the particular circumstances to probe the very nature of human value itself.

In more active, albeit still "hidden," forms, miners asserted their agency through initiation rituals and bravado. Here they created an identity and a culture that made the mine and the work of mining their own. They owned their work, in other words, in a way that coal companies never could. Whether employed or laid off, they were still miners, and mining became an essential part of their identity. Thus they humanized their world of work in a setting that was otherwise premised solely on making profits. This was important. The work of mining structured every aspect of miners' lives, so that they could not think that mining was merely a "job." Nevertheless, in the eyes of their employers it was just that, and miners were simply employees, laborers in a larger industry. "The Appalachians always had a surplus of labor," one miner said. "No matter how many got killed they could always replace them."[2] Rather than allowing their very humanity to be defined by their relationship to their employers—a very real and present danger in a world literally structured by the coal industry—miners made something else of the relationship between their work and their lives.

Resistance also took explicitly religious forms in a refusal to measure self or human value in the way that the industrial workplace insisted. Holiness religion, for instance, radically resisted the ideology of industrial progress by rejecting worldly value outright. In fact, it went further and reversed progressive ideology, interpreting the growing materialism of industry and the theologies and practices of America's dominant denominations as signs of the world's decline and the imminence of the day of judgment. Holiness was an intensified form of a more widely existing religious orientation that understood the world as a limited and transitory element of a much larger order in which material possessions and worldly power had little bearing. And Holiness transformed the pains and suffering of the work of mining into sacramental performance. In an ironic and subversive twist, Holiness was born largely from the roots of Methodism, the very form of Protestantism associated, in the eastern Kentucky mountains, with the commercial class and with ideologies of worldly progress.

All of these examples played important roles in resisting the spiritual and existential domination that was part of the world of industrial coal mining. They provided a basis for courage and human significance in the face of tremendous difficulties, and they presented a vision of a different structure of power, beyond the limits of the material world, that did not take the economic order of authority for granted. Furthermore, they provided structures of thinking and acting that lay outside of the purview of industrial control. By means of these "hidden transcripts," miners maintained cultural continuities with longer mountain traditions. As authentic religious expressions, then, they asserted a sense of humanity seen beyond the limited scope of the industrial economy that for all practical purposes measured value in terms of profits and productivity.

In 1931 these hidden transcripts began to appear in a highly public and politicized form. During that year a flurry of violent protest erupted in Harlan and Bell counties that pitted miners against the economic forces that weighed heavily on their lives, beginning a decadelong struggle for unionization and miners' rights. The events of the 1930s gave Harlan County the moniker "Bloody Harlan," and the eastern Kentucky coal fields in general developed a reputation for violent resistance. This chapter examines the first sustained period of protest, paying particular attention to the significance that miners gave to the National Miners' Union (NMU), a Communist-backed organization that was active in the area only from the summer of 1931 until January 1932. The NMU had a very short life in Harlan and Bell counties, and its membership numbers were never strong. Nevertheless, there are important reasons for examining the union's place in the history of religion in the coal fields. First, the events surrounding the NMU crystallized many of the concerns, both material and spiritual, that lay behind issues of power in the coal fields. Second, the violence that erupted in the context of this early manifestation of labor unrest caught the attention of the nation, resulting in a much-publicized "investigation" of conditions in the eastern Kentucky coal industry by liberal writers from New York. The investigative committee, led by Theodore Dreiser, interviewed a number of NMU members and transcribed the speeches that they gave at union meetings. Therefore, the records of the investigation are one of the few sources available for recovering the views of miners themselves during this period. Finally, although miners ultimately rejected the NMU, there is clear indication from the few existing records that they saw in the union the potential for redemption—with both material and spiritual resonance. This chapter first reviews the events leading up to the entrance of the NMU. Next it turns to the activities of the union before examining more closely some of the rhetorical and symbolic strategies that connected work and religion. This discussion continues with a look at the testimonies of union members recorded by Dreiser's committee, testimonies that articulate overtly the union's religious significance. Last, the chapter reviews the causes of the union's demise in eastern Kentucky. It concludes with a brief discussion about the ways in which miners used the National Miners' Union to negotiate religious and economic power, forging new ties between issues of religion and work in the industrial coal mining setting.

Organized Labor in the Coal Fields

Organized labor was never very successful in the eastern Kentucky coal fields before the 1930s. Despite attempts by the United Mine Workers of America (UMWA) to organize eastern Kentucky in 1919, 1923, 1926, and 1927, each of their efforts ultimately failed because, according to one study, union leaders "were quickly expelled from the area by operator-controlled county officials."[3] Detailed analysis of the reasons that union organization failed during the 1920s is beyond the scope of this study, as are the more widely political reasons that motivated nationally organized labor unions to increase their activities throughout the United States, including eastern Kentucky, in the 1930s. However, a few factors deserve mention. The extent to which industrialization had interrupted the traditional subsistence farming economy in eastern Kentucky, introducing the need for mountain residents to make money in order to make ends meet, surely played a role in defining the options available to miners. There were very few opportunities for "public work" other than working for coal companies by the 1920s, even as cash money became increasingly vital to daily life. Moreover, despite the dangers inherent in mining and the individual and social anxieties that came with life in coal towns, the relative stability of the coal market during that period of time ensured that miners would be able to find work with one company or another. But coal company ownership of towns, including miners' houses, and the widespread use of scrip as an official form of exchange, gave companies a high degree of control over their employees. Indeed, none other than Reinhold Niebuhr testified before the United States Senate in 1932 that these practices amounted to "essential peonage" that left miners powerless to act against the wishes of their employers.[4]

But the episodic pattern of interest that miners showed toward organized labor throughout the 1920s also suggests the need to think differently about the way that miners regarded unions. Scholars should consider the impact of a cultural style, one deeply rooted in the religious traditions of the mountains, on miners' patterns of participation. In this light, the organizational efforts of the United Mine Workers of America can be compared to revival meetings and the union itself to an organized church. Just as revival meetings gathered both sinners and saved—that is, those who had undergone the experience of conversion and those who had not—in periodic communal expressions of extraordinary worship, the organizational meetings of the UMWA took the form of revivals that attracted large numbers of miners to express their shared work experiences. In strictly religious form, it should be noted, periodic revivals alone were sufficient for most people. They did not join a church. They returned to their daily lives not without religion but without feeling the need for sustained organizational worship. When another revival took place, they likely took part. Similarly, the UMWA attracted miners during each organizational effort, but the union was unable to sustain an organizational presence over time. Studies that point to "apathy among miners" are guilty of the same methodological bias that led observers of mountain religion to conclude that low rates of church membership indicated a lack of religious interest.[5] Union participation followed the pattern of revivals, as hundreds if not thousands of miners enthusiastically took part in initial meetings, but eventually drifted away from participating in the slow building process and gradual work toward change. And this was another indication of a similarity with religious cultural style. In the episodic model of conversion held by mountain traditions, change—salvation—came all at once, rather than as a gradual process of growth and cultivation of salvation through education or maturation. Against this background, and in the context of a cultural style familiar to native miners, the "failed" attempts by unions to organize can be interpreted quite differently. It is not reaching too far to suggest that miners related to the union in much the same way that they related to revival meetings.

Continuing in this interpretive direction, it is important to notice the way that miner and Old Regular Baptist preacher Talmadge Allen described the eventual success of labor organization in 1930s. Allen said that the environment in coal camps was "completely degraded and getting worser and worser conditions till it got down to where it [was] nearly unbearable."

> There *had* to be a change, there *had* to come a change. And when this change begin to take place, the moral and determined side of life, and the determination to have a better life. . . . We don't have to live in no such conditions as this. Let's make our community, let's make our camp, let's make it a better place to live. You began to see churches begin to spring up in the coal camps, and people began a-goin' out to church. They began to see the need of a better side of life, a better way of living. Because if they had hard times, or if their families was starving, they were determined to help one another. It give them the determination, "we're gonna stick

together, we're gonna overcome this kind of life." And they did. They did. I've seen it. I've seen it happen in my lifetime. I can clearly see the upgrading and a spark begin to flare up among people.[6]

Forty years later, Allen constructed a narrative of history that had its poetic roots in the conversion style of mountain religious traditions. It spoke of an increasing intensification of troubles until they became unbearable, compelling a change—just as the moment of conversion was experienced as the increasing weight of sinfulness to the point where a sudden reversal, in the form of the grace of the Holy Spirit, lifted that burden away. Just as in the revival style, central Appalachian preaching in the Holiness and Old Regular Baptist traditions followed this format as well, compelling emotional response through the repetition and intensification of images of sin and trouble and their implications. As the images piled higher and higher and the preacher's vocal delivery grew more and more passionate, congregants felt their force in a tactile and emotional way and responded with a change of heart. *Crisis* lay at the bottom of change, whether it was a physical or emotional crisis that compelled an individual to experience the Spirit suddenly and turn to God, or a crisis poetically created by a preacher through the intensification and repetition of images of sin and trouble. Allen's narrative transcribed that structure onto history itself, giving historical events a religious significance that would be recognizable to those familiar with local cultural poetics but that might be missed by those who looked for religion in other forms.

Allen constructed his narrative with the benefit of hindsight. However, at least some miners interpreted the labor movement in a similar idiom at the time of the events themselves. Organized labor did not make sustainable inroads during the 1920s as long as miners were caught up in the everyday struggles of working and living that were difficult, but not impossible. Life, after all, was a struggle, and suffering could be articulated as a positive and necessary aspect of being human. However, in 1931 the constant background of hardship intensified into a sustained period of crisis, and the difficulties of life were no longer bearable. There had to come a change.

When the national demand for coal declined in the late 1920s, followed shortly thereafter by the Great Depression, any semblance of stability within the eastern Kentucky coal fields disappeared. By 1931 many local mines had gone bankrupt and shut down. Wages were low at those mines that remained open, and the smaller number of employees worked fewer days per week at lower wages. Miners found it increasingly difficult to earn enough money to provide basic necessities for themselves and their families. In fact, there was enough need for alternative sources of food and clothing that in February Harlan County officials appealed to the National Red Cross for aid when local coal operators announced an additional wage cut. The United Mine Workers of America, seeing an opportunity to organize, once again began a campaign to build the union in eastern Kentucky. Union leaders were successful initially, drawing over 2,000 Harlan and Bell County miners to a rally at a Pineville theater, at which they emphasized that they were not a radical organization and would work closely with the coal industry so as not to "create an industrial catastrophe." However, coal operators kept a watchful eye on the meeting and took down names of miners who participated. The next day nearly 300 miners were fired from their jobs—and unemployment also meant eviction from company-owned homes.[7] Coal companies used the control that they had over every aspect of life in company towns to thwart unionization and any other activity that went against the wishes of company officials. In so doing, they escalated what was already a difficult time into a situation of significant crisis.

Miners embraced the UMWA's organizing efforts primarily as a way to find relief from hard times. Miner Tillman Cadle recalled that "in the early months of 1931, the men had just about come to the end of their ropes and began to talk union again."[8] However, against the background of the Depression, there was likely little that companies could do to increase wages. Some of them stayed open, company officials said, despite losing money, just to provide a small amount of employment and shelter for their workers. Tensions were high. An indication that miners were responding to their situation on their own, without turning to the aid of organized labor, was the frequency of "wildcat" strikes. Although the UMWA would refuse to sanction a strike, miners would act without the union's authority. Moreover, those who had been evicted from their homes for supporting the UMWA found themselves in a desperate position, caught precariously between the two institutional powers of the industry and the union. Coal companies asserted power over miners through their control of jobs and houses, but the union also imposed its wishes. Feeling the pinch of the Depression itself, the union refused to provide relief for miners who took part in unsanctioned strikes. The Red Cross, too, refused to give food and clothing to those who were willingly out of work. When UMWA District 19 president William Turnblazer visited Harlan County in 1931, he saw starvation and aggravation among miners to such an extent that he wrote to President Herbert Hoover requesting aid, fearful that miners might resort to violence. And in short order violence did erupt. Miners began robbing food stores and commissaries in the town of Evarts in April.[9]

Evarts, as one of three incorporated towns in Harlan (and therefore not company owned), became a gathering place for unemployed miners and union activists; many of the townspeople, including the mayor and the police chief, were sympathetic to the union cause. Yet as miners sought relief in Evarts, the sudden boom in population exasperated the already difficult struggle for scarce resources. One miner remembered a time when a man went to the store to get his large family some food. The store clerk said, "Charlie, everything is gone. All we have in the store is a little pepper and salt." Charlie replied, "Do you have any rope? A man might as well hang himself as starve to death working if he can't get anything to cook for his family."[10]

In response to these pressures Evarts became the scene of the first eruptions of labor-related violence in the county, which quickly spread beyond the town's borders. Bell and Harlan counties became a muddle of class lines, with operators and officials on one side, union miners on the other, and people like merchants, working miners, and others standing somewhere in between. Union members beat nonunion miners who continued to work, sometimes firing at them from behind trees on the mountainside as they went to their shifts at the mines. Yet a scab could suddenly change his mind and become a union member, converting across the divide. Townspeople held an ambiguous position in the picture, sometimes working for the relief of struggling miners, sometimes joining the deputies to fight against union activity. To miners, the greatest threat came from armed mine guards hired by coal companies to protect company property, protect working miners, and keep union organizers away from their workers. The history of Harlan and Bell counties during this period is replete with stories about the abuses that miners suffered at the hands of what they called "gun thugs." To miners, law enforcement officers were so thoroughly connected to company interests that one miner defined "law" as "a gun thug in a big automobile."[11] Indeed, John Henry Blair, the sheriff of Harlan County, maintained a force of 170 deputies of whom only 6 were not in the pay of coal companies.[12] Throughout the county evicted and out-of-work miners waged disorganized battles against nonunion miners and coal companies, blasting mine entries with explosives, shooting at working miners from hillsides, and burning down company houses where evicted miners had lived.

Tension came to a head on May 5 in Evarts when some union miners ambushed a motorcade that was transporting nonunion miners to work at the Black Mountain Coal Corporation. One of the cars in the motorcade carried a gun thug whom miners especially feared. His car was the focus of the attack, but in the end three deputy sheriffs and at least one miner lay dead. Shooting continued for two days, schools closed, and many families moved away from the area. Fearing further violence, the unlikely alliance of Sheriff John H. Blair, County Judge H. H. Howard, UMWA District 19 president William Turnblazer, and Kentucky Federation of Labor secretary Peter Campbell all called upon Kentucky governor Flem Sampson, who declared a state of terror and lawlessness in Harlan County and sent in 300 National Guard troops. The soldiers replaced private guards at local mines, partly to prevent violence and partly to control intimidation directed toward potential employees by striking men. One of their first operations, therefore, was to stop union miners from marching on company property, a common organizing practice. The troops did manage to slow the violence and temporarily bring a controlled sense of normalcy back to the coal fields, but with Sheriff Blair's May 24 announcement, after deputies broke up a large UMWA gathering with tear gas, that no further rallies would be permitted in the county, the union abandoned the eastern Kentucky fields. By mid-July the National Guard also left the county.[13]

With a lull in violence and the union's failure to provide the relief and changes that miners had been seeking, many disappointed men went back to work. Except for the violence, the pattern fit previous organization efforts. It was not the same, however. The outbreaks of violence had created an atmosphere of fear and intimidation that was much higher than the region had ever before experienced, and 900 to 1,000 Harlan and Bell County men remained unemployed as a result of the operators' blacklist. At about the same time that the National Guard was leaving Harlan County, twenty-five miners traveled to Pittsburgh to attend a convention held by the National Miners' Union, a Communist union that aimed to compete with the United Mine Workers for control of organized labor in the southern coal fields.[14] In July, they started organizing in the Straight Creek area of Bell County.

The National Miners' Union

It is not my purpose to discuss the politics or the organization of the National Miners' Union. That topic has been well covered elsewhere.[15] The importance of the NMU to the study of religion among coal miners in eastern Kentucky lies in the way that miners used the symbol and structure of the union to navigate and work through their material and spiritual interests in the midst of crisis. The union's affiliation with Communism was of great concern to the forces that opposed organized labor, but this circumstance had little meaning to miners. Jim

Garland, a miner who was an active participant and organizer in the NMU, said, "If you had at this time said to a group of average mountain men, 'I'm a Communist,' they more than likely would have answered, 'I'm a Baptist' or 'I'm a Mason.'"[16] Indeed, miners considered the union to be a resource for supplying their much-needed material needs and an expression of the experiences and desires of their community. One miner's wife remembered,

> They called 'em commúnists (as in com-mún-a-lists), which was cómmunist, but they didn't know the pronunciation of it. They called 'em commúnists, where it should have been cómmunists. . . . I don't know what they was. . . . They was trying to get something started, to have an organization, so that people could have something to live on, you know, wouldn't be so badly mistreated. . . . They even gave 'em clothes . . . like the Church of Christ . . . like when they started the Church there. They wasn't but a very few who took up with it. Everybody was scared.[17]

As far as most miners and their families were concerned, labor unions were less political entities than they were organizations for relief. Another miner's wife echoed and expanded on this notion when she testified before the U.S. Senate, saying that "the United Mine Workers stayed with the miners and helped the miners all they could for months, and then the National Mine Workers Union came to Kentucky and my husband joined them because the United Mine Workers had throwed the miners down and left them to starve, and when the National Mine Workers came in they picked the miners up."[18] Indeed, the first action that the NMU took was to provide resources for miners to open soup kitchens for community cooking. Local mountain churches took part in these programs, too, by opening their doors to NMU relief efforts. Jim Garland noted that all types of traditional mountain churches let miners use their buildings for soup kitchens, including Missionary Baptists, Primitive Baptists (which included, in Garland's parlance, Old Regular Baptists), and Holiness churches. "The new union . . . gained the support of most of the ministers in the area," Garland remembered. "One would have to have lived in the mountains to realize the importance of the churches' support to the NMU's success."[19]

Churches that were not indigenous to the mountains also aided miners by offering relief programs, but miners distrusted the association that these institutions had with coal companies. The churches of national denominations combined their relief efforts, establishing committees on relief in both Harlan and Bell Counties. From the perspective of miners, however, these sources of food and clothing were too bound up in the politics of local economic power to care truly about the miners' situation. For instance, in the cities of Harlan and Pineville the effort to aid those in need was ambivalently coupled with the desire to rid the area of those whom coal operators and commercial interests saw as troublemakers agitating for protest. As a result, both of these cities created investigative branches of their relief committees. The investigators consisted of men "of standing" in the community, including ministers of elite churches, a coal operator, and a trained specialist. Moreover, according to Effie Bly, director of relief work in Pineville, "We try to give work where possible and to manufacture jobs because of the bad social effects of direct charity."[20] For these reasons, miners associated with union activity—and those who were out of work for having associated with the union—were ineligible for help.

Whether true or rumored, the feeling that establishment churches and civic groups refused to feed union members exacerbated the struggle for power between miners and operators. The fact that NMU-associated soup kitchens immediately attracted the attention of deputy sheriffs and became primary scenes of searches, arrests, and murders highlights their importance as both gathering places and symbolic centers of resistance. In fact, a great deal of the discourse of the struggle was focused on issues of food and health. To those in positions of power, food was the method by which the Communists were making inroads into the mining community and threatening the maintenance of order. But for miners and their families, food represented survival, and it was through the language of food and health that they brought what might otherwise have been more abstract issues of politics and economy into a discourse of immediacy and suffering. Despite the ideological issues that drove many in Harlan and Bell Counties to fight against Communism, miners experienced the National Miners' Union as a grassroots, essentially locally controlled, organization that provided much needed food and clothing, along with community, dignity, and the possibility for bringing change to what they saw as an inhuman system. As one miner put it,

> I can say this frankly—I was born and raised in Kentucky. I am a 100 percent American if there is one in the United States, and I say there ought to be a change made if the working class people have to change it, that's my feeling about it, because we are human beings. Our children has the same rights as the capitalists' children, and the coal operators' children.[21]

The language here was surely influenced by the rhetoric of the union, casting the issue in terms of "working class" and "capitalists." Even in its new form, however, the sentiment was a familiar one: before everything else, miners were human beings, and in the midst of crisis in 1931 they felt that they were not being treated as fully human. The National Miners' Union offered miners a space in which to express their full humanity, which included both spiritual and material dimensions. The union existed to critique, resist, and transform a social and economic structure that denied the humanity of mining families by treating them as something less than "capitalists" and "coal operators."

The NMU's first appeal to miners, therefore, was its ability to recognize that the labor situation was not restricted solely to workplace issues; living conditions and wage cuts, and in some situations, evictions, concerned entire families. Many women complained that before the NMU came to the region they had no way to address these matters, and they criticized the United Mine Workers as well as coal companies for disregarding the family dimensions of miners' work problems. But as Suddy Gates, a miner's wife, said,

> The good thing about the National Miners' Union is that they don't leave the women out and so, not like in other times, many times the wives would make their husbands go back to work. The wives must meet with their husbands and together plan, because it is as much to the wives as to the miners. In this National Miners' Union the wives know just as much what is going on. We are not going to say, "Go on, Johnny, go back to work."
> We are going to stand right along with them and fight.[22]

In fact, women took an active role in all aspects of union activity, from working in soup kitchens to marching on picket lines. The NMU early formed a women's auxiliary that quickly "more or less melded together" with the men's activities. According to Jim Garland, women were responsible for organizing mass meetings and "whipping up enthusiasm."[23] It is important to recall the situation of women in coal town life. In some ways the life of coal mining left women without the significant positions that they held in their families and communities on farms, where they had taken part in essential productive work. Coal towns further divided labor between men and women, but more than that, they devalued the productive role that women played in sustaining the family. Men were the breadwinners in the coal mining money economy, and it was men's work that brought food to the table. A man's labor was the link between the company and the house that his family lived in as well. On the other hand, a woman was directly affected by her husband's work because she had to rise before dawn to make the lunch that he would bring with him down into the mine and she had

Women march for the National Miners' Union. Item 36, Herndon J. Evans Collection, 1929–1982, 82M1, University of Kentucky Libraries. Used by permission.

to prepare dinner for his exhausted return. Because men were at work all day, women also had to take full responsibility for raising children. Mae Prater described the daily life of a miner's wife this way:

> Sometimes when they was working long hours and so hard in the mines I seen him leave the house about three o'clock in the morning. I got up many a morning at two o'clock for him to get ready to go to work hard all day in that mine. That's before the union come in, and it was getting pretty bad. The children wouldn't hardly see him in the daylight. See, they wouldn't be up when he'd leave and they'd maybe sometimes be in bed almost when he come in. They just didn't see him much.[24]

Recall the story about a father who spanked his son one day. The upset son ran to his mother and told her that "that old man who comes here every Sunday morning spanked me!" The message of the story reinforced Prater's comments and suggests that mining threatened to alienate family members from one another. Whereas traditional work brought families together, producing self and family as well as community, in the industrial setting work had a detrimental effect. Women found a voice in the NMU to express their dissatisfaction with this situation, and the union also gave them a sense of value and purpose that they had not found elsewhere. Suddy Gates, continuing her assessment of what the NMU meant to women, said,

> We are thankful to the National Miners' Union for [giving women an active role]. It makes you have a sensation you hardly knew what it is all about. We never had nothing to do before but cook some beans. Now we have something to do. Now we have something else to do. Now we are going to have John win the strike.[25]

Women were symbolically important, too, because they were the caretakers of families, children, and husbands. In this role, women directed the discourse about the crisis that miners faced, steering it toward issues of health and general well-being, which they linked directly to conditions of work. The importance that women played in this regard cannot be overstated. Aunt Molly Jackson is a case in point.

Work and Health

Aunt Molly Jackson's husband, brother, and father were all coal miners. Her father was also a preacher in a mountain-style Missionary Baptist church, and a brother, Jim Garland, was a deacon before his involvement in the labor struggle led him to leave the church, an issue to which I will return. She lost her father, another brother, and a son to coal mining accidents. Clearly, Aunt Molly deeply felt the destructive effects of mining in her life. In the 1930s she became active in the NMU in several ways, most famously with her singing and song-writing. When Theodore Dreiser's committee of writers from New York visited Harlan County in November to investigate reports of a "reign of terror" in the coal fields, they heard her sing this song:

> I'm sad and weary; I've got the hungry ragged blues;
> I'm sad and weary; I've got the hungry ragged blues;
> Not a penny in my pocket to buy the things I need to use.
>
> I woke up this morning with the worst blues I ever had in my life;
> I woke up this morning with the worst blues I ever had in my life;
> Not a bite to cook for breakfast, a poor coal miner's wife.

When my husband works in the coal mines, he loads a car on every trip,
When my husband works in the coal mines, he loads a car on every trip,
Then he goes to the office that evening and gits denied of scrip.

All the women in the coal camps are a-sitting with bowed-down heads,
All the women in the coal camps are a-sitting with bowed-down heads,
Ragged and barefooted, the children are a-crying for bread.

No food, no clothes for our children, I'm sure this ain't no lie,
No food, no clothes for our children, I'm sure this ain't no lie,
If we can't git more for our labor, we will starve to death and die.

Some coal operators might tell you the hungry blues are not bad;
Some coal operators might tell you the hungry blues are not bad;
They are the worst blues this poor woman ever had.[26]

These "Kentucky Miners' Wives Ragged Hungry Blues" dramatized the miners' struggle as one of suffering and starvation, effectively turning abstract economic issues into concrete images. Dreiser's committee was taken with the song and instantly made Aunt Molly a symbol of the miners' plight. She eventually moved to New York and made a career of singing songs of labor and struggle for the leftist labor movement. In Kentucky in 1931, however, her attention was squarely on her own community. Scholars have pointed out Aunt Molly's tendency to exaggerate and manipulate stories about her life and her songs. She often placed herself in important events in which truthfully she played no part, and she claimed to have invented tunes from whole cloth that had clear folkloric precedents. Nevertheless, to discount her stories as lies would fail to recognize that in their creativeness they expressed what Aunt Molly felt to be significant in her experience and the experiences of which she spoke. With this caveat in mind, a story that Aunt Molly told to a reporter for the *Daily Worker* in New York showed the important role that women played in union organizing, in symbol no less than fact. She said that women and children marched into the mines one day, singing "Kentucky Miners' Wives Ragged Hungry Blues."

Crawling out of their holes, hardly able to stand upright in the narrow passage, the men crowded together amazed. "What in god's name do they want down here?" And Aunt Molly answered. "We've come to fetch you up. You're doing no good here." They told her to go back and she said, "We've nothing to do at home, no food to cook no clothes to wash. We stay right here till you come up with us." They said that meant losing the job, and she answered them, "You've got nothing to lose. You'll live longer in fresh air and sunshine without food than you will down there. Throw down your picks, empty your water-cans and come right up and say you won't strike another pick till you get a living wage!" And they followed her.[27]

Whether or not this event actually happened the way that Aunt Molly said it did is beside the point. The message was that the work that men were doing in the mines was not providing for their families, and it took women and children to lead the men to leave their jobs—something the men were afraid to do—in order to change the situation. As before, Aunt Molly framed the labor struggle in terms of kinship and health, specifically in terms of the well-being of families, a strategy that brought the issue directly into an arena that was loaded with religious significance. If work was a duty that was prescribed by God and a responsibility to family, Aunt Molly forcefully showed that in the setting of industrial coal mining it was not functioning as designed. Aunt Molly, and the discourse of suffering and starvation, drove a wedge into the ambivalent relationship between the duty to work and the anxieties and hardship that accompanied mining. The conditions of labor in the coal mines, according to Aunt Molly's formulation, tipped the balance in favor of striking. Work itself under existing conditions was destructive.

Concern for children and health were not new to Aunt Molly in 1931. Since a young age she had been a practicing midwife. According to her brother Jim, she delivered more babies between 1910 and 1932 "than did all the doctors on both Horse Creek in Clay County and Straight Creek in Bell County." By her own estimate, she attended over 5,000 births.[28] The role of midwife placed Aunt Molly in a powerful position within traditional mountain culture, for it meant that she was a healer. Midwives, often called "Granny" or "Aunt," were expected to heal the sick as well as to deliver babies, and Aunt Molly was knowledgeable about herbal remedies and other traditional healing practices. "The greatest pleasure in this world from a little child for me was tryin' to relieve sufferin' humanity. Anybody thet was sick," she said. She believed in "ghosts, signs, tokens, and charms," and she also drew motivation from her religious background.[29]

Her father, Oliver, whose strong faith and preaching heavily influenced Aunt Molly, had been a committed union member, and his views on religion and labor often combined. He joined the Knights of Labor in 1885 and tried to talk miners in the fledgling mining industry into uniting "into one big union that Jesus Christ Himself called the brotherhood of man."[30] According to Aunt Molly, "My dad was a strong union man and a good minister . . . so he taught me to be a strong union woman."[31] From these sources, then, Aunt Molly forged her own vision of the need to change labor conditions, and her observations resonated with religious significance in the context of eastern Kentucky's cultural background.

Aunt Molly's sister, Sarah Ogan Gunning, also wrote songs that spoke of the conditions of mining and their effects. Gunning's songs, like her sister's, painted visceral pictures of the physical effects of coal mining, but one in particular displayed the stark equation between economic forces and suffering bodies:

> I hate the company bosses,
> I'll tell you the reason why.
> They cause me so much suffering
> And my dearest friends to die.
>
> Oh yes, I guess you wonder
> What they have done to me.
> I'm going to tell you, mister,
> My husband had T.B.
>
> Brought on by hard work and low wages
> And not enough to eat,
> Going naked and hungry,
> No shoes on his feet.
>
> I guess you'll say he's lazy
> And did not want to work.
> But I must say you're crazy,
> For work he did not shirk.
>
> My husband was a coal miner,
> He worked and risked his life
> To support three children,
> Himself, his mother, and wife
>
> I had a blue-eyed baby,
> The darling of my heart.
> But from my little darling
> Her mother had to part.
>
> These mighty company bosses,
> They dress in jewels and silk.
> But my darling blue-eyed baby,
> She starved to death for milk.[32]

According to folklorist Archie Green, who spoke to her about the song, Gunning did not think of it as a protest song but rather saw it autobiographically as "a response to the death of her loved ones."[33] There was no doubt a union—probably Communist—influence on the sentiment, as the original title, "I Hate the Capitalist System," hints. The song does not assert a politics, however, as much as it locates the cause of death and suffering directly in the structures of exchange that made up industrial capitalism. The song is densely packed with elements that were significant to miners' religious consciousness, including the assertion that her husband was not lazy and therefore was not neglecting his biblical responsibility to work in order to eat; he faced many challenges trying to provide for his family. The juxtaposition of company bosses dressed in their finery while a baby starved for lack of milk vividly portrayed a lack of social equality as one group of people gained at the expense of another—literally acquiring privilege at the cost of others' lives. In this song, like Aunt Molly's "Kentucky Miners' Wives Ragged and Hungry Blues," the strongest shock came from the heavy irony that the biblical injunction to earn one's bread by the sweat of one's brow not only went unfulfilled but was inverted. Work instead led to starvation.

What both Aunt Molly Jackson and Sarah Ogan Gunning accomplished with their songs—and these are only two examples among many others—was to force the discourse of power away from economic and political abstractions into a commentary on the effects of exchanges on individual human bodies. By recovering the human dimensions of the economic system, these women and their songs focused attention on the inherent value of human beings that was denied and rejected by the industrial system. In doing this, they were merely making public a structure of feeling that had been hidden in the everyday experiences and expressions of miners. Publicizing the human dimension of suffering wrought by coal mining had two important effects. First, it caught the notice of a wider audience, calling national attention to the conditions of labor in eastern Kentucky in a way that touched off moral outrage throughout the United States. While industrial powers in the coal fields could continue to see local labor struggles in terms of maintaining civic order and economic productivity, from a greater distance the images that drew the public's notice were those of helpless, suffering miners who were at the mercy of overwhelming powers even as they fought to feed their families. That image drew Theodore Dreiser and his committee to Kentucky as it also drew Reinhold Niebuhr and other "foreign" ministers, a group of students from Columbia University and Union Theological Seminary, and sundry others. These outside visitors did not find favor with coal operators, law enforcement officials, or local clergy, but their visits did result in a series of Senate hearings.[34]

Second, songs and other public expressions of the suffering experienced by miners had the effect of dramatizing and intensifying the troubles that miners faced daily. The images they conjured joined with the realities of hunger, anxieties about work and family, fear of gun thugs, violence and shootings, and the dangers that already existed in coal mining life. On top of all this, rumors and innuendo spread throughout the coal fields and created an atmosphere of uncertainty, if not terror, where "reality" and fantasy had equal footing. Stories circulated like the one that surfaced at the murder trial of William B. Jones, a local UMWA secretary who was arrested for his participation in the Battle of Evarts but was not tried until November. At the trial some witnesses claimed that miners had been required to take a "black oath," signed in blood, denouncing America and the Bible when they joined the union.[35] Another rumor concerned the "Three Foot Gangster," a gun thug supposedly called in from Chicago to act as a deputy sheriff. A wife of an unemployed miner claimed that this man threatened her while she "was reading the New Testament to some ladies" at a mass meeting on the Harlan Court House steps. She said some men said that they were going to throw teargas hand grenades to break up the meeting, and they "asked me if I wanted to cry. I told them if God Almighty saw fit for me to cry I would cry."[36] Jim Garland's uncle even said that the blacklist that coal companies kept to refuse work to union-affiliated miners did not exist; he said that it was elaborated by union organizers to foment anger and pass the blame on to coal operators for the union's failure to secure jobs.[37]

The effect of all of this can be compared to that of the preaching of revival preacher caught up in the Spirit: it intensified the atmosphere of crisis. As in a Holiness meeting, the building energy carried also an expectation of transformation. In the context of the religious culture of mountains, the moment of crisis was lifted out of the regular flow of history and appeared to be a special and significant time. Jackson and Gunning and others were, in effect, playing their parts in a cultural performance of a familiar religious idiom that transformed the struggles of everyday life into a ritualized structure that ideally progressed through crisis to healing and salvation.

The Redemptive Union

When Theodore Dreiser's investigative committee attended a meeting of miners associated with the National Miners' Union in November 1931, they recorded a series of testimonies that clearly expressed the overt religious significance that miners found in the union.

"It surprises me to face a congregation like this under the present conditions that we know slaving miners in Kentucky are existing under," said Billie Meeks before the gathered audience at the Glendon Baptist Church in Wallins Creek.[38] Meeks, a preacher and also the district president of the NMU, was not leading a church service this November night. He was at a meeting of miners called together by Dreiser's committee of New York writers to talk about conditions in the coal fields. A good deal of his testimony related directly to events that had happened in the area recently. Taken as a whole, however, in style and narrative structure his talk took the form of a sermon. He began by positing the dualistic terms of class struggle that would drive his narrative in structures of oppositions, pitting the moral against the immoral or the right against the sinful. But he was careful to circumvent the charge that the NMU was un-American; instead, the struggle was between "red-blooded Americans" like himself and the "blue-blooded Americans" of the ruling class.[39] The values of freedom and independence at the core of the idea of America were, in other words, exactly the values for which the miners were fighting. Yet the coal industry stood in the way of this freedom, especially in the behavior of company officials and gun thugs during these difficult times, since "anything that is to the benefit of our starving wives and children, Capitalists is [sic] absolutely against it." (To this his audience replied in antiphonal style, "That is the truth.") Meeks's emphasis on the inability of miners to carry through on the responsibility to care for family members under the then-current state of the economy ran throughout his talk, bringing labor issues to the bar for moral judgment and identifying capitalism as an oppressive force that stood in the way of responsibility.

Theodore Dreiser had commented that "a worker cannot turn to his church, because his church will not listen to his economic ills here on earth; it calls attention to a Paradise which is to come hereafter." But Meeks, the preacher, illustrated that the union was a specifically *earthly* mechanism through which miners could work toward meeting moral obligations.[40] It was not the church's duty, as a church, to get involved with worldly things, but there were other avenues that God provided. Speaking in terms that resonated with the claim that the Gospel was "freely given" to individuals to accept or reject, Meeks combined language that he probably absorbed from Communist rhetoric with his preacherly style: "Now listen, Comrades," he said, "there is only one way in the world for us laboring class of people out [sic], and it has been handed to you and if you don't accept it, no wonder starvation is looking you in the face, it ought to. The National Miners' Union has walked down here and offered us help."

As he continued, Meeks returned again and again to the redemptive possibilities of the union movement for restoring order to the chaos that had come to the coal fields. But he was not implying that order would return in the form in which it had existed earlier as coal operators wished. Instead, it was a new state of affairs that Meeks saw coming out of the chaos if people chose the right path of action. After evoking contrasting images of injustice and possibility, he brought home the choice as a challenge: to choose the right, to choose the way of moral responsibility over the structures of industry that had stood in the way of freedom. "It has been presented to the laboring people in Bell County that we have got to walk out from under Capitalism and if you don't take hold and work shoulder to shoulder and stand for your wives' and children's rights, it is no wonder you are slapped in jail and your brothers shot down and this condition [is] existing in Kentucky." The situation, Meeks testified, had its analogue in the Old Testament:

> The time is presented to you in the days when the Children of Israel was under bondage, when Moses went to lead them out and he came to the Red Sea and the Children got scared and said, "We would rather have died back there than to perish here in this Wilderness," and he said, "Stand still and let the Salvation of the Lord appear," and they thought they could not go through, they walked through dry sod, and Pharaoh's hosts came on and the water closed upon them. What became of them? They were drowned. We have the same opportunity presented to us, laboring men, by the National Miners' Union to walk out as the Children of Israel did, and if you don't drown these Capitalists and this Capitalism, it is your own bad luck. You can't blame any one but yourself.

Finley Donaldson, a Holiness preacher and union organizer, preached a similar message. His statement echoed that of Meeks and also speeches by others who focused on the duty that a man had to care for his family—and the way in which the existing situation impeded the accomplishment of that duty by forcing workers to walk "that lonesome road that goes between starvation and Hooverism."

> Don't think you are going to starve me to death. If you starve me on Hooverism, I will steal all you have got—I am not going to let my little children starve—you can't scare me. Never! You can build rock walls and gates but it won't keep me from getting in. I am going to feed my little children—steal, kill, rob and everything before I will have them starve, because I feel it is my duty. If you don't want me to do that, don't shut me down.... As sure as you take my muscle and the

sweat of my brow is all I have to swap for a living, as sure as you rob me of that, I will get it anyhow.[41]

Donaldson was greatly concerned with his ability to obey the laws of God as he understood them, but in this case religious duty and earthly powers came into conflict. When they conflicted, there was no doubt in his mind that he would disobey earthly laws to fulfill his duties to his family. Killing was surely sinful, but for Donaldson the people who were responsible for standing in the way of his duty to family were greater sinners. "We have told them our starving conditions and they won't divide with us," he complained. "If they will divide and give us a living, we will give them the rest and let them go to Hell, where they have started." Donaldson was even more clear than Meeks about how the industrial quest for profit constituted, in its current condition, a sinful practice that stood between miners and a godly life:

> We don't want to get rich. I hate the name of money because it led me into a bad life. I used to have some money and it led me down in Sin further than anything that ever happened. . . . If you put a man in privation you are driving him into sin, but if you give him something to live on, he can stand up to help the Christian world, but if you deprive him of food and raiment, you cause that man to commit in his heart murder and robbery and stealing, and they have almost starved me.

In each of these statements what comes across is not only how miners cast the labor movement as an urgent religious issue but also the manner in which that urgency was conveyed through narratives of conversion to union activism that offered the emotional authenticity of personal conviction as a resource to convert others. Here union members were doing more than arguing rationally for a particular political stance. They were calling forth lived realities in which conditions, by working on their bodies and convicting them, had compelled them to turn their lives toward a path that would better their conditions. The speeches and testimonies were, moreover, calls for others to do the same—not only because they *ought* to, but because the narratives themselves propelled an emotionally and physically charged sense of urgency that sought to move people from within, leaving almost no choice but the right path. And that path was not only in the hands of men, but, as Billy Meeks implied, part of God's grace for his chosen people. In this light, the NMU took on the aura of a millenarian movement.

Aunt Molly Jackson put the situation plainly in her testimony. She began by reciting from the fifth chapter of the biblical book of James, which she said she was "glad that the Lord has blessed me to see the fulfilling of." Records do not indicate what portion of the scripture she recited, but the entire chapter was directly relevant to the miners' situation. It spoke of the suffering of laborers at the hands of the wealthy who gained from the misery of others, and it promised divine justice and redemption, "for the coming of the Lord is at hand." The chapter opened with these condemning verses:

> Go now, ye rich men, weep and howl for your miseries that shall come upon you. Your riches are corrupted, and your garments are motheaten. Your gold and silver is cankered; and the rust of them shall be a witness against you, and shall eat your flesh as it were fire. Ye have heaped treasure together for the last days. Behold, the hire of the labourers who have reaped down your fields, which is of you kept back by fraud, crieth: and the cries of them which have reaped are entered into the ears of the Lord of Sabaoth.[42]

The passage went on to state that God would reward those who had suffered and had patience to await his imminent coming, and it emphasized God's power to heal the sick and suffering through prayer and anointing. That Aunt Molly chose this passage was significant not only for its appropriate message, but because it was the same passage that served as the basis for a strongly pro-labor sermon that her father had preached years before.[43] After her recitation Aunt Molly declared, "Now, we are under bondage, we have been under bondage for a long time but God is going to redeem his people. He is fixing a way and a plan for them to be redeemed from this bondage through this great organization."[44]

The testimonies of union members at this meeting that took place in an independent Baptist church are richly suggestive. A close inspection reveals that the religious significance of the labor struggle was not restricted to only one theological perspective nor even one form of religion. Both Meeks and Donaldson were preachers, so their statements should be interpreted as being congruous with their Christian orientations. Donaldson, in particular, was a Holiness preacher, and it is likely that he heard in Aunt Molly's testimony a premillennialist message that was quite literal in its expectation of the imminent day of divine judgment. Aunt Molly herself is harder to decipher. Her subsequent move to New York City and participation in leftist organizations suggests that she had transformed her mountain church background into a new religious orientation that was essentially materialist. She continued to use the idioms of her mountain Baptist tradition to comment incisively on material matters, but she turned her attention increasingly toward the power of human agency to correct injustices. This did not mean that she was any less religious, necessarily, only that her religion took a form that emphasized the ordinary and worldly as opposed to the extraordinary and otherworldly. Her songs of suffering, for instance, did not include the conclusion so common in other songs of that tradition, invoking images of a peaceful rest in heaven. As a midwife, Aunt Molly had long held a religious orientation that directed attention more toward the alleviation of suffering through available worldly resources than toward divine intervention or otherworldly rewards. In terms of the divide between world and spirit, her religion was on the side of the world.

In his autobiography, *Welcome the Traveler Home*, Jim Garland spoke directly to the way that the struggle against industrial power changed his long-held religious orientation. "You must remember that I was a religious man at this time, a deacon of the church, and that most of my family was quite religious. But when a person gets involved, truly involved, in a labor struggle, it's hard to keep his religious beliefs primary, mainly because he gets so damn mad." So he left the church. But in two important ways he never gave up on religion. First, religion remained important to him as a cultural form of mountain identity. "I seldom go to church," he wrote in his autobiography, "except when I return to the hills where I was raised. Then I go often in that this is the mountain life, the custom I knew as I was growing up, and the sociability I have returned for." Second, his reason for turning away from an active role in the church reveals that the labor struggle led him to ask important questions about the structures of power that caused suffering in the industrial setting. The church was the traditional institutional locus for the alleviation of suffering, but Garland found that in these new structures of power the church was unable to address the real human sources of suffering to his satisfaction. He recalled one time when Harry Simms, a National Miners' Union organizer from Massachusetts, said to him, "Jim, remember everything has a material base." Garland wrote, "And that was the one comment that got me thinking about the bases of my religion and the bases of my politics. It led me at that time, 1931, to believe in the Communist party as the organization that might change things for the mountain people." So Garland, in effect, switched churches.[45]

All of these examples indicate the power of work, as a fundamental and necessary human activity, to become the occasion for deeply religious questions about power, value, and ultimately of human meaning. And miners used the religious idioms of their mountain culture to express these issues regardless of their theological orientation. Recall that mountain religious traditions shared common practices and idioms even when they diverged wildly on issues of doctrine or theology. The recurrent observation, made by missionaries and others, that mountain residents argued about theology and scripture almost as a pastime suggests that what they shared as a religious culture was not theological agreement but a common set of idioms for expressing ultimate questions. Indeed, for many, final answers were humanly unknowable.

Anthropologist Kathleen Stewart has noted that "the ecstatic evangelical hell-and-damnation preaching of sectarian tent revivals developed cheek to cheek with dramatic, incendiary organizing speeches, songs, and stories. Since then the linked religious-political rhetoric has been reproduced in use in frequent strikes as well as in regular union meetings." Religion, in other words, provided a "way of talking" that linked material and spiritual concerns in a dense performative style that had significance and effect as a rhetorical form aside from any underlying doctrine. The testimonies of National Miners' Union members were polyvalent, speaking simultaneously of ordinary and extraordinary powers and possibilities, and therefore articulating the ordinary in a way that made it dense with significance. Miners shared a cultural familiarity with the testimonial and preacherly style of rhetoric and therefore knew that such speech was designed to elicit a response. In other words, "an implicit model of social action is negotiated and enacted in and through the forms of concrete practices of speech and action."[46] Likewise, the use of images of suffering and broken bodies, so prevalent in union testimonies and songs, was a part of this style of speech that implied a model of action. The world's troubles settled onto bodies in the form of pain and nerves. Abstract social relations and concepts of fairness, justice, and social power were thereby made concrete and entered into the rhetorical style that piled up visceral images designed to make others feel the weight of the situation until it compelled a response. Speech intensified and focused crisis in a familiar rhetorical structure.

Atheism

Mode of speech was thus a key element of cultural practice that tied together the ordinary with the extraordinary. But it would be oversimplifying to say that the theological perspectives that were also bound up in the expressive forms of union testimonies were inconsequential. In fact, they had dire consequences. So long as miners could interpret the meaning and significance of the union on their own

National Miners' Union rally. Item 50, Herndon J. Evans Collection, 1929–1982, 82M1, University of Kentucky Libraries. Used by permission.

terms, they could see in it redemptive potential that had religious as well as political efficacy. Indeed, the efforts of coal operators and other opposing forces to turn miners against the NMU by emphasizing its Communist connections were interpreted by union members as further examples of the desire of industrialists to control them.

The most commonly voiced charges against the union pointed to its atheism. "Communism breeds a contempt of God and all religion; corrodes the steel of society and industry; and strives to place the United States in the same plane of organization as the country in which it originated," read an editorial in the *Harlan Daily Enterprise*. Most important, Communism struck "at the very root of America's foundation—Religion."[47] The commercial and elite interests in Harlan and Bell Counties continually pitted the symbols of religion, America, and industry against the specter of Communism, which signified their opposite. Their own rhetoric made sacred significance of the industrial order and existing structures of power, intensifying a discourse that began with the earliest developments of the coal fields. On another occasion, the *Harlan Daily Enterprise* published a letter that clearly revealed the sacred dimensions of industry as its advocates understood them:

> The coal operators, bitterly and falsely maligned and abused by Red agitators, Communistic speakers and irresponsible news writers, are, in the main, responsible for the progress of Harlan County. . . . Standing there above the clouds and looking into miles of space, our mind went back to Bible days and there came before us the description of the mountain upon which Moses went to talk with God, and we thought that here in the hills of Kentucky there is a peak similar to that of Mount Sinai. If you have never been there, lay aside your rush for pleasure and go look at the indescribable work of the Almighty. You will then have a far better opinion of those men and women who live close to God and commune with Him every day in the playground of nature up in the hills of Harlan County.[48]

The difference in perspective between this view and that of union miners was striking. The miners spoke from the depths of the mines where they worked in darkness all day long, sometimes not seeing daylight for days at a time. Here, the sympathizers of industry spoke from the top of the mountain. These different locations gave each group a different perspective on the experience of the labor struggle. Newspaper editorials notwithstanding, coal miners and their families asserted that their union was not against God and America (although it was guilty of being against industry as it was then structured). Indeed, it was sent by

God. Union members' own experiences told them a different story from the one told by operators.

If anything, the strong opposition to the NMU only made the union stronger. Opposition drew the lines dividing the conflicting groups more sharply, and perhaps, especially for those union members with premillennialist leanings, proved that coal interests were persecuting miners with false religion. It was in the context of the miners' labor struggle of 1931 that Florence Reece wrote her famous protest song, "Which Side Are You On?" The song's message resonated with Jesus's assertion that "he who is not with me is against me" (Luke 23:11) and mobilized a familiar Christian idiom of the persecution of the righteous. The union grew stronger and in January 1932 staged a widespread strike.

But everything changed in February. Four NMU leaders—including Finley Donaldson—returned from union-sponsored training in Chicago and points north with the urgent message that, in fact, what their opposition had been saying was true. In a pamphlet containing their statements sworn before the official reporter of the Bell Circuit Court, they turned against the union. "Fellow workers and citizens," Donaldson's statement read, "the teachings of the Communist party would destroy our religious beliefs, our government and our homes. In teachings they demand their members to teach their children that there is no God; no Jesus; no Hereafter; no resurrection of the dead; all there is for anybody is what they get in this world. I heard them in a mass meeting and a big demonstration in Chicago denounce our government and our flag and our religion."[49]

Claiming that he had never heard such statements by NMU organizers while in Kentucky, Donaldson saw the veil lifted from his eyes in Chicago. The statement of Harvey Collett, another local organizer, revealed a racialist side to his reasons for rejecting Communist ideology. It was not only "un-American and absolutely for the purpose of destroying the teachings of Jesus Christ," but "they teach that there is no God, that a white woman is equal to a colored woman, that a negro had a right to marry a white woman, that Christ is a myth and that there is nothing in the resurrection." Despite the strong words in favor of the struggle for freedom in the testimonies of those at the Dreiser Committee hearings, freedom apparently only went so far. Black miners had participated in the union effort, but their white counterparts still considered the idea of interracial marriage beyond the pale.

Revelations of godlessness and miscegenation had a profound effect on union membership, especially since the statements came from religious men who had been intensely involved in local union leadership. Donaldson claimed that "more than a thousand members in Bell and Harlan Counties quit after I made my statement."[50] A week later 750 to 1,000 miners paraded around the Pineville courthouse, led by a preacher and singing hymns, as nine NMU members, including outside organizer Doris Parks, stood trial inside for criminal syndicalism. Parks's statement strikingly articulated what Donaldson, Collett, and other leaders had learned in the North. County Attorney Smith questioned her:

> SMITH: Do you believe in any form of religion?
> PARKS: I believe in the religion of the workers.
> SMITH: Do you believe in the Bible and that Christ was crucified?
> PARKS: I affirmed, didn't I, that I believe in the working class and their right to organize and to teach them they can be led out of this oppression by the Communist Party.[51]

Jim Garland recalled that "once [Pineville newspaper editor] Herndon Evans reproduced this statement in the *Pineville Sun* . . . we lost more than half our members. The local papers continued to hammer on the religious theme to such an extent that, I believe, this issue bruised us more than had any other."[52] The organizational efforts of the NMU ground to a halt, and leaders who were not native residents left Harlan and Bell counties. With the Depression and the aftermath of disclosures of atheism, organized labor did not make any inroads into the region for the rest of 1932. However, this was not the defeat of the labor movement. The plight of Kentucky's miners was now national news. And in 1933, following the passage of the National Recovery Act, the United Mine Workers of America reentered the eastern Kentucky coal fields and quickly attracted thousands of members. In the context of Allen Talmadge's statement earlier in this chapter, the NMU appeared as just the last straw in a long movement of conditions "getting worser and worser." They were the occasion for the crisis that, in his narrative, compelled the change that had to come. And in their short-lived struggle, they forged a connection between traditional religious rhetorical forms and practices that would shape future expressions of labor struggle in eastern Kentucky.

According to folklorist Alessandro Portelli, the events in 1931 and 1932 were a contest over the symbols of religion and America that were shared by both miners and coal operators. "In the face of unprecedented conditions and finding themselves led to unprecedented actions, miners attempted to legitimize their choices in terms of their traditional culture, of religion, and patriotism," Portelli wrote. "The symbols, words, and sources of legitimacy of this culture were shared with the operators, and the institutions of the state. The consequence was a fierce class struggle for the control of meaning."[53] Portelli's analysis is rich and insightful. A careful study of the religious significance of miners' experiences adds a deeper resonance to his observations. For miners and their religious culture, material concerns could always connect to spiritual concerns. Suffering, death, and fear led directly to matters of human value and the connection between world and spirit. Exchanges that involved relations of power made themselves known in tactile ways that also led directly to moral questions and, ultimately, to the nature of human relations. Seen in this light, the events of 1931 and early 1932 were certainly struggles over power, but that power was religious as well as political and economic. In the world of miners the forces of power and capital were felt directly on the body, and bodily feelings resonated in a religious key. Miners and their families used the appearance of the National Miners' Union as an occasion for continued experimentation, so to speak, in being human, working with and through the varieties of power in their industrial setting. The union became the locus of new formations and expressions of the dual crisis—material and spiritual—that made up the structures of feeling of the coal fields.

Sociologist Dwight Billings has argued that it is important, in settings such as this, to understand religion as a "mediating variable" in social conflicts rather than simply as a superstructural reflection of material interests.[54] It might be just as important, in the context of the eastern Kentucky coal fields, to see the labor movement as a mediating variable as well: religion mediating responses to material or political crisis, and organized labor mediating responses to religious crisis. In the process, the union provided resources for addressing a number of the tensions and challenges of coal mining life, even if its final goals were not achieved. For example, the NMU provided an institutional space to address issues that impacted mining families' sense of humanity but that were not encompassed by the worship practices or doctrines of the church. Mountain churches addressed spiritual problems in relation to divine power, but the union's resources organized the chaotic violence and suffering that impacted their daily lives and directed miners' grievances toward the industrial economic source of their troubles. The union gave miners a language and conceptual framework that allowed them to identify the cause of their situation as the institution of industrial capitalism and its forms of human and material relations. Furthermore, it provided a democratically elected system of officers who could lead them in their protests. In many cases those leaders were preachers who saw religious significance in the material concerns of the labor union. The union thus offered an institutional forum for voicing the spiritual concerns of new material conditions.

Second, through the union, miners set up soup kitchens and relief programs to interrupt temporarily the immediate problem of hunger. By stressing that the miners' struggle was fundamentally a concern for everyday physical suffering, the union again linked issues of economic power with the traditionally religious issues of survival and health. In carrying out their relief work, then, the union entered into close relations with independent churches who hosted soup kitchens and union meetings, thereby creating a visible connection between labor struggle, traditional cultural forms, relief from suffering, and the community of miners. The link was strengthened when gun thugs and deputies shot at soup kitchens and made them the targets of harassment, heightening the "us/them" dichotomy.

Third, through the National Miners' Union, miners mobilized the concern for human value in the industrial setting that was expressed in the "hidden transcripts" of talk and folklore as well as in religious worship. They asserted that industrial coal mining conditions deprived them of their full humanity, reducing them to disposable and replaceable employees and denying them the basic necessities of shelter and food. They resisted classifications and practices that reduced miners to something less than fully human, or humans valued less than others. In the context of their labor situation, miners were forced to confront a system of exchange and power that tied human value to work in an unfamiliar and seemingly inhuman way by mediating the relation between work and life with abstract economic principles. Too often, miners learned, the profit-seeking priorities of industry came between a person's work and its fruits. Miners therefore had to craft new relationships to the practical and symbolic significance of work, which nevertheless remained a defining and fundamental aspect of their humanity. Through the union and the labor struggle, mining families began to forge new understandings of their human nature—new subjectivities—in relation to the structures of industrial capitalist power. The NMU, and later the United Mine Workers of America, provided institutional structures through which miners could assert agency in a form that was meant to be recognizable and efficacious in the industrial economy.

Finally, through union activity miners and their families fashioned new gender roles. In the transition from farm to coal town, women's work often no longer directly contributed to providing materially for their families. This was not true in every case, since some women made an income by running boarding-houses, working as maids, teaching, and so forth. But the majority of coal miners' wives were left out of the structures of power that defined their living conditions. In the union, women showed that coal mining affected them, too, and that they had a stake in changing conditions. They did so by restaging tradi-tional women's roles in new arenas, focusing their criticism on issues of health, caring for children, and food. Women clearly showed that the labor movement was not only about wages and masculine power; through the union they forced attention to the ways that industrial capitalism pervaded all aspects of life and well-being.

But the short life of the National Miners' Union in eastern Kentucky also revealed the limitations of the intersections of mountain religious culture and organized labor. Assertions of equality were fine to an extent, but many miners rejected interracial marriage outright. Likewise, for the majority of miners the rejection of God was simply unacceptable. They were unwilling to leave aside re-ligious implications for practical political and economic concerns. After all, they had invested the union with a great deal of religious significance and articulated its importance through religious idioms. The revelation that the NMU denied the reality of miners' religious beliefs undercut an essential element of the meaning that the union held to mining families who were struggling to recover and retain their humanity in the face of increasing opposition to the religious culture of the eastern Kentucky mountains and its patterns of life and work. In eastern Ken-tucky's coal fields, the struggles of labor were also, in large part, religious strug-gles, and the two issues could not and would not be separated. The industrial coal fields vastly complicated the relationship between work and human value.

CONCLUSION

WHEN THE UNITED MINE WORKERS OF AMERICAN reentered the eastern Kentucky coal fields in 1933, miners embraced the union. Miners saw the new National Recovery Act as federal legitimization of organized labor, a feeling that was boosted by union organizers who plastered coal towns with posters and billboards declaring, "The president wants you to join the union."[1] Any residual questions that workers might have had concerning whether or not organized labor was anti-American were laid to rest by Franklin D. Roosevelt's official stamp of approval. In Harlan County, however, coal operators continued to resist unionization, and the struggle that began in 1931 continued throughout the decade. Some of their resistance may have been the result of the violence of the National Miners' Union struggle. Labor historians, though, point instead to the high percentage of "captive mines" as a primary reason for organized labor's difficulties breaking into the eastern Kentucky fields—that is, mines owned by large corporations like U.S. Steel, who used the coal their mines produced in other aspects of their own operations rather than selling it on the open market. Labor scholars also note the widespread use of private mine guards who continued to eject union organizers forcibly. The remainder of the 1930s saw violent struggles between miners and gun thugs much like those at the beginning of the decade. But miner-preachers continued to be involved in the labor movement, playing important leadership roles and opening their churches to union meetings and relief workers. Holiness and independent Baptist preachers alike made it clear that the union might be understood as the worldly counterpart to the church, working to relieve the suffering caused by what were widely felt to be unfair labor practices.

For miners throughout eastern Kentucky, labor issues remained an important dimension of religious concern. With creative innovation they continued to navigate the terrain of power as material conditions affected both their ordinary and extraordinary realities. From the rural farm to the industrial coal town, *work* remained a fundamental human experience that linked self, society, and the world, and extended into spiritual issues. This lived dimension of religion in the eastern Kentucky coal fields has remained invisible for the most part in religious history, largely because recovering it requires looking for religion in unexpected places. Historians are habituated to look primarily to churches, doctrines, and organized worship to find religion, but it is not restricted to those venues. The greater part of religion's work takes place in people's everyday lives as they confront, embrace, and reject significance and meaning through their daily routines. Indeed, religion is itself a form of work, involving constant production and reproduction with old and new resources. In the coal fields, the work of mining brought miners face to face with the human limit experiences of death and suffering; it placed miners in relationships of social and material exchange that were fraught with destructive power; it produced anxieties and tensions within families. But it also held the potential to fulfill religious obligations to family and community and, if sometimes it was hard to see, to provide a better life in the future. All of these circumstances at various times required miners to reformulate their identities, their sense of value, their understanding of the relationship between the particular and the eternal, and the significance of work. And this they did primarily through religious idioms—indeed, they were religious problems—even when it meant that the meanings of those idioms might change dramatically or even falter.

Since the beginning of the coal industry in eastern Kentucky it has been impossible for miners not to take their material circumstances into account in one fashion or another when they think or act religiously. Materiality simply will not disappear, even into allegedly "otherworldly" religious escape. After all, as the miners have shown, power is something that has concrete and tactile effects when experienced from the depths of a coal mine or in an atmosphere of constantly falling dust, and those effects have existential and spiritual dimensions. In 1903, W. E. B. Du Bois wrote in his influential book *The Souls of Black Folk* of the "spiritual strivings" of African Americans.[2] Yet his contents do not tell a story of churches and worship, at least not in the main. Instead, they tell of slavery's social and material repercussions, of schools, of factories, of jobs, of the concept of progress, and of the conditions of houses. It is in these arenas that identity, self-value, notions of community and belonging, and relations of exchange are constructed and deconstructed, affirmed and denied. The reader is implicitly instructed to recognize that the *spiritual* strivings of black folk are simultaneously material strivings, and that the aspects of the existential and internal history of African Americans that might be most significant for recovering the religious dimensions of their experience might also easily be overlooked by someone who is not attuned to them. Eastern Kentucky's native white coal miners have a different history and a different set of concerns from African Americans (although the story of African American coal miners remains to be told in full detail, as does the story of relations between black and white miners in eastern Kentucky); but Du Bois's lesson applies to them as well. The spiritual strivings of this community have been expressed in churches and revival meetings, at funerals and family reunions—but also in union meetings, on picket lines, in company stores, on dust-covered porches, on baseball fields, in movie theaters, and deep beneath mountains in coal mines. Sometimes they have found formal expression, but most of the time they remain hidden in stories, gossip, songs, and gestures.

The process of industrialization turned out to be religiously productive. Indeed, for the economy of eastern Kentucky, and central Appalachia more generally, it may have been more productive religiously than economically. The murals that decorated the walls of John C. C. Mayo's Paintsville mansion at the dawn of industrial mining envisioned the power of coal to unleash the forces of social and economic progress, bringing banks, businesses, and cities to the mountains. For a short time, his vision appeared to be coming true. But by the middle of the twentieth century it became clear that most of the profits from industrial mining were flowing to companies and individuals outside of coal fields and were not being reinvested in the mountains. The coal industry transformed the mountain landscape, economy, and society, but not in the way that Mayo had imagined. Likewise, Mayo's murals depicted churches springing up in the wake of industrial mining; he was right, "progress" did produce religion, but not only or even primarily of the type that he foresaw. The religious landscape became more complex and diverse, not only because "railroad religions" entered the field creating more choices but also because religious innovations flourished in the midst of the social, cultural, and material changes that impacted the rhythms and patterns of everyday life through the everyday experiences of work.

In the dynamic activity of forging meaning and value in a changing world, religious idioms proved to be powerful resources for orienting and reorienting to the particular dilemmas experienced by those whose daily labor produced the coal that powered the nation's vision of progress. Holiness religion is a powerful case in point. By intensifying some of the practices and concerns traditional to mountain forms of Christianity such as the autonomy of churches, the felt experience of the Holy Spirit, and the power of the Spirit to overcome worldly limitations and ailments, Holiness resisted forms of religious practice (and their conceptions of power and humanity) that were associated with modernization while simultaneously speaking to the structures of feeling that emerged from the world of coal mining. Its premillennial orientation found religious significance in the breakdown of traditional social values, and its emphasis on bodily experience likewise offered an idiom through which to engage the hard and dangerous physical labor of mining. Holiness religion was especially well poised to address the relationship between mortality and immortality that miners daily confronted in their work lives. Using the limitations of the body to point beyond the material world to a more enduring and eternal dimension of life, Holiness resisted the perceived tendency of industrial capitalism to reduce human significance to economic concerns. Holiness, then, used the material and existential crises that were part of the structure of feeling of industrial coal mining to resist the notion that material circumstances were the final source of human value. It enabled miners to transcend the limitations of materiality while not negating the fact of materiality. For those who did not embrace Holiness, the issues that this religious orientation expressed were still central. The highly charged nature of the debates both for and against Holiness signal the extent to which Holiness touched a nerve, as well as the emergent nature of the ongoing work of figuring and refiguring relationships of power and meaning in the industrial setting.

For miners and their families, the National Miners' Union offered a surprisingly similar critique of the new world of industrial mining in more material terms. Many miners considered the economic and social issues that the union addressed as part of the same religious problem that Holiness and other mountain traditions were confronting. A major source of existential and religious crisis was, after all, the meaning and value of *work* in the industrial capitalist setting and how it structured value, community, purpose, and identity through the embodied activities and exchanges of everyday life. The history of the NMU revealed miners articulating their economic and social problems in religious terms, and resisting and protesting in the name of religious as well as economic power. When it became clear that the union's concerns did not ultimately coincide with the miners' religious crisis, miners abandoned the union—or, in some cases, reevaluated their religious views. In either case, it was clear that religious and material concerns were tightly interwoven. Religious idioms would be an important mode of articulating labor issues into the future.

An especially interesting indication of the cultural and religious significance of the development of industrial mining, one that deserves more sustained attention than this study permits, is the way that miners have incorporated the history of the development of the coal industry—from its inception to the present, including the experience of moving from farms to coal towns, the conditions of mining, and the changes that came with the labor movement—into a religiously inflected world-view. Talmadge Allen's reflections on his life of mining are an example. He looked back and saw the time of union organization as an inevitable response to conditions "getting worser and worser" until they hit rock bottom and "a change had to come." His narrative, shaped by the contours of the conversion experience testimony and premillennial eschatology, was echoed by many others. The figure of John L. Lewis, president of the United Mine Workers of America from 1920 to 1960, also acquired iconic, if not salvific, significance in coal miners' memories. He is often thanked right beside Jesus for redeeming the work of miners. "The average coal miner thought just about as much about John L. Lewis as they did the Lord," said one miner. "He was kind of head-and-shoulders above everybody else on this earth, salute of the coal miners. . . . I thought he was one of the greatest men that I ever knew."[3] Another recalled, "We have seen the time that we felt like John L. Lewis was our father, our mother, and sister, and brother, because if it hadn't have been for him, well, I guess somebody would a come on and maybe not, but at that time it was organized, we'd a never had it without John L. Lewis."[4] According to a third miner, Franklin D. Roosevelt should also be included in that company:

> I'm glad we don't live like we did then—don't even want to think about it. Thanks to the mercy of the Lord we overcame it. Thank the Lord he's made a way through . . . John L. Lewis, I believe, and Franklin D. Roosevelt was the man that freed the working man. He give John L. Lewis the right to organize the union. That people could have the union. And he freed the working man. John L. Lewis is dead and gone, and if it hadn't been for him, Franklin D. Roosevelt, and the Lord givin' him a mind what to do, there's many a person today that's livin' that woulda been under the ground. Because we've been worked to death.[5]

There is much left to explore regarding the religion of coal miners. Still, I hope that this study has begun clearing a path, setting a framework, and indicating some directions of analysis. The lack of available sources has made recovering the every-day lives of miners and their families difficult, but the use of songs, oral histories, folklore, and recorded testimonies has given some measure of access to their inner history. As I listened to the voices of miners recorded on cassette tapes and turned to transform these individual lives and stories into a more general picture, I was constantly haunted by the recognition that each person's story was different and highly personal, even if it shared elements and structures with others. There is a certain violence that scholarship perpetuates as it tries to find more general pat-terns among individual cases. It is therefore important to say that the patterns that I have found and written about here do not apply to all miners—like all patterns, they should rather be understood as open to contestation and negotiation.

The spiritual strivings of eastern Kentucky's coal miners are only one case among countless other stories of individuals and communities in America whose lives have been shaped materially and socially by physical labor. From farmworkers to sailors, from the experiences of slavery and migrant workers to the transforma-tions wrought by industrialization, and on into the "service" and "information" economies and the dynamics of globalization, issues of work have structured American lives. These stories have seldom found a place in American religious history, even though they make up a significant part of the whole cloth of the American experience. These stories are also important because they compel those who hear them to think differently about the forms, functions, and locations of religion. Experiences and structures of life that are born in labor and work inform and are informed by religious idioms no less than any other aspect of life. Human labor finds significance through and in tension with available religious discourses, and in turn religious idioms are transformed and find new resonances in response to experiences of labor. As enduring and essential categories of humanity and soci-ety, therefore, labor and work should be recognized as important sites of religious negotiation and expression. The history of religion in the United States of America will remain incomplete until the importance of work as a central religious concern is adequately taken into account.

Notes

Introduction

Talmadge Allen's words were recorded as part of the Appalachian Oral History Project (henceforth AOHP), tape ALC #1140A.

1. From a typed transcript of Billy Meeks's testimony before the Dreiser Committee, November 7, 1931. Scrapbook, box 6, item 2, Herndon J. Evans Collection, 1929–1982, 82M1, Special Collections and Digital Programs, University of Kentucky Libraries, Lexington.

2. A classic study of serpent handlers, Weston La Barre's *They Shall Take Up Serpents* (Minneapolis: University of Minnesota Press, 1962), is a case in point.

3. See Hannah Arendt, *The Human Condition,* 2nd ed. (Chicago: University of Chicago Press, 1998), 79–172.

4. There are exceptions to historians' neglect of work and labor in the study of religion in the United States. One has been the case of communal groups such as the Shakers and the Oneida Community. Groups such as these highlighted the relationship between religion and labor, focusing attention on the religious dimensions of work and labor as a fundamental concern in the development of a religious community. Although it is possible to approach communal societies as crystallizations of concerns present but unspoken or repressed in the wider society and culture that they belong to, historians of American religion have not tended to make this overwhelming problem of work and labor a central concern in their studies of religion in U.S. history more generally. There have also been a

small number of studies of religion and working-class history in which the focus is not on work per se but on religion in connection with issues of class or class consciousness. Some examples are Clark D. Halker, *For Democracy, Workers, and God: Labor Song-Poems and Labor Protest, 1865–95* (Urbana: University of Illinois Press, 1991); Paul E. Johnson, *A Shopkeeper's Millennium: Society and Revivals in Rochester, New York, 1815–1837* (New York: Hill and Wang, 1978); James Lazerow, *Religion and the Working Class in Antebellum America* (Washington, D.C.: Smithsonian Institution Press, 1995); Teresa Anne Murphy, *Ten Hours' Labor: Religion, Reform, and Gender in Early New England* (Ithaca, N.Y.: Cornell University Press, 1992); William R. Sutten, *Journeymen for Jesus: Evangelical Artisans Confront Capitalism in Jacksonian Baltimore* (University Park: Pennsylvania State University Press, 1998). These studies tend to cover the antebellum period.

5. In the context of American religious history, see, e.g., Jon Butler, "Historiographical Heresy: Catholicism as a Model for American Religious History," in *Belief in History: Innovative Approaches to European and American Religion,* ed. Thomas Kselman (Notre Dame, Ind.: University of Notre Dame Press, 1991), 286–309; Colleen McDannell, *Material Christianity: Religion and Popular Culture in America* (New Haven, Conn.: Yale University Press, 1995), especially the introduction; Robert Orsi, *Between Heaven and Earth: The Religious Worlds People Make and the Scholars Who Study Them* (Princeton, N.J.: Princeton University Press, 2005), 177–204. For discussions of the ways that religion has been conceptualized and constructed more generally, see Talal Asad, *Genealogies of Religion: Discipline and Reasons of Power in Christianity and Islam* (Baltimore: Johns Hopkins University Press, 1993); David Chidester, *Savage Systems: Colonialism and Comparative Religion in Southern Africa* (Charlottesville: University Press of Virginia, 1996); Russell T. McCutcheon, *Manufacturing Religion: The Discourse on Sui Generis Religion and the Politics of Nostalgia* (New York: Oxford University Press, 1997).

6. For collections of work indicative of this trend toward reexamining American religious history, see Jon Butler and Harry S. Stout, eds., *Religion in American History: A Reader* (Oxford: Oxford University Press, 1998); David G. Hackett, ed., *Religion and American Culture: A Reader* (New York: Routledge, 1995); David D. Hall, ed., *Lived Religion in America: Toward a History of Practice* (Princeton, N.J.: Princeton University Press, 1997); Robert A. Orsi, ed., *Gods of the City* (Bloomington: Indiana University Press, 1999); Thomas A. Tweed, ed., *Retelling U.S. Religious History* (Berkeley: University of California Press, 1997); Peter W. Williams, ed., *Perspectives on American Religion and Culture* (Malden, Mass.: Blackwell, 1999); Peter W. Williams, *Popular Religion in America: Symbolic Change and the Modernization Process in Historical Perspective* (Urbana: University of Illinois Press, 1989).

7. Robert Orsi, "Everyday Miracles: The Study of Lived Religion," in Hall, ed., *Lived Religion in America,* 7.

8. Geographer David Harvey has written powerfully and extensively on capitalism's inherent tendency to expand across space. See *The Condition of Postmodernity:*

An Enquiry into the Origins of Cultural Change (Oxford: Blackwell, 1990), and *The Urban Experience* (Baltimore: Johns Hopkins University Press, 1989).

9. Orsi, "Everyday Miracles," 10.

10. On the perpetual creativity of religious expression that results from cultural exchanges and contacts in the United States, see especially Catherine L. Albanese, "Exchanging Selves, Exchanging Souls: Contact, Combination, and American Religious History," in Tweed, ed., *Retelling U.S. Religious History,* 200–226.

11. Scholars disagree over the precise geographic boundaries that define the Appalachian cultural area. Most would agree that southern Appalachia, a common term popularly used to refer to the Appalachian cultural region, includes the state of West Virginia, the eastern parts of Kentucky, Tennessee, and northern Georgia, and the western sections of Virginia, North Carolina, South Carolina, and northern Alabama. However, the Appalachian Regional Commission (a federal-state partnership for economic development) extends its boundaries into southwestern New York to the north, Ohio in the west, and Mississippi in the southwest; their justification is one of cultural similarities that overrule geological formations. The name central Appalachia narrows the area to southern West Virginia, eastern Kentucky, eastern Tennessee, and western Virginia—the location of abundant deposits of coal. Throughout this book, I use the general name Appalachia to refer to central Appalachia in particular. Catherine L. Albanese's textbook survey of American religious history, *America: Religions and Religion,* 3rd ed. (Belmont, Calif.: Wadsworth, 1999), includes a chapter that uses central Appalachia as an example of "regional religion." It is the only such survey I am aware of that treats Appalachia in this manner. This chapter has been omitted in the book's fourth edition.

12. For studies of images of Appalachia in the popular and scholarly imagination, see Dwight B. Billings, Gurney Norman, and Katherine Ledford, eds., *Back Talk from Appalachia: Confronting Stereotypes* (Lexington: University Press of Kentucky, 2001); Henry D. Shapiro, *Appalachia on Our Mind: The Southern Mountains and Mountaineers in the American Consciousness, 1879–1920* (Chapel Hill: University of North Carolina Press, 1978); Cratis D. Williams, "The Southern Mountaineer in Fact and Fiction" (Ph.D. diss., New York University, 1961); and W. K. McNeil, ed., *Appalachian Images in Folk and Popular Culture* (Knoxville: University of Tennessee Press, 1995).

13. Deborah Vansau McCauley, *Appalachian Mountain Religion: A History* (Urbana: University of Illinois Press, 1995), 7.

14. Shapiro, *Appalachia on Our Mind,* xi.

15. See Benedict Anderson, *Imagined Communities: Reflections on the Origin and Spread of Nationalism* (London: Verso, 1983).

16. Allen W. Batteau, *The Invention of Appalachia* (Tucson: University of Arizona Press, 1990).

17. On the "local color movement" and its central role in the "discovery" of Appalachia, see Shapiro, *Appalachia on Our Mind,* 3–31.

18. George E. Vincent, "A Retarded Frontier," *American Journal of Sociology* 4 (July 1898): 1–20.

19. William Goodell Frost, "Our Contemporary Ancestors in the Southern Mountains," *Atlantic Monthly* 83 (March 1899): 311.

20. Olive Dame Campbell, "Flame of a New Future for the Highlands," *Southern Mountain Life and Work* 1 (April 1925): 11.

21. Ronald D. Eller, *Miners, Millhands, and Mountaineers: Industrialization of the Appalachian South, 1880–1930* (Knoxville: University of Tennessee Press, 1982), 43.

22. See, e.g., Thomas Ford, ed., *The Southern Appalachian Region: A Survey* (Lexington: University Press of Kentucky, 1967); Jack E. Weller, *Yesterday's People: Life in Contemporary Appalachia* (Lexington: University Press of Kentucky, 1965).

23. See, e.g., Helen Matthews Lewis, Sue Easterling Kobak, and Linda Johnson, "Family, Religion, and Colonialism in Central Appalachia, or Bury My Rifle at Big Stone Gap," in *Colonialism in Modern America: The Appalachian Case,* ed. Helen Matthews Lewis, Linda Johnson, and Donald Askins (Boone, N.C.: Appalachian Consortium Press, 1978), 114–39; John Gaventa, *Power and Powerlessness: Quiescence and Rebellion in an Appalachian Valley* (Urbana: University of Illinois Press, 1980); Dwight B. Billings, "Religion as Opposition: A Gramscian Analysis," *American Journal of Sociology* 96 (1990): 1–31; Liston Pope, *Millhands and Preachers: A Study of Gastonia* (New Haven, Conn.: Yale University Press, 1942), 262–63.

24. See, e.g., Roger D. Abrahams, *Everyday Life: A Poetics of Vernacular Practices* (Philadelphia: University of Pennsylvania Press, 2005); Pierre Bourdieu, *The Logic of Practice* (Stanford, Calif.: Stanford University Press, 1990); Michel de Certeau, *The Practice of Everyday Life* (Berkeley: University of California Press, 1984); John Comaroff and Jean Comaroff, *Ethnography and the Historical Imagination* (Boulder, Colo.: Westview Press, 1992); Ben Highmore, *Everyday Life and Cultural Theory: An Introduction* (New York: Routledge, 2002); Alf Luedtke, ed., *The History of Everyday Life: Reconstructing Historical Experiences and Ways of Life* (Princeton, N.J.: Princeton University Press, 1995).

25. Emile Durkheim, *The Elementary Forms of Religious Life* (New York: Free Press, 1995); Mircea Eliade, *The Sacred and the Profane: The Nature of Religion* (New York: Harcourt, Brace, 1959).

26. Robert Orsi enthusiastically makes this point in "Everyday Miracles."

27. The 1990s witnessed an explosion of scholarly interest in "the body," but the body of the 1990s was predominantly a discursive body, a socially constructed sign or text to be deconstructed or "read" by scholars. The senses—the "lived body"—did not receive as much notice, but what notice it did receive was highly suggestive and innovative. Work on the senses in social and cultural theory is exemplified by such works as Constance Classen, *Worlds of Sense: Exploring the Senses in History and across Cultures* (New York: Routledge, 1993); Thomas J. Csordas, ed., *Embodiment and Experi-*

ence: *The Existential Ground of Culture and Self* (Cambridge: Cambridge University Press, 1994); David Howes, ed., *The Varieties of Sensory Experience: A Sourcebook in the Anthropology of the Senses* (Toronto: University of Toronto Press, 1991); David Howes, ed., *Empire of the Senses: The Sensual Culture Reader* (New York: Berg, 2005); and C. Nadia Seremetakis, ed., *The Senses Still: Perception and Memory as Material Culture in Modernity* (Boulder, Colo.: Westview Press, 1994). For two excellent articles discussing approaches to the body in scholarship, see Terrence Turner, "Bodies and Anti-bodies: Flesh and Fetish in Contemporary Social Theory," in *Embodiment and Experience,* ed. Csordas, 27–47; and Paul Christopher Johnson, "Models of 'the Body' in the Ethnographic Field: Garífuna and Candomblé Case Studies," *Method and Theory in the Study of Religion* 14 (2002): 170–95.

28. Talmadge Allen, AOHP, ALC #1140A.

29. See Comaroff and Comaroff, *Ethnography,* 7–21.

30. See Barbara Allen and William Lynwood Montell, *From Memory to History: Using Oral Sources in Local Historical Research* (Nashville, Tenn.: American Association for State and Local History, 1981); Alessandro Portelli, *The Death of Luigi Trastulli and Other Stories: Form and Meaning in Oral History* (Albany: State University of New York Press, 1991).

31. The work of the historian of religion in everyday life is closely connected to what C. Wright Mills called "the sociological imagination." *Sociological Imagination* (New York: Oxford University Press, 1959). See also Comaroff and Comaroff, *Ethnography.*

32. In 1932 Congress passed the Norris-LaGuardia Act protecting union activities against attempts by management to quash them. Then, in 1933, President Franklin Delano Roosevelt initiated the National Industrial Recovery Act, which promoted the formation of labor unions. It was declared unconstitutional by the Supreme Court in 1935, but the National Labor Relations Act (also known as the Wagner Act), passed that same year, protected the rights of organized labor to engage in collective bargaining and to take part in strikes.

1. Appalachian Mountain Religion

1. Flannery O'Connor, *Mystery and Manners: Occasional Prose* (New York: Farrar, Straus and Giroux, 1972), x.

2. See Shaunna L. Scott, *Two Sides to Everything: The Cultural Construction of Class Consciousness in Harlan County, Kentucky* (New York: State University of New York Press, 1995) for a fascinating account of the planning and implementation of Harlan County's memorial. The current memorial, which I have described above, replaced one that Scott helped to implement. The original was more three-dimensional, shaped in the form of a broken cross that created a "ground-breaking ambivalence" (215). That ambivalence, and the ambivalent relation of the memorial to issues of class, conflict, history, and representation in Harlan County, led to the eventual replacement of the original

memorial (designed and implemented by the Jaycees) with the more simply monumental (less symbolically ambivalent) and elite-sponsored one that stands there today.

3. Historian Henry D. Shapiro maintains that Appalachia was "discovered"—or, perhaps more appropriately, "invented"—as a distinct region in a process of description and definition that developed between 1870 and 1890. See his *Appalachia on Our Mind*, xi–xv.

4. Vincent, "A Retarded Frontier." Although turn-of-the-century studies of Appalachia made the most use of the trope of isolation in their interpretations, isolation has still remained a powerful and prevalent way of defining and explaining what is seen as Appalachian distinctiveness.

5. See, e.g., James Lane Allen, "Through the Cumberland Gap on Horseback." *Harper's Magazine* 73 (June 1886): 50–66; Vincent, "A Retarded Frontier"; Frost, "Our Contemporary Ancestors," 311.

6. See John C. Campbell, *The Southern Highlander and His Homeland* (New York: Russell Sage Foundation, 1921), 22–30, and Elizabeth R. Hooker, *Religion in the Highlands: Native Churches and Missionary Enterprises in the Southern Appalachian Area* (New York: Home Missions Council, 1933), 25–33, as good examples of the foundation of this demographic history.

7. See Nathan Hatch, *The Democratization of American Christianity* (New Haven, Conn.: Yale University Press, 1989).

8. See Leigh Eric Schmidt, *Holy Fairs: Scottish Communions and American Revivals in the Early Modern Period* (Princeton, N.J.: Princeton University Press, 1989); Marilyn J. Westerkamp, *Triumph of the Laity: Scots-Irish Piety and the Great Awakening, 1625–1760* (New York: Oxford University Press, 1988). It is important to note that revivalism's roots went beyond Presbyterianism as well, finding sources in the First Great Awakening through Anglican George Whitefield and Congregationalist Jonathan Edwards. The history of revivalism in the United States, and in Appalachia, is complex, drawing from a variety of influences and cultural combinations.

9. Albanese, *America*, 332.

10. Campbell, *The Southern Highlander*, 168–69; Hooker, *Religion in the Highlands*, 41–42; McCauley, *Appalachian Mountain Religion*, 201–37.

11. Dickson D. Bruce Jr., *And They All Sang Hallelujah: Plain-Folk Camp-Meeting Religion, 1800–1845* (Knoxville: University of Tennessee Press, 1974), 37; Campbell, *The Southern Highlander*, 163–64.

12. My discussion of the history of the New Salem Association is based upon McCauley, *Appalachian Mountain Religion*, 90–100.

13. Classical Calvinism can be summarized by five main points that make up the acronym TULIP: "Total depravity" (human beings are sinners and cannot save themselves); "Unconditional Election" (the elect are chosen unconditionally, not on the basis of their own actions); "Limited atonement" (atonement is limited the elect, not

available to all people); "Irresistible grace" (the elect cannot resist God's grace); "Perseverance of the saints" (the elect cannot lose their salvation; they will persevere). Arminianism emphasized the role of free will in atonement, putting the burden of salvation on the individual's choice. Peter W. Williams, *America's Religions: From Their Origins to the Twenty-first Century* (Urbana: University of Illinois Press, 2002), 96.

14. McCauley, *Appalachian Mountain Religion,* 97.

15. Ibid. See also Howard Dorgan, *Giving Glory to God in Appalachia: Worship Practices of Six Baptist Subdenominations* (Knoxville: University of Tennessee Press, 1987), 28.

16. McCauley, *Appalachian Mountain Religion,* 97.

17. Ibid., 99.

18. Albanese, *America,* 345.

19. Allen, "Through the Cumberland Gap on Horseback"; Frost, "Our Contemporary Ancestors"; Will Wallace Harney, "A Strange Land and a Peculiar People, *Lippincott's Magazine* 12 (October 1873): 429–38. Other examples include Ellen Churchill Semple, "The Anglo-Saxons of the Kentucky Mountains: A Study in Anthropogeography," *Geographical Journal* 17 (June 1901): 588–623; James Watt Raine, *The Land of the Saddle-Bags: A Study of the Mountain People of Appalachia* (New York: Council of Women for Home Missions and Missionary Education Movement of the United States and Canada, 1924).

20. See, e.g., Bill J. Leonard, *Christianity in Appalachia: Profiles in Regional Pluralism* (Knoxville: University of Tennessee Press, 1999), xxii–xxix; McCauley, *Appalachian Mountain Religion,* 1–3; and Emma Bell Miles, *The Spirit of the Mountains* (1905; reprint, Knoxville: University of Tennessee Press, 1975), 138.

21. See Dorgan, *Giving Glory to God in Appalachia,* for an excellent descriptive study of the differences and similarities among some of these groups.

22. For a general discussion of forms of religion that exceed or exist outside of the boundaries of organized religious institutions in the American setting, see Albanese, *America,* esp. 324–48. See also Hall, *Lived Religion in America,* and David Chidester and Edward T. Linenthal, *American Sacred Space* (Bloomington: Indiana University Press, 1995). Peter W. Williams has produced a theoretical and historical study of popular or, as he terms it, "extra-ecclesiastical" religion, titled *Popular Religion in America: Symbolic Change and the Modernization Process in Historical Perspective.*

23. For an interesting study of the process of "folklorization," by which what has at one time been considered religion or science is reclassified as folklore or superstition when it is no longer widely practiced or believed by the dominant social powers, see Herbert Leventhal, *In the Shadow of the Enlightenment: Occultism and Renaissance Science in Eighteenth-Century America* (New York: New York University Press, 1976).

24. Verna Mae Slone, in *Our Appalachia: An Oral History,* ed. Laurel Shackelford and Bill Weinberg (Lexington: University Press of Kentucky, 1988), 75.

25. John C. Campbell noted the prevalence of Bible quoting in everyday life in his study but made little of it other than the fact that it was a peculiarity of mountain religious life. See Campbell, *The Southern Highlander*, 177.

26. Several such examples are collected in Eliot Wigginton, ed, *The Foxfire Book* (Garden City, N.Y.: Doubleday, Anchor Books, 1972), 346–68. For more examples of this and other healing, divining, and planting practices and beliefs, see Wayland D. Hand, ed., *Frank C. Brown Collection of North Carolina Folklore*, vols. 6 and 7 (Durham, N.C.: Duke University Press, 1964); Leonard Roberts, ed. *Old Greasybeard: Tales from the Cumberland Gap* (Detroit: Folklore Association, 1969); and Eliot Wigginton, ed. *Foxfire 2* (Garden City, N.Y.: Doubleday, Anchor Books, 1973).

27. See Anthony Cavender, *Folk Medicine in Southern Appalachia* (Chapel Hill: University of North Carolina Press, 2003), 126. Folklorist Richard Dorson wrote on bloodstopping traditions in Michigan in *Bloodstoppers and Bearwalkers: Folk Traditions of the Upper Peninsula* (Cambridge, Mass.: Harvard University Press, 1972).

28. Cavender, *Folk Medicine*, 97.

29. Wigginton, ed. *The Foxfire Book*, 225.

30. In his 1873 observations on life in the Kentucky mountains, Will Wallace Harney discussed the prevalence of the practice of planting by phases of the moon. He also noted the practice of water-witching or dowsing, which he called "unadulterated humbug." Harney, "A Strange Land and a Peculiar People," 3.

31. See Albanese, *America*, 330–31, 339–40. Albanese is perhaps the only historian of Appalachian religion who has paid attention to these beliefs and practices as part of the religious world that pervades the mountains outside of the context of organized worship.

32. Lynwood Montell, ed., *Monroe County Folklife* (Monroe County, Ky.: privately published, 1975), 90.

33. For an excellent study of the varieties of southern Appalachian healing and their systems of practice and belief, see Cavender, *Folk Medicine*.

34. See Shelly Romalis, *Pistol Packin' Mama: Aunt Molly Jackson and the Politics of Folksong* (Urbana: University of Illinois Press, 1999), 61.

35. Charles H. Faulkner and Carol K. Buckles, eds., *Glimpses of Southern Appalachian Folk Culture: Papers in Memory of Norbert F. Riedl* (Knoxville: Tennessee Anthropological Association, 1978), 2–3, 6–8; Charles H. Murphy, "A Collection of Birth Marking Beliefs from Eastern Kentucky," *Kentucky Folklore Record* 10 (1964): 36–38; Daniel Lindsey Thomas, *Kentucky Superstitions* (Princeton, N.J.: Princeton University Press, 1920), 9–10.

36. Samuel S. Hill, "The Virtue of Hope," in *Christianity in Appalachia*, ed. Leonard, 308.

37. Charles H. Lippy, "Popular Religiosity in Central Appalachia," in *Christianity in Appalachia*, ed. Leonard, 41–42

38. Haunted places were not unique to southern and central Appalachian culture, of course. Southern African Americans also talked of "haunts"—see, e.g., "I am Blessed but You are Damned," in Clifton H. Johnson, ed., *God Struck Me Dead: Voices of Ex-Slaves* (Cleveland, Ohio: Pilgrim Press, 1993), 15–18. The Appalachian form of "haints" shared similarities with "haunts" but was specific to the cultural context of the mountains. Appalachia was therefore different, but not totally different, from other culture groups in the United States.

39. See David D. Hall, *Worlds of Wonder, Days of Judgment: Popular Religious Belief in Early New England* (Cambridge, Mass.: Harvard University Press, 1989). Contrary to current popular images, strict Puritan theology was only one source of religious authority and knowledge—and even Puritan clergy looked to the stars for omens and worried about witches and ghosts. New Englanders learned about the visible and invisible worlds from books, tracts, folklore, hearsay, songs, travelers, observations of nature, and a host of other sources in addition to their own interpretations of the Bible and the pronouncements of clergy and theologians. Hall makes much of the high rate of literacy in colonial New England and the influence of popular literature like tracts and chapbooks on belief. In Appalachia, literacy was quite a bit lower, but oral tradition was an important source of knowledge and information.

40. Kathleen Stewart, *A Space on the Side of the Road: Cultural Poetics in an "Other" America* (Princeton, N.J.: Princeton University Press, 1996), 162.

2. Patterns of Life and Work

1. Mary Beth Pudup, "The Limits of Subsistence: Agriculture and Industry in Central Appalachia," *Agricultural History* 64 (1990): 83.

2. See the interview with Teamus Bartley, University of Kentucky Library, Social History and Cultural Change in the Elkhorn Coal Field Oral History Project, 1987–88 (henceforth ECFOHP), 87OH-191 App 114.

3. Pudup, "Limits of Subsistence," 68, 74–78.

4. See, e.g., Horace Kephart, *Our Southern Highlanders* (Knoxville: University of Tennessee Press, 1976).

5. Mary Beth Pudup, "The Boundaries of Class in Preindustrial Appalachia," *Journal of American Geography* 15, no. 2 (1989): 155–56.

6. See, e.g., Semple, "The Anglo-Saxons of the Kentucky Mountains," 597–98.

7. Robert S. Weise, *Grasping at Independence: Debt, Male Authority, and Mineral Rights in Appalachian Kentucky, 1850–1915* (Knoxville: University of Tennessee Press, 2001), 11, 56.

8. Mae Prater, AOHP, ALC #1092 AB.

9. James F. Collins, AOHP, ALC #160.

10. Verna Mae Slone, *What My Heart Wants to Tell* (Lexington: University Press of Kentucky, 1979), 60.

11. Ibid., 61–62.

12. Flora Rife, AOHP, ALC #388.

13. Worley Johnson, AOHP, ALC #157.

14. James F. Collins, AOHP, ALC #160.

15. Henry Glassie, *Passing the Time in Ballymenone* (Bloomington: Indiana University Press, 1982), 325.

16. Josephine Kidd, AOHP, ALC #413.

17. Jeff Todd Titon, *Powerhouse for God: Speech, Chant, and Song in an Appalachian Baptist Church* (Austin: University of Texas Press, 1988), 75.

18. Miles, *The Spirit of the Mountains,* 127.

19. Pudup, "Boundaries of Class," 152–55.

20. Shapiro surveys the image of Appalachia in late nineteenth-century local color writing in *Appalachia on Our Mind.* The region was also a privileged site for folklore and folksong collecting in the early twentieth century, a practice that often carried with it the assumption that premodern organic forms of community and culture that had become fragmented with the growth of industrialization had been retained in this out-of-the-way place. Thus the story of Appalachian economic and social transformations in the twentieth century could serve for some as an allegory of the destructive forces of modernity and industry. Ronald D. Eller, for instance, might be criticized for painting too romantic and egalitarian a picture of preindustrial mountain life for this reason in his *Miners.*

21. Weise, *Grasping at Independence,* 68.

22. Slone, *What My Heart Wants to Tell,* 41.

23. In this sense, what I am calling a pattern of life or the everyday religious orientation of the eastern Kentucky farm has a good deal in common with Clifford Geertz's definition of religion as a "model of" and a "model for" reality. Clifford Geertz, "Religion as a Cultural System," in his *Interpretation of Cultures* (New York: Basic Books, 1973), 87–125.

24. Shackelford and Weinberg, eds., *Our Appalachia,* 86. This reference is to the Seven Sleepers of Ephesus, a Christian legend.

25. Ibid., 66.

26. Miles, *The Spirit of the Mountains,* 101.

27. The records, even when they exist, of small churches in eastern Kentucky are of questionable value for determining actual participation in church life. Surveys and censuses often overlooked these churches because they did not belong to the more visible national denominations; moreover, many Appalachian churches were relatively invisible to those from outside the area. Finally, as the text suggests, the relationship between church membership (which might have been recorded at times) and church attendance (which was not) is highly problematic, considering the meaning of membership and the

social role of the church in mountain communities. See McCauley, *Appalachian Mountain Religion,* on the problems involved in recovering Appalachian religious history.

28. On the Old Regular Baptists as the main denomination in rural eastern Kentucky prior to industrial development, see W. T. Francis (AOHP, ALC #414), Henry Hall (ALC #183), Ben Noble (ALC #143), Sallie Sowards (ALC #214), Josie Tackett (ALC #276), and Everet Tharpe (#420A). In an address on the occasion of Perry County's centennial in 1921, Samuel M. Wilson noted that Old Regular Baptists erected the first churches in the county in the early nineteenth century, followed by Methodists who built a church in Hazard in 1892 ("Centennial Address," Hazard, Ky., July 4, 1921, located in the Perry County Historical Records, Special Collections, University of Kentucky). See also Howard Dorgan, *The Old Regular Baptists of Southern Appalachia: Brothers and Sisters in Hope* (Knoxville: University of Tennessee Press, 1989) and Dorgan, *Giving Glory to God in Appalachia.*

29. Worley Johnson, AOHP, ALC #157.

30. Miles, *The Spirit of the Mountains,* 131.

31. Historical minutes from the annual meetings of Old Regular Baptist associations show that reprimands for individual behavior were not uncommon.

32. For more on the tradition of declaring the church at peace, see Dorgan, *Old Regular Baptists.*

33. See McCauley, *Appalachian Mountain Religion,* 93.

34. See also Eller, *Miners,* 33–35.

35. The "fatalistic" bent of mountain character and mountain culture has been noted from the earliest histories to the present. Themes of fatalism and individualism are most evident in stereotypes of mountain people produced and disseminated in popular culture. For a study of such stereotypes, see Dwight B. Billings, Gurney Norman, and Katherine Ledford, eds., *Confronting Appalachian Stereotypes: Back Talk from an American Region* (Lexington: University Press of Kentucky, 1999). For a collection of primary sources from both the popular press and scholarly studies that have helped to produce and maintain such stereotypes, see McNeil, *Appalachian Images in Folk and Popular Culture.* For an inquiry into the origins of mountain stereotypes that locates them in growing differences between town and country, see David C. Hsiung, *Two Worlds in the Tennessee Mountains: Exploring the Origins of Appalachian Stereotypes* (Lexington: University Press of Kentucky, 1997).

36. Miles, *The Spirit of the Mountains,* 140–41.

37. See Dwight B. Billings and Kathleen M. Blee, *The Road to Poverty: The Making of Wealth and Hardship in Appalachia* (New York: Cambridge University Press, 2000), for an analysis of the effects of population growth on the farm economy in eastern Kentucky.

38. Eller discusses public work in *Miners,* 121–22. The term appears frequently in oral history accounts of eastern Kentucky.

39. Crandall A. Shifflett, *Coal Towns: Life, Work, and Culture in Company Towns of Southern Appalachia, 1880–1960* (Knoxville: University of Tennessee Press, 1991), 16, 23.

40. Worley Johnson, AOHP, ALC #157.

41. Henry McIntosh, AOHP, ALC #411. See also Eller, *Miners,* 21–22.

42. Josiah Henry Combs, "Sympathetic Magic in the Kentucky Mountains: Some Curious Folk-Survivals," *Journal of American Folklore* 27 (1914): 328–30; Elizabeth B. Cornett, "Down Our Way: Belief Tales of Knott and Perry Counties," *Kentucky Folklore Record* 2, no. 3 (1956): 71–72; J. Hampden Porter, "Notes on the Folk-Lore of the Mountain Whites of the Alleghenies," *Journal of American Folklore* 7 (1894): 105–17.

43. On witchcraft accusations in an earlier American setting of dramatic socio-economic change, see Paul Boyer and Stephen Nissenbaum, *Salem Possessed: The Social Origins of Witchcraft* (Cambridge, Mass.: Harvard University Press, 1974). The classic study of witchcraft from an anthropological perspective is E. E. Evans-Pritchard, *Witchcraft, Oracles, and Magic among the Azande* (Oxford: Clarendon Press, 1837). For an interesting look at the occurrence of witchcraft accusations in thoroughly "modern" settings of shifting patterns of power, authority, and exchange, see Peter Geschiere, ed., *The Modernity of Witchcraft: Politics and the Occult in Postcolonial Africa* (Charlottesville: University of Virginia Press, 1997).

44. Altina L. Waller, *Feud: Hatfields, McCoys, and Social Change in Appalachia, 1860–1900* (Chapel Hill: University of North Carolina Press, 1988). Anthropologist Michael Taussig has written an intriguing study in which the devil also plays an important role in religious articulations of socioeconomic change in a very different setting. His book *The Devil and Commodity Fetishism in South America* (Chapel Hill: University of North Carolina Press, 1980) explores the penetration of capitalism into South American indigenous communities. There, Catholicism and indigenous practices relating to spirits of place provided resources for engaging the new powers and patterns of exchange and transformation that accompanied capitalism.

45. Waller, *Feud,* 40.

46. Ibid., 50.

47. Ibid., 29.

48. See Johnson, *A Shopkeeper's Millennium;* George M. Thomas, *Revivalism and Culture Change: Christianity, Nation Building, and the Market in the Nineteenth-Century United States* (Chicago: University of Chicago Press, 1989).

49. Waller, *Feud,* 51.

50. Devil John Wright's son, William T. Wright, published a biography titled *Devil John Wright of the Cumberlands* (Pound, Va.: W. T. Wright, 1932). More recently, Devil John's grandson, Coleman C. Hatfield, also published a biography with Robert Y. Spence, *The Tale of the Devil: The Biography of Devil Anse Hatfield* (Champmanville, W.Va.: Woodland Press, 2003). Other information comes from Henry P. Scalf, *Four Men of the Cumberlands* (Prestonburg, Ky.: privately published, 1958). Wright's exploits were

fictionalized, drawing on some fact, some legend, and artistic imagination, in John Fox Jr., *The Trail of the Lonesome Pine* (New York: Charles Scribner's Sons, 1908).

51. The higher number comes from Devil John's son, W. T. "Chid" Wright, who was talking about how people exaggerated stories about his father. The younger Wright said that his father "did everything that was lawful and maybe was like Thomas Jefferson, he might have stretched the thing just a bit in a place or two." Shackelford and Weinberg, eds., *Our Appalachia,* 61.

52. Ibid., 62.

53. Waller, *Feud,* 237.

54. On early coal mining, see Willard Rouse Jillson, *The Coal Industry in Kentucky: An Historical Sketch* (Frankfort, Ky.: State Journal, 1922).

55. Much of my information in this section comes from Eller, *Miners;* Gaventa, *Power and Powerlessness;* and Shifflett, *Coal Towns.*

56. Eller, *Miners,* 47.

57. Ibid., 53–54.

58. Mary Beth Pudup explores these developments in "Social Class and Economic Development in Southeast Kentucky, 1820–1880," in *Appalachian Frontiers: Settlement, Society, and Development in the Preindustrial Era,* ed. Robert D. Mitchell (Lexington: University Press of Kentucky, 1991), 235–60.

59. James Vaughn, *Blue Moon over Kentucky: A Biography of Kentucky's Troubled Highlands* (Delaplaine, Ark.: Delapress, 1985), 44.

60. Unless otherwise noted, the biographical information on Mayo that follows is drawn from John E. Buckingham, "A Sketch of the Life of John C. C. Mayo," manuscript, Appalachian Collection, Special Collections, King Library, University of Kentucky.

61. Harry Caudill, *Theirs Be the Power: The Moguls of Eastern Kentucky* (Urbana: University of Illinois Press, 1983), 66. John C. C. Mayo Jr. mentioned this in an oral history interview. "The natives at that time were still pretty wary of greenbacks. Gold was the language they understood," he said. "She was the bearer of the goodies that seemed to turn the trick in a few places." AOHP, ALC #1095A.

62. Eller, *Miners,* 63.

63. Caudill, *Theirs Be the Power,* 69.

64. Henry Adams, *The Education of Henry Adams,* quoted in Robert Muccigrosso, *Celebrating the New World: Chicago's Columbian Exposition of 1893* (Chicago: Ivan R. Dee, 1993), 179.

65. See Shapiro, *Appalachia on Our Mind.*

66. *John C. C. Mayo College, Annual Catalog, 1921–22* (Louisa, Ky.: Big Sandy News, Job Department, 1921), 19. I discovered this quotation in Carolyn Clay Turner and Carolyn Hay Traum, *John C. C. Mayo: Cumberland Capitalist* (Pikeville, Ky.: Pikeville College Press, 1983), 79. The artist who painted these murals is noted only as "a Mr. McAffey," also uncertainly named in a newspaper article, "Building of Mayo

Manor Took Seven Full Years," *Daily Independent* (Ashland, Ky.), December 31, 1967. Caudill, *Theirs Be the Power,* 80, indicates that the murals were painted in Rome.

67. "Tribute from One Who Knew Mr. Mayo's Career Intimately," p. 13 of a typescript of an article that appeared in the *Ashland Independent,* n.d., box 93, folder 6, Anne and Harry M. Caudill Collection, 1854–1996, 91M2, Special Collections and Digital Programs, University of Kentucky Libraries, Lexington.

68. McCauley, *Appalachian Mountain Religion,* 238–40.

69. On Methodism's relationship to Appalachian mountain religion, see McCauley, *Appalachian Mountain Religion,* 238–53.

70. The "discovery" and "invention" of Appalachia by missionaries and local color writers is well documented by Shapiro in *Appalachia on Our Mind.*

71. Campbell, "Flame of a New Future for the Highlands," 11.

72. See Helen Matthews Lewis, Sue Easterling Kobak, and Linda Johnson, "Family, Religion, and Colonialism in Central Appalachia." The same authors explored the connection between Episcopalian missionaries and the coal industry in southwestern Virginia in "The Missionary Movement in the Southern Mountains: A Case Study of the Episcopal Church in Southwest Virginia," paper presented at the Society for Religion in Higher Education, Maryville, Tenn., 1974.

73. Gaventa, *Power and Powerlessness,* 61–68.

74. Vincent, "A Retarded Frontier."

75. See T. J. Jackson Lears, *No Place of Grace: Antimodernism and the Transformation of American Culture, 1880–1920* (New York: Pantheon, 1981), for an excellent analysis of antimodernism. On women settlement workers in Appalachia in particular in relation to antimodernism, see Nancy K. Forderhase, "Eve Returns to the Garden: Women Reformers in Appalachian Kentucky in the Early Twentieth Century," *Register of the Kentucky Historical Society* 85 (1987): 237–61. On the ideas and practices of missionaries and social reformers in southern Appalachia in general during this period, see David E. Whisnant, *All That Is Native and Fine: The Politics of Culture in an American Region* (Chapel Hill: University of North Carolina Press, 1983).

76. *Superstition* was modern observers' term for the beliefs and practices related to "irrational" understanding of causality. All forms of magic, use of charms, or scanning for signs and patterns that would influence action (such as portents or planting by the signs) fell under this classification. Folklorists have long argued that *superstition* is a pejorative term for folk beliefs and practices. For instance, Alexander H. Krappe wrote in 1930, "Superstition, in common parlance, designates the sum of beliefs and practices shared by other people in so far as they differ from our own. What we believe and practice ourselves is, of course, Religion." See Krappe, *The Science of Folklore* (1930; reprint, New York: W. W. Norton, 1964), 203. For a more recent discussion on this topic, see Patrick B. Mullen, "Belief and the American Folk," *Journal of American Folklore* 113 (2000): 119–43.

77. Folklorist Josiah Henry Combs, born in Hazard in 1886, provides a good example of this strategy of differentiation. In *The Kentucky Highlanders from a Native Mountaineer's Viewpoint* (Lexington: J. L. Richardson, 1913), written after he graduated from college and before he went on to earn his Ph.D. in Paris, Combs described Regular and Primitive Baptists as churches organized "to combat everything that seemed modern and progressive in the other denominations: to fight Sunday Schools, missionary movements, all sorts of church societies, and centralization in church circles. Many of them believe in infant damnation, and practically all of them believe in predestination." These denominations were destined to disappear, however, because they were "not in accord with the spirit of modern progress and enlightenment" (37–39).

78. See Edward E. Knipe and Helen M. Lewis, "The Impact of Coal Mining on the Traditional Mountain Subculture," in *The Not So Solid South: Anthropological Studies in a Regional Subculture,* ed. J. Kenneth Morland (Athens: University of Georgia Press, 1971), 33.

79. Hooker, *Religion in the Highlands,* 214.

80. The terms *town* and *camp* were used interchangeably, and they are synonymous for the purposes of this study.

3. Coal Town Life

1. Flora Rife, AOHP, ALC #388.

2. Eller, *Miners,* 197; Shifflett, *Coal Towns,* 23.

3. James Still, *River of Earth* (1940; reprint, Lexington: University Press of Kentucky, 1978), 51–52.

4. U.S. Department of Agriculture, Bureau of Agricultural Economics, *Economic and Social Problems and Conditions of the Southern Appalachians,* Miscellaneous Publication 205 (Washington, D.C.: Government Printing Office, 1935), 19–20, 86–87, 121–24 (cited in Eller, *Miners,* 155); U.S. Senate, *Report of the U.S. Coal Commission,* S. Doc. 195, 68th Cong., 2nd sess., 1925, table 14, p. 1467 (cited in Eller, *Miners,* 162).

Oral history interviews with miners and their family members are filled with tales of movement from coal town to coal town. It would appear that the average miner worked for several companies at several mines. Shifflett makes the point, too, that mobility was one way that miners retained some degree of agency and control over their conditions, although the limits of this sort of "control" are evident. Shifflett, *Coal Towns,* 11–17.

5. I use the terms *camp* and *town* more or less interchangeably in this book when referring in general to company-owned and developed residential areas. The term *camp* generally refers to such areas that are less developed, while *town* is used for more developed places. Miners often used the term *coal camp* regardless of the level of development.

6. William D. Forester, *Before We Forget: Harlan County—1920 through 1930, with Background Dating Further Back in Time* (Harlan, Ky.: privately published, 1983), 5.

7. Shifflett, *Coal Towns*, 48.

8. "The Little Towns within Jenkins," *Letcher Heritage News* 18 (2004): 23–29.

9. See, e.g., Jenkins Area Jaycees, *History of Jenkins, Kentucky* (Jenkins, Ky.: Jenkins Area Jaycees, 1973). See also Wanda Stewart, ed., *The Book of Lynch* (Lynch, Ky.: Mine Portal 31 Project, n.d.); Eller, *Miners*, 143–47.

10. Margaret Ripley Wolfe, "Putting Them in Their Places: Industrial Housing in Southern Appalachia, 1900–1930," *Appalachian Heritage* 7 (1979): 27–36.

11. On model towns and what one company called the policy of "contentment sociology," see Shifflett, *Coal Towns*, 54–58. Shifflett's study concentrated mainly on model towns because of the availability of records that are scant for most coal towns. Shifflett only mentions coal towns in Kentucky briefly, focusing more on those in Virginia and other states.

12. Mae Prater, AOHP, ALC #1092A.

13. Marvin Gullett, in *Our Appalachia*, ed. Shackelford and Weinberg, 218, 221.

14. Melvin Profitt, in *Our Appalachia*, ed. Shackelford and Weinberg, 207.

15. Shifflett, *Coal Towns*, 56–57.

16. Gabe Newsome, in *Our Appalachia*, ed. Shackelford and Weinberg, 266.

17. Autie Stiltner, ECFOHP 870H186 App 109; Simon Swiney, ECFOHP 880H87 App 133.

18. Ermine Hall, AOHP, ALC #30.

19. Autie Stiltner, ECFOHP 870H186 App 109. Stiltner was probably referring to the coal town of Millard, owned by the J. E. Polley Coal Company from 1921 through 1926. Millard was at the opposite end of the spectrum from model towns like Lynch and Jenkins, employing under 100 miners, according to James B. Goode's Internet Coal Camp Database (www.coaleducation.org/coalhistory/coaltowns/coal_towns.htm).

20. Shifflett, *Coal Towns*, 183.

21. Ibid., 176–78.

22. Frances Turner, in *Our Appalachia*, ed. Shackelford and Weinberg, 214.

23. Shifflett, *Coal Towns*, 164; Everett Hall, AOHP, ALC #7b.

24. On the importance and centrality of theaters, sometimes called opera houses, in Appalachian coal towns, see William Faricy Condee, *Coal and Culture: Opera Houses in Appalachia* (Athens: Ohio University Press, 2005). See also Gregory A. Waller, *Main Street Amusements: Movies and Commercial Entertainment in a Southern City, 1896–1930* (Washington, D.C.: Smithsonian Institution Press, 1995) for a study on the ways that movies shaped cultural changes in a different, non-Appalachian area of Kentucky.

25. Frances Turner, in *Our Appalachia*, ed. Shackelford and Weinberg, 212.

26. Paris Goble remembers listening to the Grand Ol' Opry on the radio in the 1920s. According to Goble, they were able to pick up only two to three stations. By the 1930s, the number of stations received in the coal fields was quickly growing. Paris Goble, ECFOHP 880H127 App109.

27. Listen, e.g., to the Holiness music of Ernest Phipps, a coal miner and Holiness preacher from Corbin, Kentucky, who recorded on the Victor label in 1927. He was only one among many central Appalachian residents, many of them coal miners or touched by the coal industry, who recorded albums on labels like Victor and Brunswick in Bristol, Tennessee, in the late 1920s.

28. Frances Turner, in *Our Appalachia*, ed. Shackelford and Weinberg, 216.

29. Interview with George McCoy in Jenkins Area Jaycees, *History of Jenkins*, G-3.

30. Interview with Mrs. G. C. Johnson, *History of Jenkins*, G-11.

31. Stephen Clark King, "Wheelwright, Kentucky: Community in Transition" manuscript in the University of Kentucky's Appalachian Collection, 1982, 21.

32. For more on the central Appalachian coal fields as a destination during the Great Migration, see Michael H. Burchett, "Promise and Prejudice: Wise County, Virginia, and the Great Migration, 1910–1920," *Journal of Negro History* 82 (1997): 312–27.

33. Doug Cantrell, "Immigrants and Community in Harlan County, 1910–1930," *Register of the Kentucky Historical Society* 86 (1988): 126. The countywide population in 1920 was 31,546.

34. Shifflett, *Coal Towns*, 68.

35. Frances Turner, in *Our Appalachia*, ed. Shackelford and Weinberg, 211.

36. Everett Hall, AOHP, ALC #7B.

37. In his study of West Virginia miners, *Life, Work, and Rebellion in the Coal Fields: The Southern West Virginia Miners, 1880–1922* (Urbana: University of Illinois Press, 1981), David Alan Corbin has argued that class was more important than race in coal towns. Forced to undergo the same experiences of exploitation, black and white miners found that their common identification in opposition to company authorities was more powerful than their racial differences. In eastern Kentucky the situation was complex. Black, white, and immigrant miners worked side by side in the mines and seem to have treated each other equally. Yet social segregation was strikingly apparent. Moreover, in some cases black miners were brought in by coal companies to work as strike breakers, thereby driving a racial wedge directly into class unity. I have not undertaken a full study of race and ethnicity in the social and power dynamics of eastern Kentucky's coal town life, but it is clear that such a study would add much to the social and cultural history of coal mining and American labor. A few good studies of black coal miners in Appalachia exist: Daniel Letwin, *The Challenge of Interracial Unionism: Alabama Coal Miners, 1878–1921* (Chapel Hill: University of North Carolina Press, 1998); Ronald L. Lewis, *Black Coal Miners in America: Race, Class, and Community Conflict, 1780–1980* (Lexington: University Press of Kentucky, 1987); Joe William Trotter, *Coal, Class, and Color: Blacks in Southern West Virginia, 1915–1932* (Urbana: University of Illinois Press, 1990); Phillip J. Obermiller and Thomas J. Wagner, *African American Miners and Migrants: The Eastern Kentucky Social Club* (Urbana: University of Illinois Press, 2004).

38. Nellie and Victor Gibson, ECOPH, 87OH195 App 118; Frank Stewart, EC-FOHP, 87OH198 App 121.

39. Marvin Gullett, in *Our Appalachia,* ed. Shackelford and Weinberg, 261.

40. Ibid., 262. Many miners recall African Americans being paid the same wages as white miners, but there were occasions when black prisoners were brought in to work in mines as strikebreakers or for less pay, and stories of these events fed stereotypes and anxieties.

41. Miner Tommy Hall discussed this term and a Jew store near Wheelwright or Weeksbury in the 1920s. AOHP, ALC #7a.

42. Marvin Gullett, in *Our Appalachia,* ed. Shackelford and Weinberg, 222.

43. Father Ambrose Reger, cited in Margaret Ripley Wolfe, "Aliens in Southern Appalachia: Catholics in the Coal Camps, 1900–1940," *Appalachian Heritage* 6 (1978): 48.

44. Frances Turner, in *Our Appalachia,* ed. Shackelford and Weinberg, 210–11, 215; Mae Prater, AOHP, ALC #1092AB.

45. Martha Clark, AOHP, ALC #37; Melvin Profitt, AOHP, ALC #1110.

46. Marvin Gullett, AOHP, ALC #1128

47. See Allen Batteau, "Mosbys and Broomsedge: The Semantics of Class in an Appalachian Kinship System," *American Ethnologist* 9 (1982): 445–66.

48. Mae Prater, AOHP, ALC #1092A.

49. Florence Ramey, ECFOHP 87OH190 App 113.

50. Marvin Gullett, in *Our Appalachia,* ed. Shackelford and Weinberg, 219–20.

51. Talmadge Allen, in *Our Appalachia,* ed. Shackelford and Weinberg, 237–8.

52. Louellen had such a program, as did Lynch and Jenkins. See Everett Davis, "Louellen Camp Was Created in 1919," *Harlan Enterprise,* February 28, 1985, 26 (special issue: Harlan's Heritage II).

53. Mae Prater, AOHP, ALC #1092AB

54. Marvin Gullett, AOHP, ALC #1128.

55. Flora Rife, AOHP, ALC#388a-b.

56. Talmadge Allen, in *Our Appalachia,* ed. Shackelford and Weinberg, 239.

57. Marvin Gullett, AOHP, ALC #1128.

58. Melvin Profitt, AOHP, ALC #1110.

59. Mae Prater, AOHP, ALC #1092AB.

60. Marvin Gullett, AOHP, ALC #1128.

61. Cited in Glenna Horne Graves, "In the Morning We Had Bulldog Gravy: Women in Coal Camps of the Appalachian South, 1890–1940" (Ph.D. diss., University of Kentucky, 1993), 110.

62. Talmadge Allen, AOHP, ALC #1140A.

63. Hooker, *Religion in the Highlands,* 100; Warren Wright, AOHP, ALC #1132.

64. Crandall A. Shifflett has remarked that it is not surprising that Baptist and Methodist churches were predominant in coal towns, because they were the main denomina-

tions in Appalachia. He failed to take into consideration the variety of Baptist churches in the mountains and their historical relationship to the Southern Baptist Convention associated churches that grew in number with the coal industry. He also neglected to account for denominational and subdenominational variations within Appalachian areas, treating southern Appalachia as one unit. See Shifflett, *Coal Towns,* 191–92.

65. Jenkins Area Jaycees, *History of Jenkins.*

66. Davis, "Louellen Camp."

67. Rose C. Feld, "What I Found in Lynch," *Success* 10 (1921): 118. In some cases, the company would retain title to the church and lease it to the congregations, thus maintaining control over its use and earning revenue. See Stewart, *The Book of Lynch,* 88; Thomas Keleman, "A History of Lynch, Kentucky, 1917–1930" (M.A. thesis, University of Kentucky, 1972), 41; Shifflett, *Coal Towns,* 193.

68. Keleman, "A History of Lynch," 44; Stewart, *The Book of Lynch,* 90.

69. *Tri-City* (Cumberland, Benham, Lynch) *News,* March 28, 1930, 1.

70. *Tri-City News,* May 17, 1929, 1.

71. This is not to say that scholars have adequately recovered the story of immigrant miners. They have only scratched the surface.

72. On Catholic and Orthodox churches in eastern Kentucky coal towns, see Cantrell, "Immigrants and Community," 130–32; Keleman, "A History of Lynch," 42–44; Wolfe, "Aliens in Southern Appalachia." Following World War I, the robust market for coal dropped rapidly. Although in other coal-producing areas the boom ended in the early 1920s, the Appalachian fields remained highly productive into the later years of the decade. By 1928 and 1929, however, the Appalachian fields were also forced to slow production, resulting in mine closures, layoffs, and work reduction. See Eller, *Miners,* 157–59. The sale of Lynch's Greek Orthodox Church to the Lynch Baptist Church is recorded in a front-page story in the *Tri-City News,* April 5, 1929.

73. The Diocese of Covington, Kentucky, covered eastern Kentucky at the time, but Margaret Ripley Wolfe has noted that Benedictines from St. Bernard's Abbey in Cullman, Alabama, were particularly important early on in tending to Catholic immigrants in eastern Kentucky and western Virginia coal towns. See Wolfe, "Aliens in Southern Appalachia."

74. Mary Jo Wolfe, "St. George Catholic Church," in *History of Jenkins,* E-1.

75. Shifflett, *Coal Towns,* 193; *History of Jenkins,* H-9.

76. Shifflett, *Coal Towns,* 192–93. The *Harlan Daily Enterprise* and the *Tri-City News* regularly included stories and announcements throughout the 1920s concerning area churches, including those in the larger coal towns. They illustrate that most of the pastors of Baptist and Methodist churches and visiting preachers had seminary educations and came from outside the central Appalachian area.

77. See, e.g., Ruth Huston, *Observations of God's Timing in the Kentucky Mountains* (Salisbury, N.C.: Rowan Printing Co., 1962); Nan Trantham Poe, *Beautiful upon*

the Mountains: The Story of a Kentucky Missionary (Kentucky Women's Missionary Union, n.d.), and stories related in the missionary periodical *Mountain Life and Work* throughout the years of industrialization.

78. E. V. Tadlock, "Coal Camps and Character," *Mountain Life and Work* 4 (1929): 21–22.

79. See Shifflett, *Coal Towns,* 195; Corbin, *Life, Work, and Rebellion;* Gaventa, *Power and Powerlessness;* McCauley, *Appalachian Mountain Religion,* 239; Lewis, Kobak, and Johnson, "Family, Religion and Colonialism in Central Appalachia."

80. Hooker, *Religion in the Highlands,* 100.

81. "Jenkins Is a Model Mining Town of Kentucky," *Lexington Herald,* January 9, 1928, n.p.

82. James F. Collins, AOHP, ALC #160.

83. *Tri-City News,* August 30, 1929, 2.

84. The *Tri-City News* and the *Harlan Daily Enterprise* regularly announced revivals throughout the area in the 1920s, most often taking place in the late summer and fall—traditional revival and homecoming season in the mountains.

85. Flora Rife, AOHP, ALC #388A-B.

86. *History of Jenkins,* H-7.

87. Graves, "In the Morning We Had Bulldog Gravy," 255. Holiness-Pentecostal practices will be discussed further in chapter 5.

88. Shifflett, *Coal Towns,* 196. Prater's interview from which Shifflett drew this excerpt is AOHP, ALC #1092AB

89. Tommy Hall, AOHP, ALC #7A.

90. See Sandra Lee Barney, *Authorized to Heal: Gender, Class, and the Transformation of Medicine in Appalachia, 1880–1930* (Chapel Hill: University of North Carolina Press, 2000), 67.

4. "It's About as Dangerous a Thing as Exists"

The variant of "The Hard Working Miner" that heads this chapter was sung by Mary Carr in Harlan County and recorded by Harvey Fuson, a Harlan County mine owner, local historian, poet, and folklore collector, sometime before August 21, 1931, the date that Fuson originally published his *Ballads of the Kentucky Highlands.* The text is reprinted in Archie Green, *Only A Miner: Studies in Recorded Coal-Mining Songs* (Urbana: University of Illinois Press, 1972), 88.

1. Monroe Quillen, in *Our Appalachia,* ed. Shackelford and Weinberg, 234.

2. Teamus Bartley, ECFOHP 87OH191 App 114.

3. Autie Stiltner, ECFOHP 87OH186 App 109.

4. Shifflett, *Coal Towns,* 85.

5. Autie Stiltner, ECFOHP 87OH186 App 109.

6. Teamus Bartley, ECFOHP 87OH191 App 114.

7. Monroe Quillen, in *Our Appalachia,* ed. Shackelford and Weinberg, 234.

8. Charlie Campbell, AOHP, ALC #798.

9. Melvin Profitt, AOHP, ALC #1110.

10. See Corbin, *Life, Work, and Rebellion,* 65; Valerie Gordon Hall, "Contrasting Female Identities: Women in Coal Mining Communities in Northumberland, England, 1900–1939," *Journal of Women's History* 13 (2001): 107–31; George Korson, *Coal Dust on the Fiddle* (Philadelphia: University of Pennsylvania Press, 1943), 201–11; June Nash, *We Eat the Mines and the Mines Eat Us: Dependency and Exploitation in Bolivian Tin Mines* (New York: Columbia University Press, 1993), 171.

11. Melvin Profitt, AOHP, ALC #1110.

12. Autie Stiltner, ECFOHP 87OH186 App 109.

13. Paris Goble, ECFOHP 88OH127 App 109.

14. Charlie Campbell, AOHP, ALC #798.

15. Green, *Only a Miner,* 312.

16. Charlie Campbell, AOHP, ALC #798.

17. Korson, *Coal Dust,* 216–29.

18. Charlie Campbell, AOHP, ALC #798.

19. Frank Fugate, AOHP, ALC #936. Fugate's words are transcribed from a tape-recorded interview. Ellipses do not indicate omitted words, but Fugate's own pauses and speech patterns.

20. Autie Stiltner, ECFOHP 87OH186 App 109.

21. Everett Davis, "Louellen Camp Was Created in 1919," *Harlan Enterprise,* February 28, 1985, 26 (special issue: Harlan's Heritage II).

22. Eller, *Miners,* 180–81.

23. Autie Stiltner, ECFOHP 87OH186 App 109.

24. Henry McIntosh, AOHP, ALC #411.

25. Simon Swiney, ECFOHP 88OH87 App 133.

26. James E. Childers, ECFOHP 87OH88 App 111.

27. Teamus Bartley, ECFOHP 87OH191 App 114.

28. Marvin Gullett, in *Our Appalachia,* ed. Shackelford and Weinberg, 221.

29. James E. Childers, ECFOHP 87OH88 App 111.

30. Charlie Campbell, AOHP, ALC #798.

31. Teamus Bartley, ECFOHP 87OH191 App 114.

32. Melvin Profitt, in *Our Appalachia,* ed. Shackelford and Weinberg, 203–204.

33. Marvin Gullett, in *Our Appalachia,* ed. Shackelford and Weinberg, 218.

34. "The Dream of the Miner's Child," originally published as "Don't Go Down in the Mine, Dad," by Robert Donnelly and Will Geddes (London: Lawrence Wright Music Company, 1910). The version transcribed here was recorded by Vernon Dalhart on Okeh 40498, in 1925. The text can be found in Green, *Only a Miner,* 121. *United Mine Workers' Journal* published a version with the title, "Don't Go Down in the Mine,

Dad," credited to J. R. Lincoln in its February 9, 1911, issue. Other versions were collected in Ethel Park Richardson, *American Mountain Songs* (New York: Greenberg, 1927), and James Taylor Adams, *Death in the Dark* (Big Laurel, Va.: Adams-Mullins Press, 1941). Additionally, folklorist Mary Elizabeth Barnicle deposited two field-recorded versions in the Library of Congress in 1938.

35. Adams, *Death in the Dark,* 120.

36. "Letters Written in Fraterville Mine," *Courier-News* (Clinton, Tenn.), n.d. [late May 1902], cited in Loyal Jones, *Faith and Meaning in the Southern Uplands* (Urbana: University of Illinois Press, 1999), 1–3.

37. From a report by the owner of the mine, cited in Shifflett, *Coal Towns,* 102.

38. Dennis Deitz, *The Layland Mine Explosion* (South Charleston, W.Va.: Mountain Memories Books, n.d.). This short publication tells the story of the explosion as told by Bill Derenge, the man who had the vision.

39. *Harlan Daily Enterprise,* September 17, 1943, 8.

40. Fred Brown, "An American Way of the Cross," Scripps Howard News Service, April 11, 1998.

41. Ben Noble, AOHP, ALC #143; James F. Collins, AOHP, ALC #160.

42. Ken Vanderpool, AOHP, ALC #598A.

43. Harry Moore, AOHP, ALC #834A.

44. Gabe Newsome, in *Our Appalachia,* ed. Shackelford and Weinberg, 267.

45. Ken Vanderpool, AOHP, ALC #598A.

46. Tom Hunter, AOHP, ALC #245.

47. Ben Foster, *On Dark and Bloody Ground: An Oral History of the UMWA in Central Appalachia, 1920–1935* (Charleston, W.Va.: Miner's Voice, 1973). The "bulletin" recorded how many tons of clean coal a miner had loaded out during his shift and thus how much pay he was owed. Because company stores often worked on a system that deducted purchases from a miner's pay, and they only accepted scrip, a miner could not make purchases without a record of how much money the company owed him.

48. Melvin Profitt, in *Our Appalachia,* ed. Shackelford and Weinberg, 207.

49. Talmadge Allen, AOHP, ALC #1140A.

50. A. M. Ludwig and R. L. Forrester, "The Condition of 'Nerves,'" *Journal of the Kentucky Medical Association* 79 (1981): 333, cited in Setha M. Low, "Embodied Metaphors: Nerves as Lived Experience," in *Embodiment and Experience,* ed. Csordas, 154. See also Jim Lantz, "Meaning, Nerves, and the Urban-Appalachian Family," *Journal of Religion and Health* 31 (1992): 129–39.

51. Low, "Embodied Metaphors," 155, 157.

52. Nancy Scheper-Hughes, *Death without Weeping: The Violence of Everyday Life in Brazil* (Berkeley: University of California Press, 1992), 167–215. Scheper-Hughes refers to the phenomenological work of Luc Boltanski, who argued that "somatic think-

ing and practice are commonly found among the working and popular classes that extract their basic subsistence from physical labor." See Luc Boltanski, *As Classes Sociais e o Corpo* (Rio de Janeiro: Graal, 1984).

53. Portelli, *The Death of Luigi Trastulli,* 195–215.

54. Raymond Williams, *Marxism and Literature* (Oxford: Oxford University Press, 1977), 130–32.

55. Frank Fugate, AOHP, ALC #936.

56. Talmadge Allen, AOHP, ALC#1140A.

57. Marvin Gullet, in *Our Appalachia,* ed. Shackelford and Weinberg, 220.

58. Frank Fugate, AOHP, ALC #936.

59. Miles, *The Spirit of the Mountains,* 140.

60. Talmadge Allen, AOHP, ALC #1140A.

61. Still, *River of Earth,* 51–52.

62. Aud Williamson, ECFOHP 88OH165 App 162.

63. See, e.g., the letters from the Fraterville Mine accident in Jones, *Faith and Meaning in the Southern Uplands.*

64. "On Jordan's Stormy Banks," lyrics by Samuel Stennett, 1787. Lyrics printed in the liner notes to *Songs of the Old Regular Baptists,* Smithsonian Folkways 40106.

65. Dock Boggs's musical career was cut short by the Depression and by tensions within himself and between him and his wife as they wrestled with concerns about the morality of making a living by playing music. Barry O'Connell, "Down a Lonesome Road: Dock Boggs' Life in Music," in the liner notes to *Dock Boggs: His Folkways Years, 1963–1968,* Smithsonian Folkways 40108.

66. "Oh, Death," transcribed from *Dock Boggs: His Folkways Years 1963–1968.*

67. Indeed, "Oh, Death" was sung at churches and revivals as an illustration of what might happen to a person at death if they were not guaranteed eternal life through salvation. According to one study, the lyrics were written by Lloyd Chandler, a Freewill Baptist preacher from North Carolina, based upon a vision he had in 1916 that he believed was sent by God. Chandler believed that he was called to use this vision to evangelize and win converts to Christ. See Carl Lindahl, "Thrills and Miracles: Legends of Lloyd Chandler," *Journal of Folklore Research* 42 (2004): 133–71. See also Barbara Chandler, "Why I Believe That Lloyd Chandler Wrote 'Conversation with Death,' Also Known as 'O Death,'" *Journal of Folklore Research* 42 (2004): 127–32.

5. Power in the Blood

1. McCauley, *Appalachian Mountain Religion,* 57.

2. Mountain Holiness-Pentecostal churches often use the term *Holy Ghost* rather than *Holy Spirit.* I use the two terms interchangeably in this chapter.

3. Hooker, *Religion in the Highlands,* 79–80.

4. Ibid., 79–82, John B. Holt noted this problem as well in "Holiness Religion:

Cultural Shock and Social Reorganization," *American Sociological Review* 5 (1940): 740–47. See also Campbell, *The Southern Highlander,* 172.

5. The main exception was the Church of God (Cleveland, Tenn.), which began as an independent Holiness church with mountain Baptist roots but developed into a denomination around 1906 and became the second largest Pentecostal denomination in the American South. But this was the exception that proved the rule, and independent Holiness churches in the mountains vastly outnumber those that are denominationally affiliated. For a history of how the Church of God (Cleveland, Tenn.) became a denomination, see Mickey Crews, *The Church of God: A Social History* (Knoxville: University of Tennessee Press, 1990). See also McCauley's very interesting survey of a number of different versions of the church's history, "How a Church Became a Denomination," *Appalachian Mountain Religion,* 276–310.

6. Deborah Vansau McCauley, "Mountain Holiness," in *Christianity in Appalachia,* ed. Leonard, 106; see also 256.

7. McCauley, *Appalachian Mountain Religion,* 265.

8. See Sydney E. Ahlstrom, *A Religious History of the American People* (New Haven, Conn.: Yale University Press, 1972), 324–27, 436–39. For a book-length study of the development of Methodism in the United States, see John H. Wigger, *Taking Heaven by Storm: Methodism and the Rise of Popular Christianity in America, 1770–1820* (New York: Oxford University Press, 1998). See also A. Gregory Schneider, *The Way of the Cross Leads Home: The Domestication of American Methodism* (Bloomington: Indiana University Press, 1993). E. P. Thompson's *The Making of the English Working Class* (New York: Vintage Books, 1963) remains the most impressive analysis of the relationship between Methodism and the development of the industrial working class. It is a history specific to England, but Thompson's insights about religion can be generalized to promote an important line of inquiry, begun in part by Max Weber, regarding social effects of religious ideas and practices. See especially 26–54 and 350–447.

9. Robert Mapes Anderson, *Vision of the Disinherited: The Making of American Pentecostalism* (Peabody, Mass.: Hendrickson, 1979), 29–32.

10. Ibid., 39–43; Williams, *America's Religions,* 273.

11. Anderson, *Vision of the Disinherited,* 31–33.

12. For an intriguing study of the early history of Pentecostalism, see Grant Wacker, *Heaven Below: Early Pentecostals and American Culture* (Cambridge, Mass.: Harvard University Press, 2001).

13. See Sheldon Annis, *God and Production in a Guatemalan Town* (Austin: University of Texas Press, 1987); Holt, "Holiness Religion"; Weston La Barre, *They Shall Take Up Serpents: Psychology of the Southern Snake-Handling Cult* (Minneapolis: University of Minnesota Press, 1962); Pope, *Millhands and Preachers;* Ellen Stekert, "The Snake-Handling Cult of Harlan County, Kentucky: Its Influence on Folk Tradition," *Southern Folklore Quarterly* 27 (1963): 316–22.

14. Anderson, *Vision of the Disinherited*, 226, 228, 229.

15. Anderson's study would have been more informative and less biased toward Pentecostalism as a compensatory movement if he had also looked into the factors that contributed to some people of Holiness, evangelical, revivalist, or "crudely superstitious" backgrounds choosing to *reject* Pentecostalism or even to embrace mainline denominations. Among natives of eastern Kentucky, this would have been a difficult and perhaps radical decision and would certainly have had something to do with the work of missionaries, educators, and the social forces of capitalism in turning people away from their "traditional" backgrounds toward "foreign" religious ideas and practices.

16. McCauley, *Appalachian Mountain Religion*, 265–67.

17. McCauley, "Mountain Holiness," 108.

18. David L. Kimbrough, *Taking Up Serpents: Snake Handlers of Eastern Kentucky* (Chapel Hill: University of North Carolina Press, 1995), 77. The Saylor family plays a central role in Kimbrough's recovery of the history of serpent-handling churches in eastern Kentucky.

19. Hooker, *Religion in the Highlands*, 79, 81.

20. Kimbrough, *Taking Up Serpents*, 80. See also Elaine Lawless, *Handmaidens of the Lord: Pentecostal Women Preachers and Traditional Religion* (Philadelphia: University of Pennsylvania Press, 1988), 29.

21. Alfred Carrier, *The Flight of the Dove: Roots of Pentecost in Eastern Kentucky* (privately printed, 1983), 192–223.

22. Kimbrough, *Taking Up Serpents*, 80–81. Kimbrough interviewed Lawson in the 1970s.

23. Carrier, *Flight of the Dove*, 170.

24. Ibid., 38–39.

25. Grant Wacker, "The Pentecostal Tradition," in *Caring and Curing: Health and Medicine in the Western Religious Traditions*, ed. Ronald L. Numbers and Darrel W. Admundsen (New York: Macmillan, 1986), 521.

26. Kimbrough, *Taking Up Serpents*, 197n1.

27. "God Still Healing," *Church of God Evangel*, November 1, 1930, 3. The *Evangel* was the primary publication of the Church of God (Cleveland, Tenn.), which eventually became one of the nation's largest and most successful Holiness-Pentecostal denominations. Its history is something of an anomaly among Appalachian mountain churches, as it did organize into a denomination and grow well beyond its mountain roots.

28. Quoted in Troy D. Abell, *Better Felt than Said: The Holiness-Pentecostal Experience in Southern Appalachia* (Waco, Tex.: Markham Press, 1982), 81–82. Abell's book contains many transcriptions of interviews in which Holiness believers speak for themselves at length. It is a valuable resource for accessing the personal stories and experiences of Holiness believers in their own words.

29. Ibid., 82–83.

30. Jonathan R. Baer, "Redeemed Bodies: The Functions of Divine Healing in Incipient Pentecostalism," *Church History* 70 (2001): 764–65. Grant Wacker has also commented on the sacramental aspects of Pentecostal healing: "The Holy Spirit occasionally flowed out beyond the tongue, transforming the whole body into a living sacrament. . . . Little realizing what they were doing, perhaps, believers effectively sacramentalized the divine power by locating it within their own bodies, within time and space" (Wacker, *Heaven Below*, 108). See also Wacker, "The Pentecostal Tradition," 532.

31. Jonathan Z. Smith, *Imagining Religion: From Babylon to Jonestown* (Chicago: University of Chicago Press, 1982), 89.

32. See Stewart, *A Space on the Side of the Road*, 4, 16–20, 179–83.

33. Williams, *Marxism and Literature*, 166.

34. Josh Armstrong, in Abell, *Better Felt than Said*, 57.

35. Jim Birckhead, "Reading 'Snake Handling': Critical Reflections," in *Anthropology of Religion: A Handbook*, ed. Stephen D. Glazier (Westport, Conn.: Greenwood Press, 1997), 32.

36. See Shaunna L. Scott, "'They Don't Have to Live by the Old Traditions': Saintly Men, Sinner Women, and an Appalachian Pentecostal Revival," *American Ethnologist* 21 (1994): 227–44, for an ethnographic description and analysis of a more recent (1986) attempt to bring serpent handling into a Pentecostal church in eastern Kentucky that did not traditionally handle snakes. Scott's analysis is interesting both for its focus on gender, class, and authority and for its example of serpent handling as a cultural and religious resource used experimentally as a tactic for reviving flagging church attendance.

37. Kimbrough, *Taking Up Serpents*, 50.

38. The story of Hensley's initial serpent handling experience is recounted in Mary Lee Daugherty, "Serpent Handlers: When the Sacrament Comes Alive," in *Christianity in Appalachia: Profiles in Regional Pluralism*, ed. Bill J. Leonard (Knoxville: University of Tennessee Press, 1999), 150. Kimbrough, in *Taking Up Serpents*, gives a more detailed description, 39–40. It is worth noting that there was a long tradition in Appalachian folklife concerning the power of rattlesnakes not only as poisonous creatures but as enchanters that could place people and animals under their spell. Verna Mae Slone, in an oral history statement published in *Our Appalachia*, Shackleford and Weinberg, eds., mentions rattlesnake folklore. She recalled that when she was a child, her job was to watch her siblings while her mother and the older children worked thinning corn. Verna Mae's job, specifically, was to keep snakes away. "Just to show you that there is responsibility there [one day] I looked up this hollow log and here was a rattlesnake coiled. Well, this is a thing I shall always remember because you do have folklore that a rattlesnake can harm you. Now birds, when a snake is around, they'll fly round and round and round the snake. I had seen a bird do that and eventually the bird simply flew into the mouth of the snake. I don't know what happened there, I was too young to analyze it. I'm not that afraid of snakes, I'd pick them up and stroke them down and back,

you know. To this day I don't mind picking up a snake, but I will choose what snake I'm going to pick up and *how* I'm going to pick it up. But this one, somehow it was different. It was huge and I called to my mother and said, 'Mama, here's a copperhead! No, it's a rattlesnake! No, it's a garter! No, it's a viper!' All the time I was running and I didn't veer that way, I didn't veer this way. And I never had my eyes off that snake's eyes, a little six-year-old. I didn't look around to call my Mother, I didn't look around for anything. My eyes and that snake's eyes were together all this time. I could get back just so far, then I stopped. Why did I stop? I don't know, but back I was pulled right up to the face of that snake. Back and forth and back and forth just like the bird. Mother would say, 'Go away!' I had no will to go away and I wasn't afraid, and so back and forth, back and forth I went. Then, of course, Mother got really worried, came over with a hoe and hauled the snake out. It was too big for Mother to kill. She had to hold it down with a hoe and my brother and I together killed the snake" (70–71). Belief in rattlesnake charming was not limited to Appalachia; Herbert Leventhal has described it in New England as well, and similar beliefs have been collected elsewhere in the United States. See Leventhal, *In the Shadow of the Enlightenment,* 137–67; Richard M. Hurst, "Snakelore Motifs in the Writings of J. Hector St. John de Crevecoeur and Other Colonial Writers," *New York Folklore* 9 (1983): 55–98; and Silas Claiborne Turnbo, typescript housed at the Springfield–Greene County Library, Springfield, Mo. It is also interesting to note that rattlesnakes, associated with the wild, the untamed hills, and uncontrolled nature, were taken up as a significant sacramental element just as industrial development was distancing people from a close connection with natural rhythms. Bringing the snake into the church might be understood as a reassertion of the powers of nature to the industrial setting that seemed to overwhelm and control natural forces.

39. Crews, *The Church of God,* 86–87.

40. According to George Hensley's granddaughter, La Creta Simmons, quoted in Kimbrough, *Taking Up Serpents,* 47.

41. In 1928 the church's General Assembly passed a resolution that officially ended its endorsement of the practice. See Crews, *The Church of God,* 87.

42. Kimbrough, *Taking Up Serpents,* 50–51.

43. Mary Lee Daugherty, "Serpent Handling as Sacrament," *Theology Today* 33 (1976): 232–43. See also Daugherty's article "Serpent Handlers: When the Sacrament Comes Alive."

44. Vernon Watson, quoted in Abell, *Better Felt than Said,* 118. For other examples, see Abell, 36–37, 53, 57, 61, and 147.

45. Wacker, *Heaven Below,* 122.

46. On the significance of Pentecostal women's hair, see Elaine Lawless, "'Your Hair Is Your Glory': Public and Private Symbology for Pentecostal Women," *New York Folklore* 12 (1986): 33–49.

47. Grant Wacker has described Pentecostalism as a dialectic of primitivism and

pragmatism. See "Searching for Eden with a Satellite Dish: Primitivism, Pragmatism, and the Pentecostal Character," in *Religion and American Culture: A Reader,* ed. David G. Hackett (New York: Routledge, 1996), 437–58.

48. Abell, *Better Felt than Said,* 86. John Burdick has reported a similar situation in Brazil, where Pentecostal churches, in rejecting worldly status competition and forbidding activities that are part of such competition, shield members from some of the social and material problems that can result from them. See John Burdick, *Looking for God in Brazil: The Progressive Catholic Church in Urban Brazil's Religious Arena* (Berkeley: University of California Press, 1993), 120–30.

49. Wacker, *Heaven Below,* 112.

50. Kimbrough, *Taking Up Serpents,* 51.

51. For more on Phipps, see Brandon H. Story, "Gospel According to Bristol: The Life, Music, and Ministry of Ernest Phipps" (M.A. thesis, East Tennessee State University, 2003).

52. Wacker, *Heaven Below,* 201; Carrier, *Flight of the Dove,* 84–85.

53. Hooker, *Religion in the Highlands,* 80.

54. McCauley, *Appalachian Mountain Religion,* 297.

55. Kimbrough, *Taking Up Serpents,* 51–52.

56. "Healed of Diphtheria," *Church of God Evangel,* August 27, 1927, 3.

57. See Barney, *Authorized to Heal.*

58. Abell, *Better Felt than Said,* 86.

59. Hooker, *Religion in the Highlands,* 81. There is evidence that damage like that described by Hooker's informant actually did occur. Reverend Alfred Carrier talked about a Holiness believer who would "get happy and stamp on the floor so hard that the flooring would break" (*Flight of the Dove,* 209).

60. Wacker, *Heaven Below,* 112.

61. Missionary and settlement school workers regularly included descriptions of the difficulties they had reaching and teaching Appalachian people because of the power of their "fatalistic" religious beliefs. See, e.g., Harold E. Dye, *The Prophet of Little Cane Creek* (Atlanta: Home Mission Board, Southern Baptist Convention, 1949); Samuel S. Greene III, "Progressives in the Kentucky Mountains: The Formative Years of the Pine Mountain Settlement School, 1913–1930" (Ph.D. diss., Ohio State University, 1982); Nan Trantham Poe, *Beautiful upon the Mountains;* Shapiro, *Appalachia on Our Mind.*

62. For an intriguing study of this problem, see Whisnant, *All That is Native and Fine.* See also McCauley, *Appalachian Mountain Religion,* 392–441.

63. *Mountain Life and Work,* the periodical of the Conference of Southern Mountain Workers, often published articles condemning industrial labor's injustices while suggesting that mountain religion and the ignorance of mountain preachers stood in the way of social and material progress. See, e.g., "A Program for the Mountains," *Mountain Life and Work* 1 (April 1925): 20–22; Warren H. Wilson, "What Are Our

Aims—Our Standards of Success?" *Mountain Life and Work* 2 (July 1926): 3–6; E. V. Tadlock, "A Mountain School in a New Mining Region," *Mountain Life and Work* 2 (July 1926): 32–33; W. L. Cooper, "Stuart Robinson School," *Mountain Life and Work* 2 (July 1926): 33–34; Charles D. Lewis, "The Changing Mountains," *Mountain Life and Work* 4 (July 1928): 14–20, 31; Eleanor Copenhaver, "Just Change or Progress?" *Mountain Life and Work* 4 (January 1929): 1–3, 29. This is just a short sampling.

64. See Karen E. Fields, "Charismatic Religion as Popular Protest: The Ordinary and Extraordinary in Social Movements," *Theory and Society* 11 (1982): 321–61, for an analysis of "speaking in tongues" as a "tactic of revolution" in northern Zambia in 1917–19. Fields argues that, placed in its very particular context, the seemingly "irrational" or simply symbolic charismatic religious expression was indeed instrumentally rational and was directed against specific agents and forms of change. For an excellent study of forms of resistance by dominated communities who often cannot protest power in direct and open ways, see James C. Scott, *Domination and the Arts of Resistance: Hidden Transcripts* (New Haven, Conn.: Yale University Press, 1990).

65. David Chidester, *Patterns of Transcendence: Religion, Death, and Dying* (Belmont, Calif.: Wadsworth, 1990), 3.

66. For example, A. J. Tomlinson, general overseer of the Church of God, Cleveland, Tenn., said that Satan controlled the "commercial system of the world" that promoted "different things that draw man away from God" (Tomlinson, "Line of Separation," *Church of God Evangel,* November 20, 1915, 2).

67. Pentecostalism and Fundamentalism, as well as movements such as New Thought and various millennialist groups, can be understood not only as "reaction against 'modernity'" (Anderson, *Vision of the Disinherited,* 223) but also as assertions of a different form of modernity that included conceptions of supernatural or extraordinary powers typically denied by the Enlightenment heritage. The competition between worldviews that denied the reality of the supernatural and those that affirmed it is a defining aspect of the development of secular modernity and one that deserves more study and articulation. See Talal Asad, *Formations of the Secular: Christianity, Islam, Modernity* (Palo Alto, Calif.: Stanford University Press, 2003).

68. Anderson, *Vision of the Disinherited,* 229, 235, 240.

69. Ibid., 211.

70. A. J. Tomlinson, "The Church of God and Its Relation to Other Organizations and Orders," *Church of God Evangel,* July 7, 1917, 1. My information on the Church of God and organized labor is drawn from Michael Szpak, "Removing the 'Mark of the Beast': The Church of God (Cleveland, Tenn.) and Organized Labor, 1908–1934," *Labor's Heritage* 6 (1994): 46–61.

71. Szpak, "Removing the 'Mark of the Beast,'" 52.

72. McCauley has noted that the "mountain churches of the Church of God" resembled independent mountain churches. *Appalachian Mountain Religion,* 307.

73. Liston Pope also found Holiness and Pentecostal preachers to be defenders of striking workers in the textile mills of Gastonia, N.C., in his study *Millhands and Preachers,* 276.

6. Suffering and Redemption

1. Scott, *Domination and the Arts of Resistance.* Scott defines "hidden transcripts" as the speeches, gestures, and practices through which subordinated peoples express their relation to, and opposition to, power. They are "hidden" because they take place outside of the gaze of superiors, or they are coded expressions that have a subversive message that those in power do not fully understand, or they are indirect. Hidden transcripts typically do not confront power directly but are important "everyday forms of resistance" nevertheless that allow subordinated groups to survive without succumbing wholly to their superiors (see 17–23). See also James C. Scott, *Weapons of the Weak: Everyday Forms of Peasant Resistance* (New Haven, Conn.: Yale University Press, 1985), 28–47.

2. Shackelford and Weinberg, eds., *Our Appalachia,* 222.

3. John W. Hevener, *Which Side Are You On? The Harlan County Coal Miners, 1931–1939* (Urbana: University of Illinois Press, 1978), 7.

4. Senate Committee on Manufactures, *Conditions in the Coal Fields in Harlan and Bell Counties, Kentucky: Hearings before a Subcommittee of the Committee on Manufactures,* S.R. 178, 72nd Cong., 1st sess., 1932, 88.

5. For an example of a study that interpreted the failure of organized labor as apathy, see Paul F. Taylor, *Bloody Harlan: The United Mine Workers of America in Harlan County, Kentucky, 1931–1941* (Lanham, Md.: University Press of America, 1990), 12.

6. Talmadge Allen, AOHP, ALC #1140AB.

7. Hevener, *Which Side Are You On?* 33–34.

8. Jim Garland, *Welcome the Traveler Home: Jim Garland's Story of the Kentucky Mountains,* ed. Julia S. Ardery (Lexington: University Press of Kentucky, 1983), 136.

9. Hevener, *Which Side Are You On?* 37–38; Senate Committee on Manufactures, *Conditions in the Coal Fields,* 182; testimony of Melvin P. Levy, ibid., 30.

10. Garland, *Welcome the Traveler Home,* 145.

11. Melvin P. Levy, "Class War in Kentucky," in Theodore Dreiser et al., *Harlan Miners Speak: Report on Terrorism in the Kentucky Coal Fields,* prepared by members of the National Committee for the Defense of Political Prisoners (New York: Harcourt, Brace, 1932), 35n1.

12. Hevener, *Which Side Are You On?* 39.

13. Ibid., 44–45, 48, 50.

14. Theodore Draper, "Communists and Miners, 1928–1933," *Dissent* 19 (1972): 381.

15. See ibid.; Dreiser, *Harlan Miners Speak;* and *Harlan & Bell Kentucky, 1931–2: The National Miner's Union* (Huntington, W.Va.: Appalachian Movement Press, 1972).

16. Garland, *Welcome the Traveler Home,* 152.

17. Gaventa, *Power and Powerlessness,* 113.

18. Senate Committee on Manufactures, *Conditions in the Coal Fields,* 101.

19. Garland, *Welcome the Traveler Home,* 146.

20. *Cincinnati Enquirer,* April 12, 1932, reprinted in Senate Committee on Manufactures, *Conditions in the Coal Fields,* 177.

21. Senate Committee on Manufactures, *Conditions in the Coal Fields,* 107.

22. Dreiser, *Harlan Miners Speak,* 292.

23. Garland, *Welcome the Traveler Home,* 147.

24. Mae Prater, AOHP, ALC #1092AB.

25. Dreiser, *Harlan Miners Speak,* 292.

26. "Aunt Molly Jackson's Kentucky Miners' Wives (Ragged Hungry Blues)," as transcribed in Dreiser, *Harlan Miners Speak,* v–vii. I have selected only six of twelve verses to conserve space.

27. Quoted in Romalis, *Pistol Packin' Mama,* 85.

28. Garland, *Welcome the Traveler Home,* 33.

29. Romalis, *Pistol Packin' Mama,* 23.

30. Garland, *Welcome the Traveler Home,* 41.

31. Romalis, *Pistol Packin' Mama,* 61.

32. Sarah Ogan Gunning, "I Hate the Company Bosses," recorded on Gunning, *Girl of Constant Sorrow,* Folk Legacy Records, FSA-26. Lyrics are transcribed in the liner notes, with comments by Archie Green. Gunning first called this song "I Hate the Capitalist System" but later changed the title and the first line to the slightly less radical "I Hate the Company Bosses." She then changed the name back because, she said, it was not the people she hated but the system. See Alessandro Portelli, review of Shelly Romalis, *Pistol Packin' Mama,* in the *Journal of American History* 87 (2000): 717.

33. Archie Green, liner notes to Gunning, *Girl of Constant Sorrow.*

34. Both Niebuhr and William B. Spofford testified before the Senate about their reception in eastern Kentucky. According to Niebuhr, the district attorney in Bell County "said he had appointed a committee of preachers who would like to talk with us, and this committee of preachers, it turned out, were kindly but had been more or less given the task of putting us through an inquisition on our theological views, and we turned out to be horrible modernists, which, from their point of view, seemed to be something very close to communism." Senate Committee on Manufactures, *Conditions in the Coal Fields,* 85.

35. *Harlan Daily Enterprise,* November 20, 1931.

36. Testimony of Flora Shackelford in Dreiser, *Harlan Miners Speak,* 206–7.

37. Garland, *Welcome the Traveler Home,* 139.

38. All quotations from Billie Meeks are from a typed transcript of his testimony before the Dreiser Committee, November 7, 1931, scrapbook, box 6, item 2, Herndon J.

Evans Collection, 1929–82, 82M1, Special Collections and Digital Programs, University of Kentucky Libraries, Lexington.

39. For an interesting discussion about the contested symbol of blood and American identity in the conflict surrounding the National Miners' Union, see Portelli, *The Death of Luigi Trastulli*, 222–25.

40. Dreiser, *Harlan Miners Speak*, 14.

41. All quotations from Finley Donaldson are from a typed transcript of his testimony before the Dreiser Committee, November 7, 1931, Evans Collection.

42. James 5:1–4. I have cited the King James Version, as that is likely the version that Jackson used.

43. Garland, *Welcome the Traveler Home*, 41.

44. Aunt Molly Jackson, typed transcript of testimony before the Dreiser Committee, November 7, 1931, Evans Collection.

45. Garland, *Welcome the Traveler Home*, 80, 152, 153.

46. Kathleen Stewart, "On the Politics of Cultural Theory: A Case for 'Contaminated' Cultural Critique," *Social Research* 58 (1991): 404.

47. *Harlan Daily Enterprise,* July 21, 1931.

48. *Harlan Daily Enterprise,* unknown date (1931–32); cited in Malcolm Ross, *Machine Age in the Hills* (New York: Macmillan, 1933), 168–69.

49. "Miners Expose Reds," Evans Collection.

50. Homer Lawrence Morris, *The Plight of the Bituminous Coal Miner* (Philadelphia: University of Pennsylvania Press, 1934), 118.

51. *Middlesboro Daily News,* February 17, 1932, cited in Gaventa, *Power and Powerlessness,* 116.

52. Garland, *Welcome the Traveler Home,* 158.

53. Portelli, *The Death of Luigi Trastulli,* 219.

54. Billings, "Religion as Opposition: A Gramscian Analysis," 27.

Conclusion

1. Hevener, *Which Side Are You On?* 95.

2. W. E. B. Du Bois, *The Souls of Black Folks* (Chicago: A. C. McClurg, 1903).

3. AOHP, ALC #798. It is also important to note that the National Miners' Union has been lost to local memory or at least has not actively been remembered. In the eyes of labor historians, the union was an important part of the coal field story. In the life of the area, it was not. Alessandro Portelli and Shaunna Scott interpret this as the intentional forgetting of an embarrassing moment (Portelli, *The Death of Luigi Trastulli,* 195–215; Scott, *Two Sides to Everything*). I would add that the NMU never gained a sustained presence in eastern Kentucky. The UMWA did. The history of unionization is therefore a history of the growth of the UMWA. The NMU was a blip in a very localized place, part of a larger story under which it becomes submerged, subordinated, and ulti-

mately erased as it is absorbed into the general upheaval of the growth of the UMWA. In local memory the events of the NMU were added to the heap of ruins and errors that preceded the transformation signaled by the coming of John L. Lewis and the UMWA.

4. William Clark, AOHP, ALC #37.

5. Harry Moore, AOHP, ALC #834A.

Bibliography

Manuscript and Tape Collections

Anne and Harry M. Caudill Collection, 1854–1996, 91M2, Special Collections and Digital Programs, University of Kentucky Libraries, Lexington.

Appalachian Oral History Project (AOHP), Alice Lloyd College, Pippa Passes, Ky.

Herndon J. Evans Collection, 1929–82, 82M1, Special Collections and Digital Programs, University of Kentucky Libraries, Lexington.

Perry County Historical Records, Special Collections, King Library, University of Kentucky.

Silas Claiborne Turnbo. Typescript. Springfield–Greene County Library, Springfield, Mo.

University of Kentucky Library, Social History and Cultural Change in the Elkhorn Coal Field Oral History Project (ECFOHP), 1987–88, Special Collections and Digital Programs, University of Kentucky Libraries, Lexington.

Government Publications

U.S. Department of Agriculture. Bureau of Agricultural Economics. *Economic and Social Problems and Conditions of the Southern Appalachians.* Miscellaneous Publication 205. Washington, D.C.: Government Printing Office, 1935.

U.S. Senate. *Report of the U.S. Coal Commission.* S. Doc. 195, 68th Cong., 2nd sess., 1925.

————. Committee on Manufactures. *Conditions in the Coal Fields in Harlan and Bell Counties, Kentucky: Hearings before a Subcommittee of the Committee on Manufactures.* S.R. 178. 72nd Cong., 1st sess., 1932.

Newspaper Articles

"A Foreign Monster." *Harlan Daily Enterprise,* July 21, 1931, 2.

Brown, Fred. "An American Way of the Cross." Scripps Howard News Service, April 11, 1998.

"Building of Mayo Manor Took Seven Full Years." *Daily Independent* (Ashland, Ky.), December 31, 1967.

Davis, Everett. "Louellen Camp Was Created in 1919." *Harlan Enterprise,* February 28, 1985, 26.

"God Still Healing." *Church of God Evangel,* November 1, 1930, 3.

"Healed of Diphtheria." *Church of God Evangel,* August 27, 1927, 3.

"Jenkins Is a Model Mining Town of Kentucky." *Lexington Herald,* January 9, 1928.

"Letters Written in Fraterville Mine." *Courier-News* (Clinton, Tenn.), May 1902.

"Witnesses Tell of Evarts Clash." *Harlan Daily Enterprise,* November 29, 1931, 1–2.

Music

"I Hate the Company Bosses." From *Sarah Ogan Gunning, Girl of Constant Sorrow.* Compact Disk 26. Folk Legacy Records, 2006.

"Oh Death." From *Dock Boggs: His Folkways Years, 1963–1968.* Compact Disk 40108. Smithsonian Folkways, 1998.

"On Jordan's Stormy Banks." Words by Samuel Stennett (c. 1787). From *Songs of the Old Regular Baptists.* Compact Disk 40106. Smithsonian Folkways, 1997.

"There Is Power in the Blood." Words and music by Lewis E. Jones, 1899.

Books and Articles

Abell, Troy D. *Better Felt than Said: The Holiness-Pentecostal Experience in Southern Appalachia.* Waco, Tex.: Markham Press, 1982.

Abrahams, Roger D. *Everyday Life: A Poetics of Vernacular Practices.* Philadelphia: University of Pennsylvania Press, 2005.

Adams, Henry. *The Education of Henry Adams.* New York: Vintage Books, 1990.

Adams, James Taylor. *Death in the Dark.* Big Laurel, Va.: Adams-Mullins Press, 1941.

Ahlstrom, Sydney E. *A Religious History of the American People.* New Haven, Conn.: Yale University Press, 1972.

Albanese, Catherine L. "Exchanging Selves, Exchanging Souls: Contact, Combination, and American Religious History." In *Retelling U.S. Religious History,* ed. Thomas A. Tweed, 200–226. Berkeley: University of California Press, 1997.

———. *America: Religions and Religion.* 3rd ed. Belmont, Calif.: Wadsworth, 1999.

Allen, Barbara, and William Lynwood Montell. *From Memory to History: Using Oral Sources in Local Historical Research.* Nashville, Tenn.: American Association for State and Local History, 1981.

Allen, James Lane. "Through the Cumberland Gap on Horseback." *Harper's Magazine* 73 (June 1886): 50–66.

Anderson, Benedict. *Imagined Communities: Reflections on the Origin and Spread of Nationalism.* London: Verso, 1983.

Anderson, Robert M. *Vision of the Disinherited: The Making of American Pentecostalism.* Peabody, Mass.: Hendrickson, 1979.

Anderson, Sherwood. "I Want to Be Counted." In Dreiser et al., *Harlan Miners Speak,* 307. New York: Harcourt, Brace, 1932.

Annis, Sheldon. *God and Production in a Guatemalan Town.* Austin: University of Texas Press, 1987.

Arendt, Hannah. *The Human Condition.* 2nd ed. Chicago: University of Chicago Press, 1998.

Asad, Talal. *Genealogies of Religion: Discipline and Reasons of Power in Christianity and Islam.* Baltimore: Johns Hopkins University Press, 1993.

———. *Formations of the Secular: Christianity, Islam, Modernity.* Palo Alto, Calif.: Stanford University Press, 2003.

Baer, Jonathan R. "Redeemed Bodies: The Functions of Divine Healing in Incipient Pentecostalism." *Church History* 70 (2001): 735–71.

Barney, Sandra Lee. *Authorized to Heal: Gender, Class, and the Transformation of Medicine in Appalachia, 1880–1930.* Chapel Hill: University of North Carolina Press, 2000.

Barrus, Ben M. "Factors Involved in the Origin of the Cumberland Presbyterian Church." *Journal of Presbyterian History* 45 (1967): 273–89.

———. "The Cumberland Presbyterian Church." *Journal of Presbyterian History* 46 (1968): 58–73.

Batteau, Allen W. "Mosbys and Broomsedge: The Semantics of Class in an Appalachian Kinship System." *American Ethnologist* 9 (1982): 445–66.

———. *The Invention of Appalachia.* Tucson: University of Arizona Press, 1990.

Billings, Dwight B. "Religion as Opposition: A Gramscian Analysis." *American Journal of Sociology* 96 (1990): 1–31.

Billings, Dwight B., and Kathleen M. Blee. *The Road to Poverty: The Making of Wealth and Hardship in Appalachia.* Cambridge: Cambridge University Press, 2000.

Billings, Dwight B., Gurney Norman, and Katherine Ledford, eds. *Back Talk from Appalachia : Confronting Stereotypes.* Lexington: University Press of Kentucky, 2001.

Birckhead, Jim. "Reading 'Snake Handling': Critical Reflections." In *Anthropology of Religion: A Handbook,* ed. Stephen D. Glazier, 19–84. Westport, Conn.: Greenwood Press, 1997.

Boltanski, Luc. *As Classes Sociais e o Corpo.* Rio de Janeiro: Graal, 1984.

Bourdieu, Pierre. *The Logic of Practice.* Stanford, Calif.: Stanford University Press, 1990.

Boyer, Paul, and Stephen Nissenbaum. *Salem Possessed: The Social Origins of Witchcraft.* Cambridge, Mass.: Harvard University Press, 1974.

Bruce, Dickson D., Jr. *And They All Sang Hallelujah: Plain-Folk Camp-Meeting Religion, 1800–1845.* Knoxville: University of Tennessee Press, 1974.

Buckingham, John E. "A Sketch of the Life of John C. C. Mayo." Manuscript, Appalachian Collection, Special Collections, King Library, University of Kentucky.

Burchett, Michael H. "Promise and Prejudice: Wise County, Virginia, and the Great Migration, 1910–1920." *Journal of Negro History* 82 (1997): 312–27.

Burdick, John. *Looking for God in Brazil: The Progressive Catholic Church in Urban Brazil's Religious Arena.* Berkeley: University of California Press, 1993.

Burton, Thomas. *Serpent-Handling Believers.* Knoxville: University of Tennessee Press, 1993.

Butler, Jon. "Historiographical Heresy: Catholicism as a Model for American Religious History." In *Belief in History: Innovative Approaches to European and American Religion,* ed. Thomas Kselman, 286–309. Notre Dame, Ind.: University of Notre Dame Press, 1991.

Butler, Jon, and Harry S. Stout, eds. *Religion in American History: A Reader.* Oxford: Oxford University Press, 1998.

Campbell, Alexander. *The Christian Baptist.* 2nd ed. Cincinnati: D. S. Burnet, 1835; reprint, Joplin, Mo.: College Press, 1983.

Campbell, John C. *The Southern Highlander and His Homeland.* New York: Russell Sage Foundation, 1921.

Campbell, Olive Dame. "Flame of a New Future for the Highlands." *Southern Mountain Life and Work* 1 (April 1925): 9–13.

Cantrell, Doug. "Immigrants and Community in Harlan County, 1910–1930." *Register of the Kentucky Historical Society* 86 (1988): 119–41.

Carrier, Alfred. *The Flight of the Dove: Roots of Pentecost in Eastern Kentucky.* Privately printed, 1983.

Caudill, Harry M. *Night Comes to the Cumberlands.* Boston: Little, Brown, 1962.

——. *Theirs Be the Power: The Moguls of Eastern Kentucky.* Urbana: University of Illinois Press, 1983.

Cavender, Anthony. *Folk Medicine in Southern Appalachia.* Chapel Hill: University of North Carolina Press, 2003.

Chandler, Barbara. "Why I Believe That Lloyd Chandler Wrote 'Conversation with Death,' Also Known as 'O Death.'" *Journal of Folklore Research* 42 (2004): 127–32.

Chidester, David. *Patterns of Transcendence: Religion, Death, and Dying.* Belmont, Calif.: Wadsworth, 1990.

———. *Shots in the Streets: Violence and Religion in South Africa.* Boston: Beacon Press, 1991.

———. *Savage Systems: Colonialism and Comparative Religion in Southern Africa.* Charlottesville: University Press of Virginia, 1996.

Chidester, David, and Edward T. Linenthal, eds. *American Sacred Space.* Bloomington: Indiana University Press, 1995.

Classen, Constance. *Worlds of Sense: Exploring the Senses in History and across Cultures.* New York: Routledge, 1993.

Comaroff, Jean. *Body of Power, Spirit of Resistance: The Culture and History of a South African People.* Chicago: University of Chicago Press, 1985.

Comaroff, John, and Jean Comaroff. *Ethnography and the Historical Imagination.* Boulder, Colo.: Westview Press, 1992.

Combs, Josiah Henry. *The Kentucky Highlanders from a Native Mountaineer's Viewpoint.* Lexington: J. L. Richardson, 1913.

———. "Sympathetic Magic in the Kentucky Mountains: Some Curious Folk-Survivals." *Journal of American Folklore* 27 (1914): 328–30.

Condee, William Faricy. *Coal and Culture: Opera Houses in Appalachia.* Athens: Ohio University Press, 2005.

Cooper, W. L. "Stuart Robinson School." *Mountain Life and Work* 2 (July 1926): 33–34.

Copenhaver, Eleanor. "Just Change or Progress?" *Mountain Life and Work* 4 (January 1929): 1–3, 29.

Corbin, David Allen. *Life, Work, and Rebellion in the Coal Fields: The Southern West Virginia Miners, 1880–1922.* Urbana: University of Illinois Press, 1981.

Cornett, Elizabeth B. "Down Our Way: Belief Tales of Knott and Perry Counties." *Kentucky Folklore Record* 2:3 (1956): 69–75.

Crews, Mickey. *The Church of God: A Social History.* Knoxville: University of Tennessee Press, 1990.

Csordas, Thomas J., ed. *Embodiment and Experience: The Existential Ground of Culture and Self.* Cambridge: Cambridge University Press, 1994.

Daugherty, Mary Lee. "Serpent Handling as Sacrament." *Theology Today* 33 (1976): 232–43.

———. "Serpent Handlers: When the Sacrament Comes Alive." In *Christianity in Appalachia: Profiles in Regional Pluralism,* ed. Bill J. Leonard, 138–52. Knoxville: University of Tennessee Press, 1999.

de Certeau, Michel. *The Practice of Everyday Life*. Berkeley: University of California Press, 1984.

Deitz, Dennis. *The Layland Mine Explosion*. South Charleson, W.Va.: Mountain Memories Books, n.d.

Dorgan, Howard. *Giving Glory to God in Appalachia: Worship Practices of Six Baptist Subdenominations*. Knoxville: University of Tennessee Press, 1987.

——. *The Old Regular Baptists of Central Appalachia: Brothers and Sisters in Hope*. Knoxville: University of Tennessee Press, 1989.

——. *The Airwaves of Zion: Radio and Religion in Appalachia*. Knoxville: University of Tennessee Press, 1993.

——. *In the Hands of a Happy God: The "No-Hellers" of Central Appalachia*. Knoxville: University of Tennessee Press, 1997.

Dorson, Richard. *Bloodstoppers and Bearwalkers: Folk Traditions of the Upper Peninsula*. Cambridge, Mass.: Harvard University Press, 1972.

Draper, Theodore. "Communists and Miners, 1928–1933." *Dissent* 19 (1972): 371–92.

Dreiser, Theodore, et al. *Harlan Miners Speak: Report on Terrorism in the Kentucky Coal Fields*. Prepared by members of the National Committee for the Defense of Political Prisoners. New York: Harcourt, Brace, 1932.

DuBois, W. E. B. *The Souls of Black Folk*. Chicago: A. C. McClurg, 1903.

Dye, Harold E. *The Prophet of Little Cane Creek*. Atlanta: Home Mission Board, Southern Baptist Convention, 1949.

Dunaway, Wilma A. *The First American Frontier: Transition to Capitalism in Southern Appalachia, 1700–1860*. Chapel Hill: University of North Carolina Press, 1996.

Durkheim, Emile. *The Elementary Forms of Religious Life*. New York: Free Press, 1995.

Eliade, Mircea. *The Sacred and the Profane: The Nature of Religion*. New York: Harcourt, Brace, 1959.

Eller, Ronald D. *Miners, Millhands, and Mountaineers: Industrialization of the Appalachian South, 1880–1930*. Knoxville: University of Tennessee Press, 1982.

Evans-Pritchard, E. E. *Witchcraft, Oracles, and Magic among the Azande*. Oxford: Clarendon Press, 1837.

Faulkner, Charles H., and Carol K. Buckles, eds. *Glimpses of Southern Appalachian Folk Culture: Papers in Memory of Norbert F. Riedl*. Knoxville: Tennessee Anthropological Association, 1978.

Feld, Rose C. "What I Found in Lynch." *Success* 10 (1921): 58–61, 114–19.

Fields, Karen E. "Charismatic Religion as Popular Protest: The Ordinary and Extraordinary in Social Movements." *Theory and Society* 11 (1982): 321–61.

Ford, Thomas. *The Southern Appalachian Region: A Survey*. Lexington: University Press of Kentucky, 1967.

Forderhase, Nancy K. "Eve Returns to the Garden: Women Reformers in Appalachian Kentucky in the Early Twentieth Century." *Register of the Kentucky Historical Society* 85 (1987): 237–61.

Forester, William D. *Before We Forget: Harlan County—1920 through 1930, with Background Dating Further Back in Time.* Harlan, Ky.: privately published, 1983.

Foster, Ben. *On Dark and Bloody Ground: An Oral History of the UMWA in Central Appalachia, 1920–1935.* Charleston, W.Va.: Miner's Voice, 1973.

Fox, John, Jr. *The Trail of the Lonesome Pine.* New York: Charles Scribner's Sons, 1908.

Friedland, Roger, and Richard D. Hecht. *To Rule Jerusalem.* New York: Cambridge University Press, 1996.

Frost, William Goodell. "Our Contemporary Ancestors in the Southern Mountains." *Atlantic Monthly* 83 (March 1899): 311–19.

Fuson, Harvey H. *Ballads of the Kentucky Highlands.* London: Mitre Press, 1931.

Garland, Jim. *Welcome the Traveler Home: Jim Garland's Story of the Kentucky Mountains.* Edited by Julia S. Ardery. Lexington: University Press of Kentucky, 1983.

Gaventa, John. *Power and Powerlessness: Quiescence and Rebellion in an Appalachian Valley.* Urbana: University of Illinois Press, 1980.

Geertz, Clifford. "Religion as a Cultural System." In *The Interpretation of Cultures,* 87–125. New York: Basic Books, 1973.

Geschiere, Peter, ed. *The Modernity of Witchcraft: Politics and the Occult in Postcolonial Africa.* Charlottesville: University of Virginia Press, 1997.

Glassie, Henry. *Passing the Time in Ballymenone.* Bloomington: Indiana University Press, 1982.

Goode, James B. Internet Coal Camp Database, www.coaleducation.org/coalhistory/coaltowns/coal_towns.htm.

Gordon, Avery. *Ghostly Matters: Haunting and the Sociological Imagination.* Minneapolis: University of Minnesota Press, 1997.

Graves, Glenna Horne. "In the Morning We Had Bulldog Gravy: Women in Coal Camps of the Appalachian South, 1890–1940." Ph.D. diss., University of Kentucky, 1993.

Green, Archie. *Only a Miner: Studies in Recorded Coal-Mining Songs.* Urbana: University of Illinois Press, 1972.

Greene, Samuel S., III. "Progressives in the Kentucky Mountains: The Formative Years of the Pine Mountain Settlement School, 1913–1930." Ph.D. diss., Ohio State University, 1982.

Hackett, David G. *The Rude Hand of Innovation: Religion and Social Order in Albany, New York, 1652–1836.* Oxford: Oxford University Press, 1991.

———, ed. *Religion and American Culture: A Reader.* New York: Routledge, 1995.

Halker, Clark D. *For Democracy, Workers, and God: Labor Song-Poems and Labor Protest, 1865–95.* Urbana: University of Illinois Press, 1991.

Hall, David D. *Worlds of Wonder, Days of Judgment: Popular Religious Belief in Early New England.* Cambridge, Mass.: Harvard University Press, 1989.

———, ed. *Lived Religion in America: Toward a History of Practice.* Princeton, N.J.: Princeton University Press, 1997.

Hall, Valerie Gordon. "Contrasting Female Identities: Women in Coal Mining Communities in Northumberland, England, 1900–1939." *Journal of Women's History* 13 (2001): 107–31.

Hand, Wayland D., ed. *Frank C. Brown Collection of North Carolina Folklore.* Durham, N.C.: Duke University Press, 1964.

Harlan & Bell Kentucky, 1931–2: The National Miner's Union. Huntington, W.Va.: Appalachian Movement Press, 1972.

Harney, Will Wallace. "A Strange Land and a Peculiar People." *Lippincott's Magazine* 12 (October 1873): 429–38.

Harvey, David. *The Urban Experience.* Baltimore: Johns Hopkins University Press, 1989.

———. *The Condition of Postmodernity: An Enquiry into the Origins of Cultural Change.* Oxford: Blackwell, 1990.

Hatch, Nathan. *The Democratization of American Christianity.* New Haven, Conn.: Yale University Press, 1989.

Hevener, John W. *Which Side Are You On? The Harlan County Coal Miners, 1931–1939.* Urbana: University of Illinois Press, 1978.

Highmore, Ben. *Everyday Life and Cultural Theory: An Introduction.* New York: Routledge, 2002.

Hill, Samuel S. "The Virtue of Hope." In *Christianity in Appalachia,* ed. Bill J. Leonard, 308. Knoxville: University of Tennessee Press, 1999.

Holt, John B. "Holiness Religion: Cultural Shock and Social Reorganization." *American Sociological Review* 5 (1940): 740–47.

Hooker, Elizabeth R. *Religion in the Highlands: Native Churches and Missionary Enterprises in the Southern Appalachian Area.* New York: Home Missions Council, 1933.

Howes, David. *The Varieties of Sensory Experience: A Sourcebook in the Anthropology of the Senses.* Toronto: University of Toronto Press, 1991.

———, ed. *Empire of the Senses: The Sensual Culture Reader.* New York: Berg, 2005.

Hsiung, David C. *Two Worlds in the Tennessee Mountains: Exploring the Origins of Appalachian Stereotypes.* Lexington: University Press of Kentucky, 1997.

Hurst, Richard M. "Snakelore Motifs in the Writings of J. Hector St. John de Crevecoeur and Other Colonial Writers." *New York Folklore* 9 (1983): 55–98.

Huston, Ruth. *Observations of God's Timing in the Kentucky Mountains.* Salisbury, N.C.: Rowan Printing Co., 1962.

Jenkins Area Jaycees. *History of Jenkins, Kentucky.* Jenkins, Ky.: Jenkins Area Jaycees, 1973.

Jillson, Willard Rouse. *The Coal Industry in Kentucky: An Historical Sketch*. Frankfort, Ky.: State Journal, 1922.

———. *The Coal Industry in Kentucky*. Frankfort: Kentucky Geological Survey, 1924.

John C. C. Mayo College, annual catalog, 1921–22. Louisa, Ky.: Big Sandy News, Job Department, 1921.

Johnson, Clifton H., ed. *God Struck Me Dead: Voices of Ex-Slaves*. Cleveland, Ohio: Pilgrim Press, 1993.

Johnson, Paul Christopher. "Models of 'the Body' in the Ethnographic Field: Garífuna and Candomblé Case Studies." *Method and Theory in the Study of Religion* 14 (2002): 170–95.

Johnson, Paul E. *A Shopkeeper's Millennium: Society and Revivals in Rochester, New York, 1815–1837*. New York: Hill and Wang, 1978.

Jones, Loyal. *Faith and Meaning in the Southern Uplands*. Urbana: University of Illinois Press, 1999.

Kane, Steven M. "Holy Ghost People: The Snake-Handlers of Southern Appalachia." *Appalachian Journal* 4 (1974): 255–62.

———. "Ritual Possession in a Southern Appalachian Religious Sect." *Journal of American Folklore* 87 (1974): 293–302.

Keleman, Thomas. "A History of Lynch, Kentucky, 1917–1930." M.A. thesis, University of Kentucky, 1972.

Kephart, Horace. *Our Southern Highlanders*. Knoxville: University of Tennessee Press, 1976.

Kimbrough, David L. *Taking Up Serpents: Snake Handlers of Eastern Kentucky*. Chapel Hill: University of North Carolina Press, 1995.

King, Stephen Clark. "Wheelwright, Kentucky: Community in Transition." Manuscript, Appalachian Collection, Special Collections, King Library, University of Kentucky, Lexington, 1982.

Knipe, Edward E., and Helen M. Lewis. "The Impact of Coal Mining on the Traditional Mountain Subculture." In *The Not So Solid South: Anthropological Studies in a Regional Subculture,* ed. J. Kenneth Morland, 25–37. Athens: University of Georgia Press, 1971.

Korson, George. *Coal Dust on the Fiddle*. Philadelphia: University of Pennsylvania Press, 1943.

La Barre, Weston. *They Shall Take Up Serpents: Psychology of the Southern Snake-Handling Cult*. Minneapolis: University of Minnesota Press, 1962.

Lantz, Jim. "Meaning, Nerves, and the Urban-Appalachian Family." *Journal of Religion and Health* 31 (1992): 129–39.

Lawless, Elaine. "'Your Hair Is Your Glory': Public and Private Symbology for Pentecostal Women." *New York Folklore* 12 (1986): 33–49.

————. *Handmaidens of the Lord: Pentecostal Women Preachers and Traditional Religion.* Philadelphia: University of Pennsylvania Press, 1988.

Lazerow, James. *Religion and the Working Class in Antebellum America.* Washington, D.C.: Smithsonian Institution Press, 1995.

Lears, T. J. Jackson. *No Place of Grace: Antimodernism and the Transformation of American Culture, 1880–1920.* New York: Pantheon, 1981.

Leonard, Bill J. *Christianity in Appalachia: Profiles in Regional Pluralism.* Knoxville: University of Tennessee Press, 1999.

Letwin, Daniel. *The Challenge of Interracial Unionism: Alabama Coal Miners, 1878–1921.* Chapel Hill: University of North Carolina Press, 1998.

Leventhal, Herbert. *In the Shadow of the Enlightenment: Occultism and Renaissance Science in Eighteenth-Century America.* New York: New York University Press, 1976.

Levy, Melvyn P. "Class War in Kentucky." In Dreiser et al., *Harlan Miners Speak,* 20–37. New York: Harcourt, Brace, 1932.

Lewis, Charles D. "The Changing Mountains." *Mountain Life and Work* 4 (July 1928): 14–20, 31.

Lewis, Helen Matthews, Linda Johnson, and Donald Askins, eds. *Colonialism in Modern America: The Appalachian Case.* Boone, N.C.: Appalachian Consortium Press, 1978.

Lewis, Helen Matthews, Sue Easterling Kobak, and Linda Johnson. "The Missionary Movement in the Southern Mountains: A Case Study of the Episcopal Church in Southwest Virginia." Paper presented at the Society for Religion in Higher Education, Maryville, Tenn., 1974.

————. "Family, Religion, and Colonialism in Central Appalachia, or Bury My Rifle at Big Stone Gap." In *Colonialism in Modern America: The Appalachian Case,* ed. Helen Matthews Lewis, Linda Johnson, and Donald Askins, 113–39. Boone, N.C.: Appalachian Consortium Press, 1978.

Lewis, Ronald L. *Black Coal Miners in America: Race, Class, and Community Conflict, 1780–1980.* Lexington: University Press of Kentucky, 1987.

Lindahl, Carl. "Thrills and Miracles: Legends of Lloyd Chandler." *Journal of Folklore Research* 42 (2004): 133–71.

Lippy, Charles H. "Popular Religiosity in Central Appalachia." In *Christianity in Appalachia,* ed. Bill J. Leonard, 41–42. Knoxville: University of Tennessee Press, 1999.

"The Little Towns within Jenkins." *Letcher Heritage News* 18 (2004): 23–29.

Long, Charles H. *Significations: Signs, Symbols, and Images in the Interpretation of Religion.* Philadelphia: Fortress Press, 1986.

Low, Setha M. "Embodied Metaphors: Nerves as Lived Experience." In *Embodiment and Experience: The Existential Ground of Culture and Self,* ed. Thomas J. Csordas, 139–62. Cambridge: Cambridge University Press, 1994.

Ludwig, A. M., and R. L. Forrester. "The Condition of 'Nerves.'" *Journal of the Kentucky Medical Association* 79 (1981): 333–36.

Luedtke, Alf, ed. *The History of Everyday Life: Reconstructing Historical Experiences and Ways of Life.* Princeton, N.J.: Princeton University Press, 1995.

McCauley, Deborah Vansau. *Appalachian Mountain Religion: A History.* Urbana: University of Illinois Press, 1995.

———. "Mountain Holiness." In *Christianity in Appalachia: Profiles in Regional Pluralism,* ed. Bill J. Leonard, 103–16. Knoxville: University of Tennessee Press, 1999.

McCutcheon, Russell T. *Manufacturing Religion: The Discourse on Sui Generis Religion and the Politics of Nostalgia.* New York: Oxford University Press, 1997.

McDannell, Colleen. *Material Christianity: Religion and Popular Culture in America.* New Haven, Conn.: Yale University Press, 1995.

McNeil, W. K., ed. *Appalachian Images in Folk and Popular Culture.* 2nd ed. Knoxville: University of Tennessee Press, 1995.

Miles, Emma Bell. *The Spirit of the Mountains.* New York: J. Pott, 1905; reprint, Knoxville: University of Tennessee Press, 1975.

Mills, C. Wright. *Sociological Imagination.* New York: Oxford University Press, 1959.

Mitchell, Robert D., ed. *Appalachian Frontiers: Settlement, Society, and Development in the Preindustrial Era.* Lexington: University Press of Kentucky, 1991.

Montell, Lynwood, ed. *Monroe County Folklife.* Monroe County, Ky.: privately published, 1975.

Morris, Homer Lawrence. *The Plight of the Bituminous Coal Miner.* Philadelphia: University of Pennsylvania Press, 1934.

Muccigrosso, Robert. *Celebrating the New World: Chicago's Columbian Exposition of 1893.* Chicago: Ivan R. Dee, 1993.

Murphy, Charles H. "A Collection of Birth Marking Beliefs from Eastern Kentucky." *Kentucky Folklore Record* 10 (1964): 36–38.

Murphy, Teresa Anne. *Ten Hours' Labor: Religion, Reform, and Gender in Early New England.* Ithaca, N.Y.: Cornell University Press, 1992.

Nash, June. *We Eat the Mines and the Mines Eat Us: Dependency and Exploitation in Bolivian Tin Mines.* New York: Columbia University Press, 1993.

Obermiller, Phillip J., and Thomas J. Wagner. *African American Miners and Migrants: The Eastern Kentucky Social Club.* Urbana: University of Illinois Press, 2004.

O'Connell, Barry. "Down a Lonesome Road: Dock Boggs' Life in Music." Liner notes, *Dock Boggs: His Folkways Years, 1963–1968.* Compact disk 40108. Smithsonian Folkways, 1998.

O'Connor, Flannery. *Mystery and Manners: Occasional Prose.* New York: Farrar, Straus and Giroux, 1972.

Ong, Aiwa. *Spirits of Resistance and Capitalist Discipline: Factory Women in Malaysia.* New York: State University of New York Press, 1987.

Orsi, Robert A. *The Madonna of 115th Street: Faith and Community in Italian Harlem, 1880–1950.* New Haven, Conn.: Yale University Press, 1985.

———. "Everyday Miracles: The Study of Lived Religion." In *Lived Religion in America: Toward a History of Practice,* ed. David D. Hall, 3–21. Princeton, N.J.: Princeton University Press, 1997.

———. *Between Heaven and Earth: The Religious Worlds People Make and the Scholars Who Study Them.* Princeton, N.J.: Princeton University Press, 2005.

———, ed. *Gods of the City.* Bloomington: Indiana University Press, 1999.

Peacock, James L., and Ruel W. Tyson Jr. *Pilgrims of Paradox: Calvinism and Experience among the Primitive Baptists of the Blue Ridge.* Washington, D.C.: Smithsonian Institution Press, 1989.

Poe, Nan Trantham. *Beautiful upon the Mountains: The Story of a Kentucky Missionary.* Kentucky Women's Missionary Union, 1952.

Pope, Liston. *Millhands and Preachers: A Study of Gastonia.* New Haven, Conn.: Yale University Press, 1942.

Portelli, Alessandro. *The Death of Luigi Trastulli and Other Stories: Form and Meaning in Oral History.* Albany: State University of New York Press, 1991.

———. Review of Shelly Romalis, *Pistol Packin' Mama. Journal of American History* 87 (2000): 717.

Porter, J. Hampden. "Notes on the Folk-Lore of the Mountain Whites of the Alleghenies." *Journal of American Folklore* 7 (1894): 105–17.

Primiano, Leonard Norman. "Intrinsically Catholic: Vernacular Religion and Philadelphia's Dignity." Ph.D. diss., University of Pennsylvania, 1993.

"A Program for the Mountains." *Mountain Life and Work* 1 (April 1925): 20–22.

Pudup, Mary Beth. "The Boundaries of Class in Preindustrial Appalachia." *Journal of American Geography* 15:2 (1989): 139–62.

———. "The Limits of Subsistence: Agriculture and Industry in Central Appalachia." *Agricultural History* 64 (1990): 61–89.

———. "Social Class and Economic Development in Southeast Kentucky, 1820–1880." In *Appalachian Frontiers: Settlement, Society, and Development in the Preindustrial Era,* ed. Robert D. Mitchell, 235–60. Lexington: University Press of Kentucky, 1991.

Pudup, Mary Beth, Dwight B. Billings, and Altina L. Waller, eds. *Appalachia in the Making: The Mountain South in the Nineteenth Century.* Chapel Hill: University of North Carolina Press, 1995.

Raine, James Watt. *The Land of the Saddle-Bags: A Study of the Mountain People of Appalachia.* New York: Council of Women for Home Missions and Missionary Education Movement of the United States and Canada, 1924.

Reid, Melanie Sovine. "On the Study of Religion in Appalachia: A Review/Essay." *Appalachian Journal* 6 (1979): 239–44.

Richardson, Ethel Park. *American Mountain Songs.* New York: Greenberg, 1927.

Ritchie, Jean. *Singing Family of the Cumberlands.* New York: Oxford University Press, 1955.

Roberts, Leonard, ed. *Old Greasybeard: Tales from the Cumberland Gap.* Detroit: Folklore Association, 1969.

Romalis, Shelly. *Pistol Packin' Mama: Aunt Molly Jackson and the Politics of Folksong.* Urbana: University of Illinois Press, 1999.

Ross, Malcolm. *Machine Age in the Hills.* New York: Macmillan, 1933.

Scalf, Henry P. *Four Men of the Cumberlands.* Prestonburg, Ky.: privately published, 1958.

Scheper-Hughes, Nancy. *Death without Weeping: The Violence of Everyday Life in Brazil.* Berkeley: University of California Press, 1992.

Schmidt, Leigh Eric. *Holy Fairs: Scottish Communions and American Revivals in the Early Modern Period.* Princeton, N.J.: Princeton University Press, 1989.

Schneider, A. Gregory. *The Way of the Cross Leads Home: The Domestication of American Methodism.* Bloomington: Indiana University Press, 1993.

Scott, James C. *Weapons of the Weak: Everyday Forms of Peasant Resistance.* New Haven, Conn.: Yale University Press, 1985.

———. *Domination and the Arts of Resistance: Hidden Transcripts.* New Haven, Conn.: Yale University Press, 1990.

Scott, Shaunna L. "'They Don't Have to Live by the Old Traditions': Saintly Men, Sinner Women, and an Appalachian Pentecostal Revival." *American Ethnologist* 21 (1994): 227–44.

———. *Two Sides to Everything: The Cultural Construction of Class Consciousness in Harlan County, Kentucky.* Albany: State University of New York Press, 1995.

Semple, Ellen Churchill. "The Anglo-Saxons of the Kentucky Mountains: A Study in Anthropogeography." *Geographical Journal* 17 (June 1901): 588–623.

Seremetakis, C. Nadia, ed. *The Senses Still: Perception and Memory as Material Culture in Modernity.* Boulder, Colo.: Westview Press, 1994.

Shackelford, Laurel, and Bill Weinberg, eds. *Our Appalachia: An Oral History.* Lexington: University Press of Kentucky, 1988.

Shapiro, Henry D. *Appalachia on Our Mind: The Southern Mountains and Mountaineers in the American Consciousness, 1879–1920.* Chapel Hill: University of North Carolina Press, 1978.

Shifflett, Crandall A. *Coal Towns: Life, Work, and Culture in Company Towns of Southern Appalachia, 1880–1960.* Knoxville: University of Tennessee Press, 1991.

Slone, Verna Mae. *What My Heart Wants to Tell*. Lexington: University Press of Kentucky, 1979.

Smith, Jonathan Z. *Imagining Religion: From Babylon to Jonestown*. Chicago: University of Chicago Press, 1982.

Stekert, Ellen. "The Snake-Handling Sect of Harlan County, Kentucky: Its Influence on Folk Tradition." *Southern Folklore Quarterly* 27 (1963): 316–22.

Stewart, Kathleen. "On the Politics of Cultural Theory: A Case for 'Contaminated' Cultural Critique." *Social Research* 58 (1991): 395–412.

———. *A Space on the Side of the Road: Cultural Poetics in an "Other" America*. Princeton, N.J.: Princeton University Press, 1996.

Stewart, Wanda, ed. *The Book of Lynch*. Lynch, Ky.: Mine Portal 31 Project, n.d.

Still, James. *River of Earth*. Lexington: University Press of Kentucky, 1978.

Story, Brandon H. "Gospel According to Bristol: The Life, Music, and Ministry of Ernest Phipps." M.A. thesis, East Tennessee State University, 2003.

Sutten, William R. *Journeymen for Jesus: Evangelical Artisans Confront Capitalism in Jacksonian Baltimore*. University Park: Pennsylvania State University Press, 1998.

Szpak, Michael. "Removing the 'Mark of the Beast': The Church of God (Cleveland, Tenn.) and Organized Labor, 1908–1934." *Labor's Heritage* 6 (1994): 46–61.

Tadlock, E. V. "A Mountain School in a New Mining Region." *Mountain Life and Work* 2 (July 1926): 32–33.

———. "Coal Camps and Character." *Mountain Life and Work* 4 (1929): 20–23.

Taussig, Michael. *The Devil and Commodity Fetishism in South America*. Chapel Hill: University of North Carolina Press, 1980.

Taylor, John. *Thoughts on Missions*. N.p., 1819.

Taylor, Paul F. *Bloody Harlan: The United Mine Workers of America in Harlan County, Kentucky, 1931–1941*. Lanham, Md.: University Press of America, 1990.

Thomas, Daniel Lindsey. *Kentucky Superstitions*. Princeton, N.J.: Princeton University Press, 1920, 9–10.

Thomas, George M. *Revivalism and Cultural Change: Christianity, Nation Building, and the Market in the Nineteenth-Century United States*. Chicago: University of Chicago Press, 1989.

Thompson, E. P. *The Making of the English Working Class*. New York: Vintage Books, 1963.

Titon, Jeff Todd. *Powerhouse for God: Sacred Speech, Chant, and Song in an Appalachian Baptist Church*. Austin: University of Texas Press, 1988.

Tomlinson, A. J. "Line of Separation." *Church of God Evangel*, November 20, 1915, 2.

———. "The Church of God and Its Relation to Other Organizations and Orders." *Church of God Evangel*, July 7, 1917, 1.

Trotter, Joe William. *Coal, Class, and Color: Blacks in Southern West Virginia, 1915–1932.* Urbana: University of Illinois Press, 1990.

Turner, Carolyn Clay, and Carolyn Hay Traum. *John C. C. Mayo: Cumberland Capitalist.* Pikeville, Ky.: Pikeville College Press, 1983.

Turner, Terrence. "Bodies and Anti-bodies: Flesh and Fetish in Contemporary Social Theory." In *Embodiment and Experience: The Existential Ground of Culture and Self,* ed. Thomas J. Csordas, 27–47. Cambridge: Cambridge University Press, 1994.

Tweed, Thomas A., ed. *Retelling U.S. Religious History.* Berkeley: University of California Press, 1997.

Vaughn, James. *Blue Moon over Kentucky: A Biography of Kentucky's Troubled Highlands.* Delaplaine, Ark.: Delapress, 1985.

Vincent, George E. "A Retarded Frontier." *American Journal of Sociology* 4 (July 1898): 1–20.

Wacker, Grant. "The Pentecostal Tradition." In *Caring and Curing: Health and Medicine in the Western Religious Traditions,* ed. Ronald L. Numbers and Darrel W. Admundsen, 516–20. New York: Macmillan, 1986.

———. "Searching for Eden with a Satellite Dish: Primitivism, Pragmatism, and the Pentecostal Character." In *Religion and American Culture: A Reader,* ed. David G. Hackett, 437–58. New York: Routledge, 1996.

———. *Heaven Below: Early Pentecostals and American Culture.* Cambridge, Mass.: Harvard University Press, 2001.

Waller, Altina L. *Feud: Hatfields, McCoys, and Social Change in Appalachia, 1860–1900.* Chapel Hill: University of North Carolina Press, 1988.

Waller, Gregory A. *Main Street Amusements: Movies and Commercial Entertainment in a Southern City, 1896–1930.* Washington, D.C.: Smithsonian Institution Press, 1995.

Weise, Robert S. *Grasping at Independence: Debt, Male Authority, and Mineral Rights in Appalachian Kentucky, 1850–1915.* Knoxville: University of Tennessee Press, 2001.

Weller, Jack E. *Yesterday's People: Life in Contemporary Appalachia.* Lexington: University Press of Kentucky, 1965.

Westerkamp, Marilyn J. *Triumph of the Laity: Scots-Irish Piety and the Great Awakening, 1625–1760.* New York: Oxford University Press, 1988.

Whisnant, David E. *All That Is Native and Fine: The Politics of Culture in an American Region.* Chapel Hill: University of North Carolina Press, 1983.

Wigger, John H. *Taking Heaven by Storm: Methodism and the Rise of Popular Christianity in America, 1770–1820.* New York: Oxford University Press, 1998.

Wigginton, Eliot, ed. *The Foxfire Book.* Garden City, N.Y.: Doubleday, Anchor Books, 1972.

———. *Foxfire 2.* Garden City, N.Y.: Doubleday, Anchor Books, 1973.

Williams, Cratis D. "The Southern Mountaineer in Fact and Fiction." Ph.D. diss., New York University, 1961.

Williams, Peter W. *Popular Religion in America: Symbolic Change and the Modernization Process in Historical Perspective.* Urbana: University of Illinois Press, 1989.

———. *America's Religions: From Their Origins to the Twenty-first Century.* Urbana: University of Illinois Press, 2002.

———, ed. *Perspectives on American Religion and Culture.* Malden, Mass.: Blackwell, 1999.

Williams, Raymond. *Marxism and Literature.* Oxford: Oxford University Press, 1977.

Wilson, Samuel M. "Centennial Address." Hazard, Ky., July 4, 1921. Manuscript, Perry County Historical Records, Special Collections, King Library, University of Kentucky.

Wilson, Warren H. "What Are Our Aims—Our Standards of Success?" *Mountain Life and Work* 2 (July 1926): 3–6.

Wolfe, Margaret Ripley. "Aliens in Southern Appalachia: Catholics in the Coal Camps, 1900–1940." *Appalachian Heritage* 6 (1978): 43–56.

———. "Putting Them in Their Places: Industrial Housing in Southern Appalachia, 1900–1930." *Appalachian Heritage* 7 (1979): m27–36.

Wright, William T. *Devil John Wright of the Cumberlands.* Pound, Va.: W. T. Wright, 1932.

Index